T0330293

A Research Agenda for Workplace Stress and Wellbeing

Elgar Research Agendas outline the future of research in a given area. Leading scholars are given the space to explore their subject in provocative ways, and map out the potential directions of travel. They are relevant but also visionary.

Forward-looking and innovative, Elgar Research Agendas are an essential resource for PhD students, scholars and anybody who wants to be at the forefront of research.

Titles in the series include:

A Research Agenda for Workplace Stress and Wellbeing

Edited by

E. KEVIN KELLOWAY

Canada Research Chair in Occupational Health Psychology, Saint Mary's University, Canada

PROFESSOR SIR CARY COOPER

Alliance Manchester Business School, University of Manchester, UK

Elgar Research Agendas

Edward Elgar
PUBLISHING

Cheltenham, UK • Northampton, MA, USA

Published by
Edward Elgar Publishing Limited
The Lypiatts
15 Lansdown Road
Cheltenham
Glos GL50 2JA
UK

Edward Elgar Publishing, Inc.
William Pratt House
9 Dewey Court
Northampton
Massachusetts 01060
USA

A catalogue record for this book
is available from the British Library

Library of Congress Control Number: 2021943592

This book is available electronically in the **Elgar**online
Business subject collection
http://dx.doi.org/10.4337/9781789905021

ISBN 978 1 78990 501 4 (cased)
ISBN 978 1 78990 502 1 (eBook)

Printed and bound by CPI Group (UK) Ltd, Croydon, CR0 4YY

Contents

Figures

Tables

Contributors

Carolyn Axtell, Senior Lecturer in Work Psychology, Institute of Work Psychology, Sheffield University Management School, University of Sheffield, UK

Julian Barling, Borden Professor of Leadership, Smith School of Business, Queen's University, Canada

James Campbell Quick, Academy of Distinguished Scholars, The University of Texas at Arlington, USA

Ryan Cook, Department of Psychology, Saint Mary's University, Halifax, Canada

Professor Sir Cary L. Cooper, Alliance Manchester Business School, University of Manchester, UK

Madeleine T. D'Agata, Defence Scientist, Defence Research and Development Canada – Toronto Centre, National Defence, Canada

Arla Day, Professor of Psychology, Saint Mary's University, Halifax, Canada

Jennifer K. Dimoff, Assistant Professor, Telfer School of Management, University of Ottawa, Ottawa, Canada

Deniz Fikretoglu, Defence Scientist, Defence Research and Development Canada – Toronto Centre, National Defence, Canada

Christine Frank, Defence Scientist, Director General Military Personnel Research and Analysis, National Defence, Canada

Eva Guérin, Defence Scientist, Director General Military Personnel Research and Analysis, National Defence, Canada

M. Sandy Hershcovis, Professor of Organizational Behavior, University of Calgary, Calgary, AB, Canada

Ute R. Hülsheger, Professor of Occupational Health Psychology, Department of Work and Social Psychology, Maastricht University, The Netherlands

Gary W. Ivey, Director Personnel Science-Policy Integration, Director General Military Personnel Research and Analysis, National Defence, Canada

Sheena Johnson, Professor of Work Psychology and Wellbeing, Alliance Manchester Business School, University of Manchester, UK

Rachael Jones-Chick, Department of Psychology, Saint Mary's University, Halifax, Canada

E. Kevin Kelloway, Canada Research Chair in Occupational Health Psychology, Saint Mary's University, Halifax, Canada

Jennifer E.C. Lee, Director Research Personnel and Family Support, Director General Military Personnel Research and Analysis, National Defence, Canada

Zhanna Lyubykh, University of Calgary, Calgary, Canada

Vanessa Myers, Department of Psychology, Saint Mary's University, Halifax, Canada

Karina Nielsen, Chair of Work Psychology, Director of the Institute of Work Psychology, Sheffield University Management School, University of Sheffield, UK

Elinor O'Connor, Professor of Occupational Psychology, Alliance Manchester Business School, University of Manchester, UK

Donna I. Pickering, Defence Scientist, Defence Research and Development Canada – Toronto Centre, National Defence, Canada

Shani Pupco, Smith School of Business, Queen's University, Canada

Maree Roche, Associate Professor & Co Director Leadership Unit, Waikato School of Management, University of Waikato, Hamilton, New Zealand

Winny Shen, Associate Professor of Organization Studies, Schulich School of Business, York University, Canada

Stacey Silins, Defence Scientist, Director General Military Personnel Research and Analysis, National Defence, Canada

Glorian Sorensen, Professor of Social and Behavioral Sciences, Harvard T.H. Chan School of Public Health, Dana-Farber Cancer Institute, USA

Kristen M. Shockley, Associate Professor of Industrial/Organizational Psychology, Department of Psychology, University of Georgia, United States of America

Megan M. Thompson, Defence Scientist, Defence Research and Development Canada – Toronto Centre, National Defence, Canada

Michelle R. Tuckey, Professor of Work & Organisational Psychology at the University of South Australia

Dr. Christian van Stolk, Executive Vice President, RAND Europe, Cambridge, UK

Whitney E.S. Vogel, Department of Psychology, Portland State University, USA

Ivana Vranjes, University of Tilburg, the Netherlands

Olivia Yoder, Department of Psychology, Portland State University, USA

PART I

SETTING THE SCENE

1. Introduction to *A Research Agenda for Workplace Stress and Wellbeing*

E. Kevin Kelloway and Cary L. Cooper

If the events of the past year (2020) have taught us anything, it is that planning for the future is an audacious act. The global pandemic and associated events (e.g., lockdowns and the move to remote work) have both stalled and enhanced research progress. On the one hand, disruptions in the workplace have led to well-developed research plans being stalled or rapidly reformulated to recognize the changing situation. On the other hand, the crisis has led to a renewed recognition of the importance of mental health issues and wellbeing in the workplace. Many are already predicting an "echo pandemic" (Dozois, 2020) of mental health problems arising from the Covid-19 pandemic and this will be part of the new reality faced by organizations and their employees.

Prior to the pandemic, the authors represented in this volume were approached with a request that, in itself, required some audacity. We asked individuals with established expertise in workplace wellbeing to consider their respective literatures, review what was known about their topic and to articulate an agenda for future researchers. Although the pandemic has created its own research needs (see, for example, Chapter 12), there is much more to be done to understand and positively influence workplace wellbeing. We are pleased that so many experts accepted our invitation and contributed their expertise to this volume.

Why work and wellbeing?

There is a clear need to focus on issues related to employee wellbeing. A frequently cited estimate is that one in four people (translating into more than 450 million people) will experience a significant mental health problem (National Alliance on Mental Illness [NAMI], 2019; World Health

Organization [WHO], 2002, 2004) and mental health issues are one of the leading causes of workplace disability (Mental Health Commission of Canada [MHCC], 2012; WHO, 2019). The cost of mental health problems has been estimated to be over 135 Euros each year (5 percent of GDP) in the European Union (McDaid, 2011), between $150 and $300 billion annually in the United States (American Institute of Stress, 2005) and $50 billion each year in Canada (MHCC, 2012).

Jones-Chick and Kelloway (in press) point to the inadequacy of "minimalist" attempts to address this issue. They argue that many organizations have been content to establish an Employee Assistance Program and trust that such a program will "fix" mental health issues. However, the available data suggest that such programs are typically underutilized (Attridge et al., 2013; Canadian Medical Association, 2013; Linnan et al., 2008; Reynolds & Lehman, 2003) and that individuals experiencing mental health issues frequently go undiagnosed (Corrigan, 2004). Indeed, the individuals who are most likely to benefit from such programs may be the least likely to use them (Dimoff & Kelloway, 2016; Hunt & Eisenberg, 2010; Linnan et al., 2008).

Kelloway (2017) has suggested that there are clear signs that organizations are changing their orientation and moving beyond a minimalist approach to mental health issues in the workplace. In conjunction with increased societal awareness of mental health issues, organizations have become involved in actively promoting employee wellbeing. Kelloway (2017, see also Jones-Chick & Kelloway, in press) has suggested that more comprehensive approaches to workplace mental health rest on the "three pillars" of prevention, intervention, and accommodation. That is, organizations are increasingly looking at means of reducing workplace stress and enhancing workplace conditions for employees (i.e., prevention), recognizing that organizations can, and should, assist individuals in crisis (i.e., intervention, see Dimoff & Kelloway, 2019), and helping individuals stay at work or return to work after a period of leave (i.e. accommodation, see Kelloway, 2017).

Definitional issues

In many cases, an organizational focus on mental health is part of the evolution of the healthy workplace movement. Healthy workplace programs are "employer sponsored initiatives directed at improving the health and wellbeing of employees" (Goetzel et al., 2008, p.4). Originally focused on physical health issues (Baicker et al., 2010), such programs have typically evolved to include issues of psychological wellbeing as well (Kelloway, 2017). Although there is evidence supporting the effectiveness of healthy workplace programs (see, for example, Goetzel & Ozminkowski, 2008), there are also significant concerns with research in this area which limits the conclusions that can be drawn (for a review see Dimoff et al., 2014).

Although organizations have begun to focus more on employee wellbeing, a concern for psychological factors in the workplace is by no means new. Kornhauser's (1965) seminal work identified the mental health concerns inherent in factory work and the *Work in America* (Secretary of Health, Education and Welfare, 1974) report drew attention to the prevalence and effects of workplace stress. In 1990, the National Institute for Occupational Safety and Health (NIOSH) identified workplace stress as one of the 10 leading causes of workplace death and declared stress to be a national epidemic (Sauter et al., 1990). The NIOSH report focused specifically on six common workplace stressors (i.e., role stress, workload and pace, work scheduling, job content and control, work–family conflict and interpersonal stressors) and a substantial body of research supports their conclusions (for a review see Kelloway & Day, 2005).

Although the initial focus of research and practice was on the identification and reduction of workplace stressors, subsequent approaches have emphasized the provision of resources that both contribute directly to wellbeing and mitigate the effects of organizational stressors. Five such resources – recognition, opportunities for growth and development, involvement, health and safety and work–family balance – provide the basis for the psychologically healthy workplace model promoted by the American Psychological Association (APA; Grawitch, Gottschalk & Munz, 2006). Consistent with this approach, recognition is associated with enhanced employee wellbeing (Gilbert & Kelloway, 2018). Moreover, Gulseren et al. (in press) drew on the APA model to formulate the R.I.G.H.T. model of leadership (i.e., recognition, involvement, growth, health and safety, teamwork). When leaders provide these opportunities, employees experience enhanced wellbeing (Gulseren et al., in press).

The enactment of a national standard for psychological health and safety (Canadian Standards Association, 2013) has largely shaped the discussion about workplace wellbeing in Canada. A psychologically healthy and safe workplace is defined in the standard as a "workplace that promotes workers' psychological wellbeing and actively works to prevent harm to worker psychological health, including in negligent, reckless, or intentional ways". There are two distinct aspects of this definition – the promotion of workers' psychological wellbeing and the prevention of harm to psychological health. The definition is consistent with the World Health Organization's definition of health as comprising "a state of complete physical, mental and social wellbeing and not merely the absence of disease or infirmity" (World Health Organization, 1948).

Similarly, common usage of the term mental health or wellbeing invokes two quite different themes. On the one hand mental health – or more accurately mental illness – refers to a set of conditions defined by diagnostic criteria as expressed in the DSM. Conditions such as clinical depression, Post-Traumatic Stress Disorder, or anxiety disorder are representative of this set of diagnosable conditions. On the other hand, the term "mental health" is also used to refer to a more positive state that goes beyond the absence of mental illness (e.g., the standard refers to the promotion of wellbeing). Ryff (1989) has offered the most well-supported model of positive functioning as comprising self-acceptance, positive relationships with others, autonomy, environmental mastery, purpose in life, and personal growth. Thus, individuals have psychological wellbeing or optimal mental health when they "like most parts of themselves, have warm and trusting relationships, see themselves developing into better people have a direction in life, are able to shape their environments and have a degree of self-determination" (Keyes, 2002, pp. 208–209).

These two aspects of mental health – mental illness and positive psychological wellbeing – do not seem to be opposite ends of a single continuum. They appear to be two moderately negatively correlated but separate dimensions of health. Moreover, these two dimensions are paralleled by discussions of physical health in which we might distinguish between being physically ill (e.g., having a flu) and being physically fit (e.g., having aerobic capacity, good cardiovascular health etc.). Thus, in discussing workplace wellbeing we are really addressing two related issues: the extent to which the organization is taking steps to reduce harm (e.g., by reducing, eliminating or mitigating the effects of workplace stressors); and the extent to which the organization is promoting the positive psychological wellbeing of employees.

Methodological issues

Even a brief perusal of the literature on work and wellbeing would evidence some common concerns with regard to research methodologies. Perhaps the most common concern is the reliance on cross-sectional self-report data that has dominated, and continues to be prevalent in, research on work and wellbeing. There is no doubt that cross-sectional research designs have a role to play in research (e.g., Taris et al., in press). However, there is also a clear need to move beyond such designs.

Spector and Pindek (2016) conducted a content analysis of articles published in the *Journal of Occupational Health Psychology* and *Work & Stress* between 2010 and 2014. As a result of their review, they made five specific recommendations for research methodology. First, they suggested there was a need for inductive or exploratory methods as used in fields such as the natural sciences, in contrast to the predominant model of theory-based deduction used in occupational health psychology. This suggestion is also reflected in Quick's (see Chapter 2) call for more inter-disciplinary approaches to the study of wellbeing. Second, Spector and Pindek (2016) point to the need to understand processes and the temporal sequence of events that lead to health-related outcomes. The emergence of diary studies, or studies based on ecological momentary assessment, are a response to this call – although Taris et al. (in press) note that the analyses of these data often do not account for temporal relations and, as a result, a promising methodology often produces data that does not go beyond understanding cross-sectional relationships. Spector and Pindek (2016) also note the potential for three specific research approaches – qualitative research, longitudinal research, and research incorporating multi-level perspectives – for advancing our understanding of workplace wellbeing.

Kelloway (2017, 2020) has argued for the need for adopting the perspective of evidence-based management in the study of workplace wellbeing. Evidence-based management has its roots in the evidence-based medicine movement (Smith, 1991), which, in turn, emerged from concerns that many medical interventions were under- or mis-used (Walshe & Rundall, 2001). Organizational researchers noted the relevance of these concerns (e.g., Pfeffer & Sutton, 2006; Rynes et al., 2002) and called for evidence-based decision making in organizations (Rousseau & Barends, 2011).

Although researchers have typically attributed the lack of evidence-based practice in organizations to a lack of knowledge on the part of managers (e.g., Charlier et al., 2011; Rynes et al., 2002, 2007), Kelloway (2017, 2020) took a different approach, suggesting that current approaches to research do not provide a basis for evidence-based practice. In short, he suggested that evidence-based management requires management-based evidence – evidence that is useful for managers to implement in organizational contexts (Kelloway, 2020).

Three suggestions for research emerged from this perspective. First, as have others, Kelloway (2020) noted the need for longitudinal research in the study of work and wellbeing. Although others have recognized the need for predictive longitudinal studies (Ployhart & Vandenburg, 2010) – research that examines the predictors of change over time – there is also a need for descriptive longitudinal studies of workplace wellbeing (Kelloway & Francis, 2012). Descriptive longitudinal studies would examine how the form, direction, and timing of changes in wellbeing changes over time (e.g., Garst et al., 2000). Such descriptive studies are necessary to understand the nature of workplace wellbeing.

Intervention studies (see also Nielsen et al.'s Chapter 11 in this volume) are notoriously difficult to conduct in organizations (Karinika-Murray & Biron, 2015) but remain the single most compelling source of knowledge about workplace wellbeing. Intervening in organizations to change a potential influence on individual wellbeing and assessing whether that intervention had the desired effect teaches us a great deal about the causes of individual wellbeing in the workplace. If we can do that intervention in the context of an experimental design that isolates the nature of the change, then we have learned even more about workplace wellbeing.

Finally, Kelloway (2020) identified the need to identify dose–response relationships as an important move forward in the study of work and wellbeing. All too often, our research leads to bromides that provide little guidance for implementation or practice. Finding that workload is a stressor that negatively affects wellbeing, for example, provides little information that would inform an organization's attempts to intervene. Most jobs have at least some periods of elevated workload and reducing workload may lead to a condition of underload which, in itself, can have deleterious consequences (e.g., Pindek et al., 2018). What is needed is evidence that supports a more precise intervention (e.g., evidence as to how much workload is "too much" in terms of wellbeing). Research methods that focus on associations or correlations between continuous measures, provide little such guidance. Techniques such as Receiver Operating Characteristic (ROC) analysis, widely used in epidemiological and medical research, may provide a means of establishing cutoffs for common organizational stressors (see for example Blanc et al., 2014).

ROC analysis requires a dichotomous outcome – classically in medical research a "diagnosis". Organizational researchers have tended to use more continuous measures of outcomes (e.g., measures of wellbeing, absenteeism etc.) and are well aware of the dangers of dichotomizing such outcomes (e.g., MacCallum et al., 2002). Although problematic in research that focuses on establishing relationships between predictors and outcomes, we suggest that such a strategy might be necessary in order to move from research to practice.

About this book

As reflected in the contributions to this volume, both methodological and substantive challenges face researchers focused on work and wellbeing. We believe that the experts who have contributed chapters have done a remarkable job of summarizing a voluminous literature and identifying research agendas that would move the field forward.

James Campbell Quick – a noted researcher and inaugural editor of the *Journal of Occupational Health Psychology* – sets the scene for the volume by reviewing the historical evolution of the field (Chapter 2). He moves beyond history to identify six innovative ways to move the study of work and wellbeing forward. First, he suggests that researchers could profitably engage in multidisciplinary research that avoids reliance on the theory and methods of a single discipline. He also points to the potential benefits that could be obtained through a focus on outliers (whether individuals or organizations) and high risk situations or occupations where the costs of failure are high. Fourth, he advocates for research focused on screening and surveillance mechanisms in the workplace to improve early identification of problems and early intervention. The final two recommendations deal with the focus of research, Quick argues that there is value in taking a segmented approach, focusing on individuals who are most at risk and those who are in the top 10 percent of performers. He also recognizes a broader view that focuses on workplaces, rather than individuals, as the unit of analysis.

Christian Van Stolk continues to set the scene by examining the costs of workplace stress in Chapter 3. His particular focus is on the costs experienced by U.K. employers and employees and he presents interesting data from the Britain's Healthiest Workplaces survey. He points to the significant costs associated with stress and impaired wellbeing in the workplace and their implication for productivity and, by extension, the economic health of society.

In Part II of the book we move to a consideration of factors that influence wellbeing in the workplace. In Chapter 4, Shani Pupco and Julian Barling offer an intriguing agenda focused on leadership in organizations. They begin by reviewing the substantial literature relating leadership and employee wellbeing, but then turn the question on its head by considering how leaders' own mental health affects leadership and, thereby, employees. This leads to their call for a greater focus on leaders' wellbeing. Following calls for multi-disciplinary approaches, they then look beyond the traditional leadership or occupational health psychology literatures to identify novel research questions. They conclude with a consideration of issues related to sex and both sexual and gender identities. In taking this diverse perspective, Pupco and Barling identify both novel and important questions that significantly expand the literature on leadership and wellbeing.

In Chapter 5, Ivana Vranjes, Zhanna Lyubykh and M. Sandy Herschovis consider the influence of workplace aggression on workplace wellbeing. Their particular focus is on the role of observers to workplace aggression. They begin with a broad view of what, in theory, observers can do in organizations and then consider the empirical evidence as to what observers actually do and when they do it. They conclude by considering identifying research questions dealing with intervention effectiveness, the consequences experienced by observers that intervene, and the consequences for observers that do not intervene.

In Chapter 6, Arla Day, Ryan Cook, Rachael Jones-Chick and Vanessa Myers examine the links between information and communications technology (ICT) and wellbeing. They begin by reviewing the extant literature showing the multiple ways in which ICT use can affect wellbeing. They develop a four-pronged framework, integrating the physical effects of ICT use, ICT as a conduit for demands and resources, the direct and indirect effects of ICT use and the directionality of the ICT use–wellbeing relationship. They articulate research questions emerging from each of these perspectives and, in doing so, provide a structured research agenda for future research on ICT use and its contribution to wellbeing in the workplace.

In Chapter 7, Winny Shen and Kristen M. Stockley consider the influence of work–family concerns on individual wellbeing. They offer a constructive critique of this literature – arguing that the field is at a crossroads and must move beyond the pervasive use of cross-sectional research designs to establish a relationship between work–family issues and strain. Specifically, they suggest three new directions for work–family research; questioning whether researchers truly understand the constructs underlying commonly used measures, whether interventions have been targeted toward the most effective points, and whether we should expect to, or try to, change individual work–family experiences.

In Part III of the book, we focus on interventions targeted toward improving wellbeing in the workplace. The section begins with Jennifer K. Dimoff, Whitney E.S. Vogel and Olivia Yoder's consideration of mental health in the workplace. They point to the prevalence of mental health issues in society that are reflected in the workplace and the need for organizations to intervene to assist employees. After highlighting organizations that have done an effective job in this area, Dimoff et al. also point to the numerous questions that remain for researchers to address.

In Chapter 9, Sheena Johnson and Elinor O'Connor consider stress management interventions. After introducing a conceptual model of stress management interventions, they identify both substantive and methodological areas in which research on stress management can be advanced. They also identify the changing nature of work as an influence on stress management interventions.

Mindfulness interventions are the focus of Maree Roche, Michelle R. Tuckey and Ute R. Hülsheger in Chapter 10. They review existing research pointing to the nature and potential benefits of mindfulness in the workplace. However, they also note the areas in which more research is needed. These include greater conceptual clarity in the nature of mindfulness, the development of a stronger evidence base through greater methodological rigor and a greater understanding of mindfulness in the context of the workplace.

Karina Nielsen, Caroline Axtell and Glorian Sorensen move beyond the focus on individual intervention to consider the nature of organizational interventions in Chapter 11. Their particular focus is participatory interventions and how the context can shape the nature and effectiveness of the intervention. They draw on the IGLOO (individual, group, leader, organizational and outer context) framework to identify the relevant contextual influences.

As mentioned at the beginning of this chapter, this volume unfolded in the midst of the worldwide Covid-19 pandemic. It quickly became apparent that issues arising from the pandemic would likely influence the nature of work – and the nature of organizational research for the future. In Chapter 12, Gary W. Ivey and his team consider the implications of the pandemic for research on work and wellbeing, identifying potential influences and research questions.

We feel fortunate to have secured the participation of these experts in creating a research agenda for research on work and wellbeing. We believe that, both individually and collectively, the contributors to this volume have posed a considerable challenge for researchers to address a myriad of issues related to work and wellbeing. We are also confident that researchers will respond to these challenges in order to create better workplaces that positively influence wellbeing.

References

American Institute of Stress (2005). *Workplace Stress*. Accessed on August 27, 2015. Retrieved from http://www.stress.org/workplace-stress/

Attridge, M., Cahill, T., Granberry, S.W., & Herlihy, P.A. (2013). The National Behavioral Consortium industry profile of external EAP vendors. *Journal of Workplace Behavioral Health*, 28(4), 251–324.

Baicker, K., Cutler, D., & Song, Z. (2010). Workplace wellness programs can generate savings. *Health Affairs*, 29(2), 304–311.

Blanc, S., Zamorski, M., Ivey, G., Edge, H. M., & Hill, K. (2014). How much distress is too much on deployed operations? Validation of the Kessler Psychological Distress Scale (K10) for application in military operational settings. Military Psychology, 26(2), 88–100. https://doi.org/10.1037/mil0000033

Canadian Medical Association (2013). *Mental Health*. Accessed on August 3, 2015. Retrieved from https://www.cma.ca/En/Pages/mental-health.aspx

Canadian Standards Association (2013). *Psychological Health and Safety in the Workplace: Prevention, Promotion, and Guidance to Staged Implementation*. Ottawa, Ontario, Canada: Canadian Standards Association.

Charlier, S., Brown, K., & Rynes, S. (2011). Teaching evidence-based management inMBA programs: What evidence is there? *Academy of Management Learning & Education*, 10(2), 222–236.

Corrigan, P. (2004). How stigma interferes with mental health care. *American Psychologist*, 59, 614.

Dimoff, J.K. and Kelloway, E.K. (2016). Resource utilization model: Organizational leaders as resource facilitators. In W.A. Gentry, C. Clerkin, P.L. Perrewé, J.R.B. Halbesleben, and C.C. Rosen (eds), *Research in Occupational Stress and Wellbeing Volume 14: The Role of Leadership in Occupational Stress*. London, UK: Emerald, pp. 141–160.

Dimoff, J.K., & Kelloway, E.K. (2019). With a little help from my boss: The impact of workplace mental health training on leader behaviors and employee resource utilization. *Journal of Occupational Health Psychology*, 24(1), 4–19.

Dimoff, J.K., Kelloway, E.K., & MacLellan, A.S. (2014). Health and performance: Science or Advocacy? *Journal of Organizational Effectiveness: People and Performance*, 1, 316–334.

Dozois, D.J. (2020). Anxiety and depression in Canada during the COVID-19 pandemic: A national survey. *Canadian Psychology/Psychologie canadienne* 62(1), 136–142.

Garst, H., Frese, M., & Molenaar, P.C.M. (2000). The temporal factor of change in stressor–strain relationships: A growth curve model on a longitudinal study in East Germany. *Journal of Applied Psychology*, 85, 417–438.

Goetzel, R.Z., & Ozminkowski, R.J. (2008). The health and cost benefits of work site health-promotion programs. *Annual Review of Public Health*, 29, 303–323.

Goetzel, R.Z., Roemer, E.C., Liss-Levinson, R.C., & Samoly, D.K. (2008). Workplace health promotion: Policy recommendations that encourage employers to support health improvement programs for their workers. A paper commissioned by Partnership for Prevention, Emory University, available at: www.prevent.org/data/files/initiatives/workplacehealtpromotionpolicyrecommendations.pdf

Gilbert, S.L., & Kelloway, E.K. (2018). Leadership, recognition and well-being: A moderated mediational model. *Canadian Journal of Administrative Sciences/Revue canadienne des sciences de l'administration*, 35(4), 523–534.

Grawitch, M., Gottschalk, M., and Munz, D. (2006). The path to a healthy workplace: A critical review linking healthy workplace practices, employee wellbeing, and organizational improvements. *Consulting Psychology Journal: Practice and Research*, 8, 129–147.

Gulseren, D.B., Thibault, T., Kelloway, E.K., Mullen, J., Teed, M., Gilbert,S., & Dimoff, J.K. (in press). R.I.G.H.T. leadership: Scale development and validation of a psychologically healthy leadership model. *Canadian Journal of Administrative Science*.

Hunt, J., & Eisenberg, D. (2010). Mental health problems and help-seeking behavior among college students. *Journal of Adolescent Health*, 46, 3–10.

Jones-Chick, R., & Kelloway, E.K. (in press). The 3 pillars of mental health in the workplace: Prevention, intervention, and accommodation. In T. Wall, C. Cooper and P. Brough (eds), *The Oxford Handbook of Organizational Wellbeing*. Oxford, UK.

Karinika-Murray, M., & Biron, C, eds (2015). *Derailed Organizational Interventions for Stress and Wellbeing: Confessions of Failure and Solutions for Success*, NewYork: Springer.

Kelloway, E.K. (2017). Mental health in the workplace: Towards evidence-based practice. *Canadian Psychology*, 58(1), 1–6. http://dx.doi.org/10.1037/cap0000084

Kelloway, E.K. (2020). Chasing the dream: The healthy and productive workplace. In P. Graf and D. Dozois (eds), *Handbook on the State of the Art in Applied Psychology*, New York: Wiley.

Kelloway, E.K., & Day, A.L. (2005). Building healthy organizations: What we know so far. *Canadian Journal of Behavioural Science*, 37, 223–235. http://dx.doi.org/10.1037/h0087259

Kelloway, E.K., & Francis, L. (2012). Longitudinal research and data analysis. In R. Sinclair, M. Wang, and L. Tetrick (eds), *Research Methods in Occupational Health Psychology*, New York: Routledge, pp. 374–394.

Keyes, C.L. (2002). The mental health continuum: From languishing to flourishing in life. *Journal of Health and Social Behavior*, 43(2), 207–222.

Kornhauser, A. (1965). *Mental Health of the Industrial Worker*, New York: Wiley

Linnan, L., Bowling, M., Childress, J., Lindsay, G., Blakey, C., Pronk, S., ... & Royall, P. (2008). Results of the 2004 national worksite health promotion survey. *American Journal of Public Health*, 98, 1503–1509.

MacCallum, R.C., Zhang, S., Preacher, K.J., & Rucker, D.D. (2002). On the practice of dichotomization of quantitative variables. *Psychological Methods*, 7(1), 19–40.

McDaid, D. (2011). *Making the Long-term Economic Case for Investing in Mental Health to Contribute to Sustainability*. European Union. Retrieved from https://www.researchgate.net/publication/303024588_Making_the_long-term_economic_case_for_investing_in_mental_health_to_contribute_to_sustainability, Accessed July 21, 2021.

Mental Health Commission of Canada [MHCC], (2012). *Changing Directions, Changing Lives: The Mental Health Strategy for Canada*, Calgary, AB.

National Alliance on Mental Illness (2019). Mental health by the numbers. Retrieved from https://www.nami.org/learn-more/mental-health-by-the-numbers, July 21, 2021.

Pfeffer, J., & Sutton, R. (2006). Evidence-based management. *Harvard Business Review*, 84(1), 63–74.

Pindek, S., Krajcevska, A., & Spector, P.E. (2018). Cyberloafing as a coping mechanism: Dealing with workplace boredom. *Computers in Human Behavior*, 86, 147–152.

Ployhart, R.E., & Vandenberg, R.K. (2010). Longitudinal research: The theory, design, and analysis of change. *Journal of Management*, 36, 94–120.

Reynolds, G.S., & Lehman, W.E. (2003). Levels of substance use and willingness to use the employee assistance program. *Journal of Behavioral Health Services & Research*, 30, 238–248.

Rousseau, D., & Barends, E. (2011). Becoming an evidence-based HR practitioner. *Human Resource Management Journal*, 21(3), 221–235.

Ryff, C.D. (1989). Happiness is everything, or is it? Explorations on the meaning of psychological wellbeing. *Journal of Personality and Social Psychology*, 57(6), 1069.

Rynes, S., Colbert, A., & Brown, K. (2002). HR professionals' beliefs about effective human resource practices: Correspondence between research and practice. *Human Resource Management*, 41, 149–174.

Rynes, S., Giluk, T., & Brown, K. (2007). The very separate worlds of academic and practitioner periodicals in human resource management: Implications for evidence-based management. *Academy of Management Journal*, 50(5), 987–1008.

Sauter, S.L., Murphy, L.R., and Hurrell, Jr., J.J. (1990). Prevention of work-related psychological disorders. *American Psychologist*, 45, 1146–1153.

Secretary of Health, Education and Welfare (1974). *Work in America (A Report of a Special Task Force to the Secretary of Health, Education, and Welfare)*. Cambridge, MA: MIT Press.

Smith, R. (1991). Where is the wisdom…? The poverty of medical evidence. *British Medical Journal*, 303, 798–799.

Spector, P.E., & Pindek, S. (2016). The future of research methods in work and occupational health psychology. *Applied Psychology*, 65(2), 412–431.

Taris, T., Kessler, S., & Kelloway, E.K. (in press). Editorial: Strategies addressing the limitations of cross-sectional designs in occupational health psychology: What they are good for (and what not). *Work & Stress*, 35(1), 1–5.

Walshe, K., & Rundall, T. G. 2001. Evidence-based management: From theory to practice in health care. *Milbank Quarterly*, 79, 429–457.

World Health Organization (1948). Preamble to the Constitution of the World Health Organization as adopted by the International Health Conference, New York, 19–22 June 1946, and entered into force on 7 April 1948. Available at https://www.who.int/about/who-we-are/constitution. Accessed June 3, 2021.

World Health Organization (2002). *Prevention and Promotion in Mental Health*. Accessed on January 20, 2020. Retrieved from https://www.who.int/mental_health/media/en/545.pdf

World Health Organization (2004). *The Summary Report on Promoting Mental Health: Concepts, Emerging Evidence, and Practice*. Geneva, Switzerland: World Health Organization.

World Health Organization (2019) Mental health in the workplace: Information sheet. Available at: https://www.who.int/mental_health/in_the_workplace/en/ (accessed 24 June 2020).

2. Workplace stress and wellbeing: pathways for future research advances

James Campbell Quick

Introduction

The purpose of this chapter is to explore pathways (i.e., plausible trajectories) for future research advances in workplace stress and wellbeing. However, before doing so it is essential to set the framework of where the field is currently and define the two key constructs under consideration. Stress and wellbeing are companion or complimentary constructs in the study of people in work organizations. They are not equivalents nor interchangeable constructs. The study of each pre-dates research on either in the context of the workplace. For this chapter, the stress research of the past century beginning with the Yerkes–Dodson Law is the principle foundation (cf., Hargrove et al., 2011). To fully appreciate and understand wellbeing research requires a modicum of knowledge about moral philosophy, one of the foundational disciplines along with physiology that laid the groundwork for the science of psychology. Moral philosophy dates to *The Theory of Moral Sentiments* (Smith, 1759).

Review of research on workplace stress and wellbeing

Stress and wellbeing are excellent rubrics for domains of study and research. However, neither term has a scientifically specific, broadly accepted definition. Therefore, before setting forth a research agenda for either it is important to explore the meaning(s) and research for each. While the stress concept is anchored in medical and physiological research of Walter B. Cannon (Benison et al., 1987), the earlier research embodied in the Yerkes–Dodson Law is key to the performance aspects of the stress concept, especially in the workplace; that is, workplace stress is not only concerned with its health consequences but also performance consequences of stress in the workplace. On the other hand, workplace wellbeing focuses on health and happiness rather than human performance. Wellbeing has both positive and negative aspects; hence, there is positive wellbeing, as in high energy and vitality, as well as negative wellbeing, as in sickness and depression (Quick & Quick, 2013). Wellbeing applies to individuals as well as groups, such as those found in the workplace (Cooper & Quick, 2017).

The concept of workplace stress

The research on workplace stress has its origins in the research and practice of Robert Kahn and his colleagues (1964), Harry Levinson (2002), and Cary Cooper and Roy Payne (1978, 1980). The focus of these early workplace stress initiatives was organizational stress, specifically studies in role conflict and ambiguity, mental health and hygiene in occupational settings, and finally occupational and work stress. Over the next several decades there was a pro-liferation of theories, constructs, and measures for workplace stress. Cooper (1998) identified 12 leading theories of organizational stress from across the world, ranging from individual burnout to organizational public health and person–environment fit to cybernetic theory of stress, coping, and wellbeing. Collectively, these stress theories give consideration (1) to the environment in terms of stressors and demands placed on individuals and groups and (2) to the individual in terms of self-imposed demands, stress responses, and psycho-physiological strain.

In spite of the normalcy of the stress response, stress can be the kiss of death as well as the spice of life (Levi, 2000). Stress is a direct contributing cause or indirectly implicated in over 50 percent of all human morbidity and mortality (Quick & Cooper, 2003). In the workplace, Goh et al. (2016) built a model to estimate the excess mortality and incremental health expenditures associated with exposure to ten workplace stressors. They argue that American business policies, practices, and the management of American workforces contribute materially to workplace stress and employee strain, including mortality. Based on epidemiological evidence, their research links specific workplace stressors to health outcomes. They conclude that over 120,000 deaths per year and approximately 5–8 percent of annual healthcare costs are attributable to American management practices, including how companies manage their workforces. The three leading causes of death were absence of health insurance for workers, unemployment, and low job control. Goh et al.'s (2016) research represents an especially significant shift from the psychosocial study of workplace stress to the public health study of causes and risks of workplace stress by relying on the science of epidemiology.

The concept of workplace wellbeing

The research on workplace wellbeing is rooted in moral philosophy by way of the broader concept of wellbeing, especially utilitarianism (Mill, 1910; *Stanford Encyclopedia of Philosophy*, 2008). The historical roots actually date back several centuries, especially to the work of Adam Smith (1759) during the Scottish Enlightenment. While best known as the founder of political economics and his most currently famous publication focused on the wealth of nations (Smith, 1910), it was his earlier *The Theory of Moral Sentiments* that established Smith (1759) as a luminary thought leader of his day. Wellbeing is concerned with health and happiness, which for Smith required the balancing of selfish, social, and unsocial passions within the individual. The social passions are the basis for collective interests while the selfish passions are the basis for individual interests. He set forth the moral sense, the conscience as the basis for what is right and wrong, sympathy, and propriety of action. For Smith, self-interest and social interest were both important.

Wellbeing in this philosophical tradition focuses primarily on the individual over the course of a lifetime. Hence, Vaillant's (1977, 2012) focus on the Harvard Class of 1942 in the Grant Study examined the wellbeing of these men over seven decades. In this philosophical tradition, wellbeing encompasses the whole life rather than focusing on short-lived states of happiness, contentment, and/or pleasure. Thus, wellbeing is concerned with what makes life good for the individual living that life; hence, positive wellbeing. Wellbeing is more commonly understood today in terms of three concepts: the state of being happy, healthy, or prosperous. This shorter-term approach to wellbeing is more compatible with the study of workplace wellbeing. Hence, Diener et al.'s (1999) concept of subjective wellbeing and happiness that enables researchers to study adaptation, goals, coping strategies, and individual dispositional influences. Wright and Cropanzano's (2004) concept of psychological wellbeing is an overlapping concept with subjective wellbeing, but not an interchangeable equivalent.

Workplace wellbeing has become an important concern of psychology, especially organizational psychology. With the three missions of repairing damage, preventing mental health problems, and building on individuals' strengths, the science of psychology has turned more focused attention to the third mission at the heart of positive psychology. As such, research on character strengths and virtues is a cornerstone for individual wellbeing (Peterson & Seligman, 2004).

Cooper and Quick (2017) identify individual wellbeing as one key category of wellbeing to consider in addition to organizational and community wellbeing. The latter includes consideration of wellbeing in neighborhoods, wellbeing in an aging population, and wellbeing in a societal context. Bennett and his colleagues (2017) bring attention to wellbeing in the arena of the workplace as distinct from wellbeing in other arenas, such as the family.

Research traditions and foundations

There are a handful of research traditions from diverse disciplines that may be used as platforms from which future stress and wellbeing research trajectories may be launched. These include the psychobiology of psychiatrist Adolph Meyer (1922); the Grant Study research of psychiatrist George Vaillant (1977, 2012); the occupational stress research of organizational psychologist Sir Cary Cooper and his collaborators (cf., Cooper & Payne, 1978, 1980); the epidemiological Army STARRS research of sociologist and psychiatric epidemiologist Ron Kessler and his collaborators (Kessler et al., 2014; Nock et al., 2014; Schoenbaum et al., 2014); and the organizational behavior/public health approach of the Quick brothers, distilled into a salient measurements approach to organizational stress (Quick, 2020).

Psychobiology – life charts and occupation therapy

Adolph Meyer was the first psychiatrist-in-chief at Johns Hopkins and well known for his very detailed work building case histories of patients. His theoretical framework was psychobiology and a distinguishing aspect of his career was the concept of life charts for patients, which identified the points of major life change events as well as medical and psychiatric histories. In addition, he was an early advocate of occupation therapy (Meyer, 1922); that is, intervening in the workplace so that work would have a salutatory effect or a means of restoring an individual to health and wellbeing. His use of life charts led to his discovery that health problems often lagged major life change events by 12–18 months. That insight led Holmes and Rahe to begin systematic research on life change events as stressors that could be predictive of a range of psychological and medical health problems (Quick & Quick, 1984). Rahe (2009) then constructed pathways to health and resilience. Hence, the critical study of individual cases laid a foundation for subsequent large-scale research in the stress domain.

The Grant Study

The Grant Study was initiated in 1940 with the Harvard men who would become the Class of 1942. This cohort of men has been studied over the past 70 plus years. Their variations in stress and wellbeing over the decades has been probed and explored in great detail, both qualitatively and quantitatively. At the 35-year point in the research, Vaillant (1977) found two distinguishing lessons, one being that every single member of the class had experiences of one or another trauma or tragedy. The other lesson was that those who appeared to cope best with these life events had more mature psychological adaptive mechanisms, such as altruism and humor. One of the key lessons from his 70-year follow-up on the class was that a class member's wellbeing was importantly influenced by how he came to grips with life's regret(s). Those who made peace with important life regrets had more positive wellbeing.

Both Meyer and Vaillant anchor their research in an idiographic or case study approach and mode of inquiry. That mode of inquiry stands in contrast to the natural scientific approach of an experimental paradigm that aims at generalizability. For workplace assessments, Levinson's (2002) organizational diagnostic or organizational assessment approach is anchored in the same scientific tradition. Levinson's rigorous approach relies on a broad set of genetic and descriptive data about the workplace as well as interpretative data about attitudes and relationships.

Occupational stress research

The occupational stress research tradition of Sir Cary Cooper and his collaborators (cf., Cooper & Payne, 1978, 1980) is a very different one from Meyer's, Vaillant's, and Levinson's. Cooper's research tradition rests on the experimental, cause–effect paradigm of the natural sciences. This reductionist approach to stress and wellbeing research offers a way of exploring a wide range of stressors and demands as causes for the many forms of strain and distress that are manifest psychologically, medically, and/or behaviorally. This research approach offers a very complimentary one for the idiographic approach of Meyer, Vaillant, and Levinson.

This tradition also offers the opportunity to examine the fit between individuals and their work (i.e., occupations). Counterintuitive findings can emerge from such a line of inquiry, such as in the study of British bomb disposal officers assigned to Northern Ireland during the Troubles (Quick, 2011). In similar research in U.S. Army deep operations showing unique personality attributes being highly functional for clandestine, risky military missions, both sets of findings underline the importance of functional person–environment fit for high-risk work environments.

Army STARRS research

The American Long War in Afghanistan, Iraq, and the Middle East more broadly has created stresses, strains, and challenges that are consequential when it comes to the human costs. By 2008, there were a rising suicide rates across the U.S.'s five armed services, especially within the U.S. Army and Marine Corps who were those most in direct contact with enemy forces in Afghanistan and Iraq, as well as the accompanying rise in PTSD (post-traumatic stress disorder) and TBI (traumatic brain injury). In response, Secretary of Defense Robert Gates appointed 13 experts on psychological health to the Defense Health Board for three-year terms (2008–2011). General Casey (2011) launched a comprehensive soldier fitness program aimed at raising psychological resilience in the U.S. Army, though the results have been less than impressive. A second initiative was to undertake the largest epidemiological study in the history of the U.S. Army, aimed at understanding the underlying causes of the suicide rates. This followed the report of the Department of Defense Task Force on the Prevention of Suicide by Members of the Armed Forces to the Defense Health Board on 14 July 2010.

Results from the Army Study to Assess Risk and Resilience in Servicemembers (Army STARRS) were released in a set of three research articles in *JAMA Psychiatry*. Schoenbaum et al. (2014) found that increased suicide risk was associated with being a man (or a woman during deployment), white race/ethnicity, junior enlisted rank, recent demotion, and current or previous deployment. Their results debunk several hypotheses but set the stage for more in-depth analyses to help the Army identify high-risk soldiers and high-risk situations. Kessler et al. (2014) examined the prevalence of mental disorders and found about 25 percent of respondents met the criteria for a mental disorder. Of significance in their conclusions is the importance of pre-enlistment risk factors, such as childhood stresses and mental disorders, that pre-date military service. They suggest consideration be given to outreach and treatment problems for soldiers. Nock et al. (2014) found that approximately one-third of post-enlistment suicide attempts are associated with pre-enlistment mental disorders. This trilogy of Army STARRS research articles underlines the importance of pre-existing stresses and mental disorders in understanding workplace stress and strain.

Public health in the workplace

Macik-Frey et al. (2007) suggest that epidemiology is for assessing the burden of suffering in the workplace, both in terms of morbidity and mortality. Further, they suggest that public health in the workplace can offer a range of preventive interventions to ameliorate stress and enhance wellbeing. Goh et al. (2016) use epidemiology to examine workplace mortality in particular. They built a model to estimate the excess mortality and incremental health expenditures associated with exposure to ten workplace stressors: unemployment, lack of health insurance, exposure to shift work, long working hours, job insecurity, work–family conflict, low job control, high job demands, low social support at work, and low organizational justice. They argue that American business policies, practices, and the ways in which U.S. businesses manage their workforces contribute to workplace stress and harm employee wellbeing. Long working hours in particular increase workforce stress; that is, work in excess becomes a hazard despite the range of social, psychological, and economic benefits that accrue from work. Quick (2020) recommends using Goh et al.'s (2016) model for workplace screening along with Cascio and Boudreau's (2011) absenteeism and voluntary turnover assessments.

While Kessler and his colleagues (2014) do not suggest estimates of high-risk soldiers in the US Army, Quick and McFadyen (2017) suggest that 1–3 percent of employees may be in the high-risk category with the potential to become dangerous. Therefore, in line with Kessler's suggestion for outreach and screening, Quick (2020) has recommended three individual screening assessments in the workplace. These are: the Trait-State Anxiety Inventory (American Psychological Association, 2019a); Beck Depression Inventory (BDI) (American Psychological Association, 2019b); and Maslach Burnout Inventory (MBI) (cf., Maslach, 2006).

Research agenda for stress and wellbeing

Articulating an agenda for research on workplace stress and wellbeing is best done from the context of the established research traditions and foundations in these domains of knowledge. From the traditions just reviewed, we can set forth six trajectories for launching into the future. Rather than being subject focused in this agenda, the six trajectories are a cross of population, situation, and process focus. The six agenda trajectories for workplace stress and wellbeing are:

1. Research that is multidisciplinary in nature and avoids the narrow confines of a single discipline.
2. Research that focuses on the outliers, be those individuals or workplaces as a whole, from a normal distribution.
3. Research focused on high-risk situations and/or occupations where the costs of failure are especially high.
4. Research that emphasizes screening and surveillance mechanisms, especially for individuals within the workplace for early identification and early intervention.
5. Research examining targeted subgroups at two ends of the population, the most at risk and the top 10 percent top performers.
6. Research that takes the entire workplace as the subject of analysis, in contrast to the individual persons within the workplace.

Multidisciplinary research collaborations

Workplace stress and wellness research will benefit from more deeply embedding multidisciplinary collaborations as the standard in our programs of research. In 1998, the Workplace Health Group (WHG) was established to conduct multidisciplinary research in worker health, safety, and organizational effectiveness (Haynes et al., 2019). The occupational health psychology domain of research concerning workplace stress and wellbeing has trended toward multidisciplinary collaborations. This is reflected across the *Handbook of Occupational Health Psychology* (Quick & Tetrick, 2011) and in Macik-Frey et al. (2007: p. 812, Figure 1) whose model of occupational health in the context of the workplace scientific shows contributions from not only psychology but also epidemiology (preventive medicine) and engineering. Another multidisciplinary example is Hammer et al.'s (2011) attention to the work–family boundary and encouragement of family-supportive supervisory behaviors that benefit all concerned by relying on psychology and family systems research. Setting a standard for multidisciplinary research teams for workplace stress and wellbeing poses challenges as well as opportunities (cf., Haynes et al., 2019).

One of the key challenges for multidisciplinary research surrounds the conflicts across disciplinary boundaries. Quick and Quick (1984) experienced substantive disciplinary conflict through the process of translating the public health notions of prevention and medicine into the workplace context of organizational stress and psychology. Psychologists from the American Psychological Association experienced a parallel conflict when in a joint meeting with public health professionals and epidemiologists in Atlanta at the Centers for Disease Control and Prevention. The constructs, the concepts, and the within-discipline knowledge bases can be so dramatically different that the process is like speaking different languages. However, these differing points of view offer the potential for a more 360-degree understanding of the workplace and the individuals therein. Thus, having preventive conflict management skills can help advance multidisciplinary research.

Another example of such a multidisciplinary research collaboration was implemented by Klunder (2008), an organizational clinical psychologist, in a six-year applied intervention in a large logistics and maintenance workplace impacting 13,000 personnel. Under the authority of the chief executive of the organization, Klunder assembled a multidisciplinary team to oversee mental health during a major realignment, restructuring, and closure process. The multidisciplinary team included: occupational medicine, social work, human resources, chaplains, security personnel, and occupational safety. This multi-disciplinary team provided a 360-degree view of the organization, workplace, and individuals within it for early intervention and distress prevention.

One of the keys to success in multidisciplinary team research is one or more conflict resolution mechanisms. Preventive conflict management is an essential interpersonal skill that can rely on structural mechanisms, such as discerning use of authority, or process mechanisms, such as reflective listening and empathy (Nelson & Quick, 2019). For Klunder (2008), the benefits were materially realized in the absence of individual fatalities and workplace violence as well as, according to HR estimates, over US$33,000,000 in cost savings over the six-year period, which equates to roughly US$5,500,000 savings on an annual basis.

Outliers and unexpected events

Outliers may be considered the "unexpected" and some might argue that they should be discounted when looking for generalizable patterns or trends. Weick and Sutcliffe (2015) argue that managing the unexpected is crucial to the success of high reliability organizations; ones that also are good stress managers and have high levels of wellbeing. Failures are a perfect example of the unexpected in organizations and should be outliers in the normal distribution of events in an organization. However, rather than discounting the failure as an outlier or random event, Weick and Sutcliffe (2015) argue that the organization should be focused on and preoccupied with these specific events, asking a host of questions such as: Why did this unexpected event happen? How did this unexpected event happen? The aim here is to focus on learning and exploring the processes surrounding the unexpected event rather than aiming to find a scapegoat to blame for the event. Scapegoating is an ancient social process that humans use to affix blame when something wrong, bad, unexpected, or harmful occurs. This social process shuts down learning, avoids the process of exploring corrective actions that may be engaged to prevent future failures, and wastes the opportunity offered by the outlier. Exploring the uniqueness and distinctiveness of the failure enables change and organizational transformation.

Organizations can either aspire to be normal or aspire to be healthy and these are not necessarily the same thing. Normal is that which falls within the center of a distribution for organizations and/or individuals. On the other hand, healthy is that which is optimally or maximally functional for the individual or the organization. Thus, costs associated with the unexpected failure as an outlier may be viewed as tuition payments for lessons yet to be learned. While failures are outliers at one end of the distribution, extraordinary human achievements are outliers at the other end of the distribution. One example would be the complex process of landing men on the moon and returning them safely to earth. So, outliers at either end of the distribution are worthy of research.

High-risk situations and high-risk occupations

Schoenbaum et al. (2014) emphasize the importance of high-risk situations in their conclusions. The study of bomb disposal officers is an example of a high-risk occupation where failure has devastating consequences for not only the individual but potentially others. Because of the mortality and morbidity costs associated with high-risk situations and high-risk occupations, research on workplace stress and wellbeing can leverage benefits for individuals, worksites, and the larger community by developing a typology of high-risk situations and high-risk occupations. Weick and Sutcliffe's (2015) approach is to create high-reliability organizations that manage unexpected events with resilience. Theirs is a response to the high-risk situations and high-risk occupations. To benefit from their work, the field of workplace stress and wellbeing needs two things: (1) dimensionality for defining and identifying high-risk situations and (2) occupational stress and wellbeing studies.

The first requirement is for a typology or classification scheme that identifies the dimensionality of high-risk situations. Some such situations are intuitively obvious, such as open steel work at high elevations in building construction.

A failure or a miss step in that work context is potentially catastrophic and fatal for the individual worker. Or, a military combatant in a war zone aiming to engage enemy combatants. Beyond that which is intuitively obvious, the field needs more discerning detail and potentially a scale against which work situations may be classified as high risk to low risk. Uncertainty would be one dimension of real importance. Weick and Sutcliffe (2015) focus on the unexpected as a key dimension for consideration. Beyond the physical dangers of a worksite, there is the host of psychosocial hazards that should be considered a dimensions of a high-risk situation. The potential for interpersonal abuse and destructive conflict, which contrasts with positive conflict leading to creative outcomes, are also dimensions to consider in defining high-risk situations (cf., Quick & McFadyen's, 2017 extensive 20-year review of sexual harassment in the workplace).

Screening and surveillance mechanisms

Research that focuses on workplace screening and surveillance mechanisms for stress and wellbeing will benefit from standardization. This might be thought of as taking the vital signs for the worksite much as a physician takes an individual patient's vital signs at the outset of a consultation, including heart rate, temperature, blood pressure, and often height and weight.

Screening and surveillance in workplaces should include three individual risk/strain indicators and three worksite risk/strain indicators.

The individual risk/strain indicators are anxiety, depression, and burnout. As early as 1980, NIOSH identified stress and psychological disorders in the workplace as among the top ten occupational health hazards in America (Sauter et al., 1990). The two leading presenting complaints for stress are anxiety disorders and depression (Quick & Cooper, 2003). In addition, burnout is an ongoing concern in the workplace (Maslach, 2006). Research in the American Orthopaedic Association using the Maslach Burnout Inventory found emergent burnout among academic leaders within the profession, offering an opportunity for early intervention and prevention (Quick et al., 2006).

The worksite risk/strain indicators are turnover, absenteeism, and high-risk employees. Cascio and Boudreau (2011) use a well-developed, systematic research approach to costing employee attitudes and behaviors for organizations. Their two key indicators are turnover and absenteeism. Turnover rates are easily monitored by an organization and then benchmarked with industry and national standards. The costs associated with turnover include separation costs and replacement costs (Cascio & Boudreau, 2011), which may escalate markedly if these is a violent workplace event following from an involuntary turnover. Cascio and Boudreau (2011) suggest that the voluntary turnover is what the organization should primarily monitor and manage. While some involuntary turnover can be healthy for the organization by removing under-performing employees and refreshing the workplace with vital and energetic newcomers, the risks of violent responses by select involuntary turnover individuals requires monitoring.

Absenteeism, including sick leave, is the second key organizational indicator of concern (Cascio & Boudreau, 2011). They estimate that 16 percent of absenteeism can be directly attributable to organizational stress and another 26 percent to family-related issues. They estimate that 60 percent may be caused by personal illness (sick leave), personal needs, and sense of entitlement. So, there may be hidden costs and hidden issues embedded within the absenteeism rates that management may need to explore more deeply below the indicator numbers themselves.

The third worksite risk/strain indicator is high-risk employees, who are estimated to compose about 1–3 percent of a work population (Quick et al., 2014). Our research suggests that these employees cannot be screened out in the recruiting process. However, early identification of high-risk employees offers an opportunity for psychological, financial, or family counselling, or other stress-related preventive intervention, precluding them from becoming dangerous (Klunder, 2008). With the levels of gun violence and drug addiction in the larger American culture, this category of surveillance and monitoring is well warranted. Research that explores the mechanisms giving rise to anxiety, depression, burnout, turnover, absenteeism, and high-risk employees has upside potential.

Targeted subgroups within the workforce

The primary focus in twentieth-century stress and wellbeing research focused on how stress could harm, compromise, impair, cause disease and dysfunction, and/or kill (cf., Quick et al., 1997). This led to an inevitable focus on subgroups within the workforce who displayed signs and symptoms of distress. The accompanying psychological and behavioral strategies for these subgroups of employees was the development of prevention and repair mechanisms for intervention and treatment. For example, the U.S. Defense Health Board circa 2009–2010 began focusing attention on the groups of soldiers from the Long War who were exhibiting PTSD and TBI symptoms, a minority of combat veterans who were distressed. In addition, the Defense Health Board attended to the subgroup of soldiers, sailors, airmen, and marines who committed suicide (cf., Kessler et al., 2014). Advancing prevention and treatment interventions for the subgroups in work populations continues to be needed but more focus needs to be placed on eustress and the positive side of the stress and wellbeing (Nelson & Simmons, 2011; Quick et al., 2013).

In the late 1990s there was a recognition that the positive aspects of stress had been overlooked or at least not fully acknowledged (Fredrickson, 2009). The flip side of distressed employees with negative wellbeing is that group of employees who are thriving, filled with vigor, vitality, and eustress. Gallup's 2008–2017 national trends data on thriving show an increase from 49 percent to 56 percent. What strengths are the groups that thrive drawing on to achieve healthy stress management and positive wellbeing? Are these strengths innate or are they amenable to teaching, learning, and development? "What do we know about the top 10% of our young men and women who are exposed to armed conflict, chronic war stress, and trauma yet keep on ticking with vigor and vitality?" (Quick, 2011: p. 645). The psychological health members of the U.S. Defense Health Board had no answer. However, this is the kind of question we need to be asking of subgroups within our workplaces that fall in this top 10 percent.

The workplace as the subject

Levinson (2002) takes the workplace as the subject of analysis and provides a framework that focuses on a detailed understanding of the workplace for the purpose of identifying stresses and strains. The purpose is not to achieve generalizability of results to other workplaces. Rather, the comprehensive approach that Levinson offers involves examining generic data, descriptive data, analysis of current workplace functioning, interpretative data focused on inferences drawn, and interpretative data about attitudes and relationships. This approach to workplace stress and wellbeing provides a foundation for scientific management of the workplace as a dynamic system, in contrast to the practice of management science which aims at research findings that can be generalized across organizations. Levinson's (2002) approach provides for a real-time assessment of the workplace and the individuals who work within it, using assessments of stress, wellbeing, and dynamic functioning as a scientific basis for then intervening to improve the health and wellbeing of the workplace.

While there is value in quantitative, nomothetic research based on cause–effect relationships that can lead to generalizable evidence (American Psychological Association, 2020: p. 77), that scientific model has the potential to discount the unique issues of the individual subject or case. Using Levinson's assessment framework places the emphasis on history, versus cause and effect, and the interpretation of the workplace as a dynamically functioning entity. This category of research falls in the categories of qualitative or mixed methods research (American Psychological Association, 2020: pp. 93, 105). Levinson's approach to assessing workplace stress and wellbeing is a complement to other research paradigms that take individuals or workplaces as subjects of analysis.

Conclusion

This chapter has taken a look back at a number of research traditions in workplace stress and wellbeing that contain within them launch points for trajectories into future research pathways that advance our knowledge and practice. The six-point research agenda offered in the chapter emphasizes multidisciplinary points of view, consideration of outliers and unexpected events, high-risk situations and occupations, screening and surveillance mechanisms, targeted subgroups within workplace populations, and the workplace itself as the subject of analysis.

References

American Psychological Association (2019a). The Trait-State Anxiety Inventory. https://www.apa.org/pi/about/publications/caregivers/practice-settings/assessment/tools/trait-state (downloaded 30 September)

American Psychological Association (2019b). Beck Depression Inventory (BDI). https://www.apa.org/depression-guideline/assessment/ (downloaded 30 September).

American Psychological Association. (2020). *Publication Manual of the American Psychological Association*, Seventh Edition. Washington, DC: American Psychological Association.

Bennett, J.B., Weaver, J., Senft, M., & Neeper, M. (2017). Creating workplace well-being. In C.L. Cooper & J.C. Quick (Eds.) *The Handbook of Stress and Health: A Guide to Research and Practice*, pp. 570–604. Chichester, UK: Wiley Blackwell.

Benison, S. Barger, A.C., & Wolfe, E.L. (1987). *Walter B. Cannon: The Life and Times of a Young Scientist*. Cambridge, MA: Belknap Press of Harvard University Press.

Cascio, W.F. & Boudreau, J.W. (2011). *Investing in People: Financial Impact of Human Resource Initiatives* (2nd Ed.). Upper Saddle Ridge, NJ: Pearson Education/FT Press.

Casey, G.W. Jr. (2011). Comprehensive soldier fitness: A vision for psychological resilience in the U.S. Army. *American Psychologist*, 66(1), 1–3.

Cooper, C. L. (1998). *Theories of Organizational Stress*. Oxford, UK: Oxford University Press.

Cooper, C.L., & Payne, R. (Eds.) (1978). *Stress at Work*. New York: John Wiley & Sons.

Cooper, C.L., & Payne, R. (Eds.) (1980). *Current Concerns in Occupational Stress*. New York: John Wiley & Sons.

Cooper, C.L., & Quick, J.C. (2017). *The Handbook of Stress and Health: A Guide to Research and Practice*. Chichester, UK: Wiley Blackwell.

Diener, E., Suh, E.M., Lucas, E.R., & Smith, H.L. (1999). Subjective well-being: Three decades of progress. *Psychological Bulletin*, 125, 276–302.

Fredrickson, B. (2009). *Positivity: Groundbreaking Research Reveals how to Embrace the Hidden Strength of Positive Emotions, Overcome Negativity, and Thrive*. New York, NY: Crown Publishers.

Goh, J., Pfeffer, J. & Zenios, S.A. (2016). The relationship between workplace stressors and mortality and health costs in the United States. *Management Science*, 62(2), 608–628.

Hammer, L.B., Kossek, E.E., Anger, W.K., Bodner, T., & Zimmerman, K.L. (2011). Clarifying work–family intervention processes: The roles of work–family conflict and family-supportive supervisor behaviors. *Journal of Applied Psychology*, 96(1), 134–150.

Hargrove, M.B., Quick, J.C., Nelson, D.L., & Quick, J.D. (2011). The theory of preventive stress management: A 33-year review and evaluation. *Stress and Health*, 27(3), 182–193.

Haynes, N.J., Vandenberg, R.J., DeJoy, D.M., Wilson, M.G., Padilla, H.M., Zuecher, H.S., & Robertson, M.M. (2019). The workplace health group: A case study of 20 years of multidisciplinary research. *American Psychologist*, 74(3), 380–393.

Kahn, R.L., Wolfe, R.P., Quinn, R.P., Snoek, J.D., & Rosenthal, R.A. (1964). *Organizational Stress: Studies in Role Conflict and Ambiguity*. New York: John Wiley & Sons.

Kessler, R.C., Heeringa, S.G., Stein, M.B., Colpe, L.J., Fullerton, C.S., Hwang, I., Naifeh, J.A., Nock, M.K., Petukhova, M., Sampson, N.A., Schoenbaum, M., Zaslavsky, A.M., & Ursano, R.J. (2014). Thirty-day prevalence of *DSM-IV* mental disorders among nondeployed soldiers in the US Army: Results from the Army Study of Assess Risk and Resilience in Servicemembers (Army STARRS). *JAMA Psychiatry*, 71(5), 504–513.

Klunder, C.S. (2008). Preventive stress management at work: The case of the San Antonio Air Logistics Center, Air Force Materiel Command (AFMC). *Managing and Leading: SPIM Conference and Institutes*, San Antonio, 29 February.

Levi, L. (2000). *Guidance on Work-Related Stress: Spice of Life or Kiss of Death?* Luxembourg: European Commission, Directorate-General for Employment and Social Affairs, Health & Safety at Work (100 pages).

Levinson, H. (2002). *Organizational Assessment*. Washington, DC: American Psychological Assocation.

Macik-Frey, M., Quick, J.C., & Nelson, D.L. (2007). Advances in occupational health: From a stressful beginning to a positive future. *Journal of Management*, 33(6), 809–840.

Maslach, C. (2006). Understanding job burnout. In A.M. Rossi, P.L. Perrewé, & S.L. Sauter (Eds.), *Stress and Quality of Working Life: Current Perspectives in Occupational Work*, pp. 37–51. Greenwich, CT: Information Age Publishing.

Meyer, A. (1922). The philosophy of occupation therapy. *Archives of Occupational Therapy*, 1, 1–10.

Mill, J.S. (1910). *Utilitarianism, Liberty, and Representative Government*. London: Dent.

Nelson, D.L., & Quick, J.C. (2019). *ORGB[6]: Organizational Behavior*. Mason, OH: Cengage/South-Western.

Nelson, D.L. & Simmons, B.L. (2011). Savoring eustress whole coping with distress: The holistic model of stress. In J.C. Quick & L.E. Tetrick (Eds.), *Handbook of Occupational Health Psychology*, pp. 37–54. Washington, DC: American Psychological Association.

Nock, M.K., Stein, M.B., Heeringa, S.G., Ursano, R.J. Colpe, L.J., Fullerton, C.S., Hwang, I., Naifeh, J.A., Petukhova, M., Sampson, N.A., Schoenbaum, M., Zaslavsky, A.M., & Kessler, R.C. (2014). Prevalence and correlates of suicidal behavior among soldiers: Results from the Army Study of Assess Risk and Resilience in Servicemembers (Army STARRS). *JAMA Psychiatry*, 71(5), 514–522.

Peterson, C. & Seligman, M.E.P. (2004). *Character Strengths and Virtues*. Oxford and New York: American Psychological Association and Oxford University Press.

Quick, J.C. (2011). Missing: Critical and skeptical perspectives on comprehensive soldier fitness. *American Psychologist*, 66(7), 645.

Quick, J.C. (2020). Organizational stress in the United States of America: Research and practice. In K. Sharma, C.L. Cooper & D.M. Pestonjee (Eds.), *Organizational Stress Around the World: Research and Practice*. Abingdon, UK: Taylor & Francis, 303–317.

Quick, J. C., & Cooper, C. L. (2003). *Stress and Strain*, Second Edition. Oxford, UK: Health Press.

Quick, J.C., & McFadyen, A. (2017). Sexual harassment: Have we made any progress? *Journal of Occupational Health Psychology*, 22(3), 286–298.

Quick, J.C. & Quick, J.D. (1984). *Organizational Stress and Preventive Management*. New York: McGraw-Hill.

Quick, J.C. & Quick, J.D. (2013). Executive well-being. In A. Caza & K.S. Cameron (Eds.), *Happiness and Organizations*, Section VII in S.A. David, I. Boniwell & A. Conley Ayers (Eds.), *The Oxford Handbook of Happiness*, pp. 798–813. Oxford, UK: Oxford University Press.

Quick, J.C., & Tetrick, L.E. (Eds.) (2011). *Handbook of Occupational Health Psychology*, Second Edition. Washington, DC: American Psychological Association.

Quick, J.C., McFadyen, A., & Nelson, D.L. (2014). No accident: Health, well-being, performance... and danger. *Journal of Organizational Effectiveness*, 1(1), 98–119.

Quick, J.C., Quick, J.D., Nelson, D.L., & Hurrell, J.J. (1997). *Preventive Stress Management in Organizations*. Washington, DC: American Psychological Association.

Quick, J.C., Saleh, K.J., Sime, W.E., Martin, W., Cooper, C.L., Quick, J.D., and Mont, M.A. (2006). Stress management skills for strong leadership: Is it worth dying for? *Journal of Bone & Joint Surgery*, 88(1), 217–225.

Quick, J.C., Wright, T.A., Adkins, J.A., Nelson, D.L. & Quick, J.D. (2013). *Preventive Stress Management in Organizations*, Second Edition. Washington, DC: American Psychological Association.

Rahe, R.H. (2009). *Paths to Health and Resilience*. Reno, NV: Health Assessment Programs. *Stanford Encyclopedia of Philosophy* (2008). Palo Alto, CA: Stanford University.

Sauter, S.L., Murphy, L.R. and Hurrell, J.J. (1990) Prevention of work-related psychological disorders: A national strategy proposed by the National Institute for Occupational Safety and Health (NIOSH), *American Psychologist*, 45(10), 1146–1158.

Schoenbaum, M., Kessler, R.C., Gilman, S.E., Colpe, L.J., Heeringa, S.G., Stein, M.B., Ursano, R.J., & Cox, K.L. (2014). Predictors of suicide and accident death in the Army Study to Assess Risk and Resilience in Servicemembers (Army STARRS). *JAMA Psychiatry*, 71(5), 493–503.

Smith, A. (1759). *The Theory of the Moral Sentiments*. Edinburgh, Scotland: A. Kincaid and J. Bell.

Smith, A. (1910). *An Inquiry into the Nature and Causes of the Wealth of Nations*. In C.J. Bullock (Ed.), *Harvard Classics, Volume 10*, New York: P.F. Collier & Son.

Vaillant, G.E. (1977). *Adaptation to Life*. Boston: Little, Brown.

Vaillant, G.E. (2012). *Triumphs of Experience: The Men of the Harvard Grant Study*. Boston: Belknap Press of Harvard University Press.

Weick, K.E. & Sutcliffe, K.M. (2015). *Managing the Unexpected*, Third Edition. Hoboken, NJ: John Wiley & Sons, Inc.

Wright, T.A., & Cropanzano, R. (2004). The role of psychological well-being in job performance. *Organizational Dynamics*, 33, 338–351.

3. The cost of stress to UK employers and employees

Christian van Stolk[1]

Employers lose a significant amount of productive time due to employees being absent from work and employees being in suboptimal health while they are at work. Sickness absence is very visible and therefore relatively straightforward to measure. Many organisations have elaborate processes to manage and reduce sickness absence over time. Presenteeism or employees losing productive time because of suboptimal health while at work is more difficult to conceptualise and therefore harder to measure. However, most estimates suggest that presenteeism is a far more significant issue for employers than the more visible sickness absence measure. The Centre for Mental Health (2018) suggested in 2011 that presenteeism costs the UK economy about double the amount lost due to sickness absence. Our own analysis using Britain's Healthiest Workplace (BHW) data, an initiative that has surveyed participating employers and employees on health and wellbeing in the workplace since 2014, suggests that presenteeism is far more significant than absenteeism, perhaps tenfold on the basis of the data that the BHW surveys collect annually. In 2018, the BHW survey of a selection of UK employers found that overall productivity loss was 13.7 per cent of working days in the UK per worker surveyed, with absenteeism accounting for 1.2 per cent of working days lost and presenteeism for 12.5 per cent.[2] The difference in these estimates between studies possibly reflects the varying approaches used to conceptualise and measure presenteeism.

These findings on absenteeism and presenteeism matter. Productivity is a salient topic internationally as governments since the crisis of 2008 worry about the slowdown of employee productivity and its impact on economic growth. Employee health and wellbeing also offers shared value between employers and society whereby employers focusing on improvements in the health and wellbeing of their employees could improve their bottom line, change their engagement with staff, and also contribute to improvement in the public health of a nation. As such, there appears to be a solid business case for all stakeholders to invest in employee health and wellbeing.

Moreover, this chapter was written at the start of the COVID-19 pandemic. It stands to reason that the pandemic will lead to profound changes in working practices that could be far-reaching and lasting. It is obvious that the COVID-19 crisis will impact employee health and wellbeing. Any impact of COVID-19 on productivity as measured by presenteeism and absenteeism will contribute to the undoubtedly significant impacts of the crisis on the workplace, employment and the economy.

The question remains what drives absenteeism and presenteeism. There are two main health conditions that are often cited (see e.g. Johns 2010) and disproportionally lead to people struggling to maintain employment: mental health and musculoskeletal conditions. At any given point in time, around one in six people of working age in England have a mental health condition.[3] Of these, the majority have either depressive disorders, anxiety disorders, or a mixture of the two (NHSIC, 2009). Musculoskeletal conditions account for about 55 per cent of all work-related illness and are the second most commonly identified cause of long-term absence for manual workers (44 per cent) (Zheltoukhova et al., 2012). The Office for National Statistics (2014) in the UK found that musculoskeletal conditions cost the UK economy more than 30 million working days in 2013. Musculoskeletal conditions also show comorbidity with a range of other conditions, including mental health.

Econometric modelling on BHW data looked in particular at the determinants of absenteeism and presenteeism (Hafner et al., 2015). The findings suggest that lack of sleep and financial concerns are negatively associated with productivity (or positively with productivity loss). Mental health problems as diagnosed in the Kessler-6 scale, a binary measure to understand whether someone is at risk of depression and anxiety, are also positively associated with productivity loss, especially in the form of presenteeism. In line with findings in other studies (see e.g. Johns, 2010; Kuoppala et al., 2008; Schultz and Edington, 2007; Waddell et al., 2006), Hafner et al. (2015) also found that employees with musculoskeletal and other chronic health conditions (e.g. diabetes, cardiovascular issues) report higher rates of absenteeism and presenteeism than workers without such conditions.

When looking at the work environment Hafner et al. (2015) find that workers who are bullied in the workplace report significantly higher levels of absenteeism and presenteeism than those who are not. Finally, the study finds that more than 45 per cent of those employees surveyed reported being subject to unrealistic time pressures, which is associated with an increase in presenteeism.

Some of these findings confirm what we broadly expect. Mental health and musculoskeletal conditions are important factors of productivity loss. However, a wider range of factors relating to the work environment show up as significant in several studies.

One variable that connects the work environment to mental health and other health conditions is workplace stress. Workplace stress is not a medical condition and can be difficult to define. However, the concept captures how the workplace is affecting individual employees, their health and wellbeing, and their productivity. In this chapter, we want to focus in particular on stress in the workplace and try to understand what data collected in BHW tell us about its impact on absenteeism and presenteeism (or broadly productivity loss).

What is BHW and how do we define stress and productivity loss?

The Britain's Healthiest Workplace (BHW) Survey has been conducted by RAND Europe since 2014. The surveys were initially designed together with the Institute of Public Health and the University of Cambridge in 2013. BHW collects responses from employers and their employees through the Organisational Health Assessment (OHA) and the Employee Health Assessment (EHA) respectively. Participation is voluntary. The initiative is advertised widely in the UK and participation is also encouraged through networks managed by Vitality Health, an insurer in the UK; Mercer, the benefits company; and the *Financial Times*, a leading business publication. Participating organisations return the OHA, including general organisational characteristics such as the size and nature of the organisation, the work environment, and information on the organisation's approach to health promotion and wellbeing interventions. This information is typically supplied by a human resources (HR) professional or finance director. Subsequently, employees are invited to respond to the EHA, which collects socio-demographic information on them (such as age, gender, income, general background); lifestyle and behavioural and clinical risk factors (including weight, diet, exercise, smoking, alcohol intake, stress, cholesterol and blood pressure); information about the work environment and culture; and how often people participate in organisational health and wellbeing interventions. The EHA has about 150 questions that aim to provide a holistic picture of health and wellbeing in the workplace.

The initiative stipulates that a minimum number of employees per organisation have to participate. This is a percentage of employees for each organisation to give us confidence in the significance of the sample. Typically, about 30,000 employees participate and about 200–250 employers. The sample is not aimed to be representative of all employers in the UK. The sample is also not consistent year on year. Some employers have participated over all the years and some participate only in a given year or return after a couple of years. BHW has a small cohort of employees who have participated consistently over the years. However, the aim of BHW is not to build a cohort over time but it aims to take the pulse of what is happening in UK workplaces.

Overall, we find an over-representation of companies with greater numbers of middle-income and middle-age employees, and/or with higher proportions of female employees. However, estimates of health measures such as the body mass index (BMI) change little after weighting, and BMI estimates from respondents are only slightly different from a nationally representative group of employees. Nevertheless, it is important to stress that in general response rates are typically lower among the very old, the very young, and those living in lower-income areas. It is also possible that employees with healthier lifestyles are more likely to respond than employees with less healthy lifestyles. The implications for this survey are that respondents may not be typical of all respondents within participating companies, nor participating companies of all employers in the UK. However, the implications of these potential biases for the analyses presented in the rest of this chapter are low. All income, age and gender groups are represented among respondents, and in the analysis we also adjust for socio-demographic and company characteristics.

BHW collects a range of outcome measures. The initiative tries to align these measures with outcome measures used in the international literature or devised by regulators. For instance, BHW's productivity loss measure is the Work Productivity Activity Impairment scale (WPAI) (Reilly et al., 1993). This measure asks respondents about their health, the amount of time they spent at work, their contracted hours, sickness absence and whether their health impacted their work. WPAI is a one week recall scale and allows researchers to calculate both absenteeism and presenteeism. The measure is widely used and comparative data are available through a wide range of studies published on the Reilly Associates website.[4]

Our stress in the workplace measure comes from the Health and Safety Executive (HSE), the main workplace health regulator in the UK. HSE defines stress as 'the adverse reaction people have to excessive pressures or other types of demand placed on them' (HSE, 2019). BHW tracks stress in the workplace by looking at management standards in the workplace around stress. In particular, BHW looks at a number of components that contribute to employees feeling stressed as defined by HSE (see e.g. 2014). These include:

- Demands: this includes workload, work patterns and the work environment.
- Control: This includes how much autonomy (choice) and say employees have.
- Support: This includes resources and support from line managers.
- Relationships: this includes avoiding conflict and dealing with unacceptable behaviour such as bullying.
- Role: this includes whether employees are clear about the role that they are performing.
- Change: This includes whether organisational change is managed and communicated well.

Our modelling approach

Broadly, the main meta-reviews on the factors of workplace absenteeism and presenteeism (or productivity loss) group determinants of workplace productivity into three broad categories.

Cancelliere et al. (2011) look at the association between workplace programmes and HR practice and presenteeism. These studies are interested in specific aspects of the work environment and the employer offer. These find that successful approaches offer organisational leadership, health risk screening, individually tailored programmes, and a supportive workplace culture. Other reviews such as Lohaus and Habermann (2019) provide a wide overview of workplace correlates and presenteeism. They start considering cause and effect and indeed the interaction between variables. So, job design and workplace related factors is broadly a first group.

Most studies see stress as an expression of the pressure that the work environment or workplace factors put on an employee. Stress has been identified as a significant factor of presenteeism. Callen et al. (2013) find that workplace stress, home stress and financial stress show a relationship with presenteeism. They do not find statistically significant relationships for other health risks. The interesting finding here is also the interaction between workplace factors and home life. Other studies also look at intermediate variables. Coutu et al. (2015) shows the negative association between presenteeism and psychological distress. Both individual and organisational factors are related to psychological distress. Krpalek et al. (2014) focus on intermediate variables that interact with stress and presenteeism. Presenteeism in and by itself can cause stress, Stress in turn impacts on presenteeism once more (see e.g. Lu et al., 2013).

In this chapter, we do not account for the dynamic relationships between workplace factors and stress but rather run variables such as the HSE management standards next to factors such as leadership and the health and wellbeing offer in a workplace.

A second group of studies focuses on the association between health and productivity. Schultz and Edington (2007) in their systematic review look at the relationship between health conditions and presenteeism. They show the costs of health conditions exceeding the cost of medical care and find statistically significant relationships between conditions such as allergies and arthritis and presenteeism. However, they also identify an association between productivity loss and lifestyle factors such as physical activity and body weight. In their subsequent review in 2009, Schultz et al. also show the relative weight of some of these conditions and start presenting a business case for employers to manage the health and wellbeing in staff in order to manage the costs associated with specific conditions. Other reviews look more explicitly at the link between conditions such as poor mental health (see e.g. Evans-Lacko and Knapp, 2016) and physical activity (Burton et al. 2014) and workplace productivity. The former is important as it was somewhat absent in the meta-reviews of Schultz and Eddington (2007). Some studies focus on lifestyle risks as well as more chronic conditions (Kowlessar et al., 2011).

In this chapter, we separate out lifestyle factors from more chronic conditions. Survey-based productivity measures are by definition short-term impressions of productivity loss and could therefore be more sensitive to lifestyle factors such as mental health and lack of sleep compared to chronic conditions. This is something that the modelling aims to test.

In the BHW surveys, many of our variables map onto these categories.

1. Job- and workplace-related factors: the HSE management standards, organisational and leadership commitment to health and wellbeing, HR practices.
2. Personal and modifiable lifestyle factors, which include financial wellbeing, caring responsibilities, obesity, mental health, sleep, alcohol use, smoking, nutrition, financial wellbeing, caring responsibilities.

3. Health and physical factors include existing (long-term) health conditions such as musculoskeletal conditions, blood pressure, glucose, cholesterol, other chronic conditions such as cancer etc.

To explore the associations between workplace productivity and the groups of factors outlined above, such as work demands, health problems, lifestyle factors, and organisations' attitudes towards health and wellbeing, we apply ordinary least squares (OLS) regression analysis. In particular, we are interested in the singular contribution of stress as measured by the HSE management standards to productivity loss as captured by the WPAI. In terms of the HSE management standards, we break this variable down into its constituent parts (the six dimensions outlined above) and look at the dimensions individually.

In reality, there is likely to be a substantial interaction between variables and as such we expect dynamic effects. It stands to reason that stress at work may contribute to mental health conditions or that poor workplace policies may lead to stress at work. To capture these effects requires a more longitudinal perspective. Our BHW data is not well set up to do this. Rather, as stated earlier, we focus on the singular contributions that variables make to productivity loss while controlling for the other factors. These factors also include, as mentioned before, many socio-demographic factors such as age, income gender and ethnicity.

A linear regression model is used to describe the relation between two or more variables in a set of data points with a line. OLS is a statistical approach to fitting a model to the observed data by finding the function which most closely approximates (or best fits) the data (Wooldridge, 2010). In technical terms, the OLS method is used to fit a straight line through a set of data points so that the sum of the squared vertical distances (called residuals) from the actual data-points is minimised. Therefore, the best fit can be represented by the line that minimises the total distance between the actual data points and the predicted values.

The statistical analysis is conducted using STATA Version 15. All results, as is common in this type of analysis, are presented at the 5 per cent significance level or lower.

Findings

We report on the relationships between what we conceptualise as the factors associated with productivity loss and the WPAI, our measure of productivity loss. Productivity loss captures the sum of absenteeism and presenteeism. This is typically reported as the number of days lost across a workplace due to absenteeism and presenteeism. In our analysis, we report this as the number of days lost due to a specific factor. This represents the number of days lost per worker that has this factor (e.g. obesity, or lack of sleep). It is important to note that some factors are more prevalent in a population than others. We group the factors in the categories outlined above. Of course, we cannot always be clear on the direction of causality. It could be that lower productivity loss in a workplace in and by itself causes less stress or better lifestyles. However, we test the relationships that have been outlined in the wider literature. In this analysis we use 2018 BHW data.

Job- and workplace-related factors

In our analysis, we find statistically significant relationships between many of the HSE dimensions and productivity loss (see Table 3.1). Those who experience bullying also report more than 11 days of productivity loss adjusting for age and income and controlling for other factors. Relationships at work are important. When those relationships are strained, we see an impact on productivity loss with those who report it losing on average about six days of productive time more compared to those who do not. Those with unrealistic time demands report about seven days. This is a broadly similar productivity loss compared to those who do not get the respect they deserve from their peers and those who are not clear what their role is at work. A good relationship with the line manager matters as well. Those who report that their line manager does not encourage them at work lose nearly five days more than those who do not. This appears to matter more than other leadership dimensions in our analysis. Change at work and control (or choice at work) are significant factors but appear to result in fewer days lost than the other HSE dimensions.

It is also important to consider the prevalence of the HSE dimensions in the population. The most prevalent dimensions that are reported by employees is not being consulted about change at work (32 per cent of those surveyed) followed by lack of choice at work or control (21.1 per cent). The more significant factors in terms of days lost per employee also tend to be somewhat less prevalent. Only 1 per cent reports being bullied, though 11.3 per cent report relationships being strained. Overall, 56.5 per cent of employees that participated in the BHW survey report one dimension of stress and 26.4 per cent report two different HSE dimensions of stress. Over 35 per cent of employees surveyed felt that work-related stress was making them feel unwell.

There are some other factors that are significant and some that we may have expected to be significant that are not. The health and wellbeing offer does not appear to be significant in our analysis. This may be due to the low levels of awareness among employees of the offer (about 50 per cent in BHW) and as a result low levels of participation in health and wellbeing programmes (about 8–9 per cent in BHW) that we find in many workplaces. As a result, we cannot be specific in this analysis about which aspects of a health and wellbeing offer contribute positively or negatively to productivity loss. Another interesting factor is the relationship between long commutes and productivity loss. Those who commute more than 60 minutes per day also report significantly higher productivity loss, close to two days lost.

Personal and modifiable lifestyle factors

BHW includes a range of personal and modifiable lifestyle factors. Our analysis finds a number of statistically significant relationships. Being at risk in most lifestyle factors show a positive association with productivity loss. For instance, not being physically active is associated with six additional days of productivity loss. Lack of physical activity is also prevalent in the population, with 33.3 per cent exercising less than 150 minutes of moderate activity a week. Lack of sleep is associated with nearly four additional productive days lost. Over 35 per cent sleep less than seven hours per day. Other factors are typically between one to two days of additional productive time lost.

There is one relationship that does not make intuitive sense. Those who report drinking more than 14 alcoholic units per week appear to have lower productivity loss than those who do not. The analysis controls for income and as such it is hard to explain or contextualise this finding.

An interesting finding concerns financial wellbeing. About 51 per cent report having some financial concerns. The econometric modelling finds that having financial concerns is associated with about 8.5 productive days lost.

One of the most significant factors impacting on overall workplace performance and wellbeing cited in studies is mental health. Here, the analysis has an interesting finding. The survey differentiates between those diagnosed with a mental health condition and those who are found to be clinically depressed on the Kessler-6 scale.[5] The latter includes about 8.5 per cent of the population surveyed and the former 2.5 per cent. Those diagnosed with depression lose over 19 days of productive time per year. However, those who have not been diagnosed lose over 45. This difference may highlight the negative impact that suffering in silence and the absence of treatment may have on a person's life. Overall, mental health is not the most prevalent condition but for those with diagnosed and undiagnosed mental health problems it is associated with the highest number of productive days lost per employee.

Health and physical factors

The analysis finds positive associations between chronic and clinical conditions and productivity loss. Our differentiation between chronic and modifiable lifestyle conditions is somewhat artificial. It stands to reason that poor nutrition can lead to high blood pressure for instance. The analysis finds that many conditions are associated with productivity loss. The main one is our all-encompassing measure of having a chronic condition. This includes cardiovascular disease, cancer, lung problems and so on. Having a chronic condition as defined by the BHW survey is associated with over 12 productive days lost. We also find that over 39 per cent of our surveyed population has a chronic condition.

Muscoloskeletal conditions are also prevalent with close to 79 per cent of the population reporting they have one condition. These are associated with 3.5 days of productive time lost per employee per year. Other conditions are less prevalent, such as high glucose or cholesterol, but again show a positive association with productivity loss. One observation is that a relatively small number of employees in the UK know their measurements (e.g. between 25–30 per cent of employees had their glucose and cholesterol checked) and as such there could be reporting error in how employees estimate blood pressure, glucose and cholesterol.

So, underlying conditions and modifiable health risks are associated with how productive employees are in the workplace. The modelling shows a very significant relationships between chronic conditions and the productivity loss measure. Underlying conditions clearly are associated with reported productivity, even in a short recall productivity measure.

Table 3.1   Days lost per year per employee

VARIABLES (prevalence in population – at risk)	All
At risk BMI >=30 (19.6%)	1.62037
	(0.39323)**
	0.848
	(2.393)
At risk physical activity >=150 minutes of moderate exercise (33.3%)	6.00954
	(0.30917)**
	5.402
	(6.617)
At risk fruit and vegetables 5 a day (65%)	1.32195
	(0.27290)**
	0.786
	(1.858)
At risk smoking (10.2%)	0.60229
	(0.26948)*
	0.073
	(1.132)
At risk alcohol 14 units per week (28%)	−0.78403
	(0.31369)*
	−1.400
	(−0.168)
At risk sleep <7 hours (35%)	4.04085
	(0.32310)**
	3.406
	(4.676)

VARIABLES (prevalence in population – at risk)	All	
Having a MSK (79%)	3.42632	
	(0.09776)**	
	3.234	
	(3.618)	
Having a chronic condition (39.4%)	12.05461	
	(0.42643)**	
	11.217	
	(12.892)	
At risk of high blood pressure above 120 (23%)	2.14627	
	(0.37142)**	
	1.417	
	(2.876)	
High glucose (1%)	7.49764	
	(1.66067)**	
	4.236	
	(10.760)	
High cholesterol (2.1%)	3.28676	
	(0.86594)**	
	1.586	
	(4.988)	
Diagnosed with depression (2%)	19.31123	
	(1.17556)**	
	17.002	
	(21.620)	
hse_control (21.1%)	2.27837	* Control (choice): I have a choice in deciding what I do at work (never or seldom)
	(0.41152)**	
	1.470	
	(3.087)	

VARIABLES (prevalence in population – at risk)	All	
hse_demands (16.4%)	6.81259	* Demands (time_pressure): I have unrealistic time pressures (often/always)
	(0.32654)**	
	6.171	
	(7.454)	
hse_peersup (4.6%)	6.45213	* I receive the respect at work I deserve from my colleagues (disagree/strongly disagree)
	(0.71274)**	
	5.052	
	(7.852)	
hse_role (6.6%)	7.04934	* I am clear what my duties and responsibilities are (never/seldom)
	(0.83759)**	
	5.404	
	(8.695)	
hse_change (32%)	2.52682	*Staff are always consulted about change at work (disagree/strongly disagree)
	(0.40128)**	
	1.739	
	(3.315)	
hse_relation1 (1%)	11.14810	* Relationships1 (bullying): I am subject to bullying at work (often/always)
	(1.01709)**	
	9.150	
	(13.146)	
hse_relation2 (11.3%)	5.93901	* Relationships2: at work are strained (agree/strongly agree)
	(0.48530)**	
	4.986	
	(6.892)	
hse_mgrsup (8.6%)	4.85977	*My line manager encourages me at work (disagree/strongly disagree)
	(0.63109)**	
	3.620	
	(6.099)	

VARIABLES (prevalence in population – at risk)	All
Reporting poor financial wellbeing (51%)	8.58094
	(0.30409)**
	7.984
	(9.178)
At risk on the Kessler scale (8.5%)	45.42319
	(0.89804)**
	43.659
	(47.187)
Commuting for more than 60 minutes (13%)	1.72556
	(0.31910)**
	1.099
	(2.352)
Constant	3.08853
	(4.44906)
	−5.651
	(11.828)
Observations	120,287
R-squared	0.21907

Notes: robust standard errors (se) in parentheses; ** $p<0.01$, * $p<0.05$. Analysis based on the BHW survey. Rows Beta and Se report the standardized coefficient and corresponding standard error from a regression using the WPAI score as predictor variable.

Discussion

HSE statistics (2019) show that work-related stress is a significant issue with more than 15.4 million working days lost as a result of stress, anxiety or depression at a conservative estimated cost of £5.2 billion to industry, individuals and the government.

Our econometric model confirms that stress is prevalent in the population that we sampled and leads to productive time being lost. In 2018, over 56 per cent of those surveyed reported one HSE dimension of work-related stress. The most prevalent single HSE dimension is not being consulted about change at work with its associated loss of 2.5 days lost per worker who reports this dimension. This represents about 1 per cent of annual days lost (if we assume a working year of 260 days). The most significant, though less prevalent, dimension is those subject to bullying with over 11 productive days lost or about 4.2 per cent of working days lost per year. These are significant costs to employers and raise the question on how the prevalence of these dimensions can be reduced.

Our model suggests that this may be less about the health and wellbeing offer and putting specific interventions in place. Rather, it may be more about looking holistically at 'job design' and 'work culture'. The latter is of course more difficult to conceptualise and operationalise. However, interventions such as improving communications, having zero tolerance to bullying, flexible working, training line managers and allowing workers autonomy in their work could be building blocks in managing stress better in the workplace. Ultimately, it comes down to principles of 'good' work. The business case to employers seems obvious. Better workplaces are more productive workplaces.

Stress is a bellwether for the overall health of a workplace. However, our approach possibly underplays the significance of stress. Our analysis is not set up to capture the interaction between variables. It stands to reason that various factors contribute to stress and that stress contributes to other factors. These may include factors such as sleep, mental health, financial wellbeing, and indeed more traditional physical health indicators. It is likely that those with stress sleep less and have poorer mental and physical health. Therefore, the interaction between these variables matters and suggests that the overall productivity loss of those affected by stress may be much more significant when taking other factors into account. The average productivity loss per employee in BHW in 2018 is 13.7 per cent of working days lost (35 days per employee per year). This suggests a very significant interplay between factors, with many being at risk in multiple categories. An interesting finding in our model is that various lifestyle and more clinical factors are associated with productivity loss suggesting a wider interplay between long-term and perhaps more modifiable conditions and factors. Stress and musculoskeletal conditions are some of the most prevalent factors in the survey. We know that there are comorbidities between stress, mental health and musculoskeletal conditions (Zheltoukhova et al., 2012).

The prevalence of some of these factors changes over time. There is evidence to suggest that psychosocial wellbeing in the UK is deteriorating across recent years. According to the Skills Employment Survey, insecurity and pressure at work in the UK reached their highest point for twenty years in 2012 (SES, 2012). The report found that public sector workers no longer feel more secure than those in the private sector: more than half of employees were worried about reductions in pay and job status, stress has gone up and wellbeing has gone down, and employees report working harder than before. The 2012 data compares directly with data collected in 2006 and with previous cycles of the survey.

Our own analysis of BHW survey data between 2014 and 2018 suggests that those reporting two HSE stress dimensions is virtually unchanged between those years from 27 per cent to 26.4 per cent. However, the mental health and sleep of respondents in particular seem to have deteriorated. In 2018, over 8 per cent were determined to be in distress on the Kessler-6 scale compared to 4 per cent of all surveyed in 2014. The prevalence of lack of sleep went from 26 per cent to 35 per cent in 2018. At the same time, overall productivity loss went from 9 per cent to 13.7 per cent, mostly made up by presenteeism. BHW is not a cohort study. Different employers and employees participate over time. So, we need to be cautious in interpreting these numbers. Nonetheless, given that the same types of employers participate over time, BHW takes the pulse of large UK employers and suggests worsening psychological wellbeing among employees over time associated with more productive time being lost. Psychological wellbeing appears worst among younger workers and those on lower incomes.

Our modelling suggests that workplace stress is prevalent. The model sets out specifically the amount of productive time lost per HSE dimension. These add up to significant costs for employers and society, especially when taking associated conditions into account. There are indications in our survey that these costs might be increasing over time. This presents a challenge to employers and society. There appears shared value for employers and governments to reduce the impact of workplace stress and related conditions. However, the reality in the UK is that there is significant divergence between workplaces that promote 'good' work and the health and wellbeing of employees and those that do not have the knowledge, motivation or perhaps resources to do the same. The latter can be the case in smaller employers. There is an additional risk in the present COVID-19 crisis that the importance of managing stress in the workplace or promoting 'good' work can be drowned out by the wider employment challenges that society faces. This would be a mistake. There is a significant productivity challenge in the UK already. Stress contributes to lower productivity. A good outcome of this present health crisis would be a renewed appreciation of the importance of health and wellbeing in the workplace. This could help offset the productivity impact of stress and anxiety among the workforce that the current crisis will likely have.

Notes

1. Christian van Stolk is Executive Vice President at RAND Europe.
2. Based on BHW data available at https://www.rand.org/randeurope/research/projects/britains-healthiest-workplace.html (accessed May 2020).
3. Based on data from: National Centre for Social Research, University of Leicester. Adult Psychiatric Morbidity Survey, 2007. Third edition. London: UK Data Service; 2011. Available from: http://discover.ukdataservice.ac.uk/catalogue/?sn=6379&type=Data%20catalogue#variables.
4. See http://www.reillyassociates.net/WPAI_General.html (accessed March 2020).
5. See https://www.statisticssolutions.com/kessler-psychological-distress-scale-k6/ (accessed May 2020)

References

Burton, W. N., Chen, C. Y., Li, X., Schultz, A. B., & Abrahamsson, H. (2014). The association of self-reported employee physical activity with metabolic syndrome, health care costs, absenteeism, and presenteeism. *Journal of Occupational and Environmental Medicine*, 56(9), 919–926.

Callen, B. L., Lindley, L. C., & Niederhauser, V. P. (2013). Health risk factors associated with presenteeism in the workplace. *Journal of Occupational and Environmental Medicine*, 55(11), 1312–1317.

Cancelliere, C., Cassidy, J. D., Ammendolia, C., & Côté, P. (2011). Are workplace health promotion programs effective at improving presenteeism in workers? A systematic review and best evidence synthesis of the literature. *BMC Public Health*, 11(1), 395.

Centre for Mental Health (2018). Managing presenteeism: A discussion paper. Available at: https://www.centreformentalhealth.org.uk/publications/managing -presenteeism.

Coutu, M. F., Corbiere, M., Durand, M. J., Nastasia, I., Labrecque, M. E., Berbiche, D., & Albert, V. (2015). Factors associated with presenteeism and psychological distress using a theory-driven approach. *Journal of Occupational and Environmental Medicine*, 57(6), 617–626.

Evans-Lacko, S., & Knapp, M. (2016). Global patterns of workplace productivity for people with depression: Absenteeism and presenteeism costs across eight diverse countries. *Social Psychiatry and Psychiatric Epidemiology*, 51(11), 1525–1537.

Hafner, M., van Stolk, C., Saunders, C.L., Krapels, J. and Baruch, B. (2015). Health, well-being and productivity in the workplace: A Britain's Healthiest Company summary report. RAND. Available at: https://www.rand.org/pubs/research_reports/RR1084 .html.

HSE (2019), Tackling work-related stress using the Management Standards approach: A step-by-step workbook. HSE. Available at: https://www.hse.gov.uk/pubns/wbk01 .htm.

Johns, G. (2010). Presenteeism in the workplace: A review and research agenda. *Journal of Organizational Behavior*, 31(4), 519–542.

Kowlessar, N. M., Goetzel, R. Z., Carls, G. S., Tabrizi, M. J., & Guindon, A. (2011). The relationship between 11 health risks and medical and productivity costs for a large employer. *Journal of Occupational and Environmental Medicine*, 53(5), 468–477.

Krpalek, D., Meredith, P., & Ziviani, J. (2014). Investigating mediated pathways between adult attachment patterns and reported rates of absenteeism and presenteeism. *Journal of Workplace Behavioral Health*, 29(4), 259–280.

Kuoppala, J., Lamminpää, A., & Husman, P. (2008). Work health promotion, job well-being, and sickness absences: A systematic review and meta-analysis. *Journal of Occupational and Environmental Medicine*, 50(11), 1216–1227.

Lohaus, D., & Habermann, W. (2019). Presenteeism: A review and research directions. *Human Resource Management Review*, 29(1), 43–58.

Lu, L., Cooper, C. L., & Lin, H. Y. (2013). A cross-cultural examination of presenteeism and supervisory support. *Career Development International*, 18, 440–456.

NHS Information Centre for Health and Social Care (NHSIC) (2009). Adult psychiatric morbidity in England, 2007: Results of a household survey. London: The Health & Social Care Information Centre.

Office for National Statistics (ONS) (2014). *Sickness Absence in the Labour Market*. London: ONS. Available from: www.ons.gov.uk/employmentandlabourmarket/peopleinwork/employmentandemployeetypes/datasets/sicknessabsenceinthelabourmarket.

Reilly, M. C., Zbrozek, A. S., & Dukes, E. (1993). The validity and reproducibility of a work productivity and activity impairment measure. *PharmacoEconomics*, 4(5), 353–365.

Schultz, A. B., & Edington, D. W. (2007). Employee health and presenteeism: A systematic review. *Journal of Occupational Rehabilitation*, 17(3), 547–579.

Schultz, A. B., Chen, C. Y., & Edington, D. W. (2009). The cost and impact of health conditions on presenteeism to employers. *Pharmacoeconomics*, 27(5), 365–378.

SES (2012). Skills Employment Survey 2012. Available at: https://www.cardiff.ac.uk/research/explore/find-a-project/view/117804-skills-and-employment-survey-2012.

Waddell, G., Burton, K., & Aylward, M. (2006). Work and common health problems. *Journal of Insurance Medicine (New York, NY)*, 39, 109–120.

Wooldridge, J.M., (2010). *Econometric Analysis of Cross Section and Panel Data*. Cambridge, MA: MIT Press.

Zheltoukhova, K., O'Dea, L., & Bevan, S. (2012). Taking the strain: The impact of musculoskeletal disorders on work and home life. Lancaster: The Work Foundation, Lancaster University. Available from: www.theworkfoundation.com/DownloadPublication/Report/326_FFW%20UK%20survey%20FINAL.pdf.

PART II

SPECIFIC INFLUENCES

4. Leadership and well-being

Shani Pupco and Julian Barling

Leadership and well-being

Employees' well-being has been of considerable interest to organizational researchers for decades. Kornhauser's (1965) interview-based study of the mental health of workers in mass-production jobs in Detroit, conducted more than half a century ago, was probably the first major exploration of this topic. Since that time, concern for employees' psychological and physical well-being has only grown among policy makers and the lay public. Importantly, a focus on leaders has never been absent from this concern. However, the dominant concern is whether and how leaders negatively (and sometimes positively) affect their employees' well-being. As one of the earliest examples, more than a decade before he published his seminal study in 1965, Kornhauser and Sharp (1932) had shown that poor supervision resulted in employee dissatisfaction, which in turn affected employees' emotional adjustment.

Evidence of the vibrant interest in leadership and well-being currently is evident in different ways. First, several qualitative review articles, all of which include thoughts about possible directions for research, have been published in the past several years. As examples, Arnold (2017) reviewed 40 articles and established that transformational leadership indirectly affects employees' well-being through mediators such as trust in leadership, meaningful work and self-efficacy. Arnold went on to note that we now need to know more about the moderators of these indirect effects. Inceoglu et al. (2018) go beyond the effects of transformational leadership in their review, and examine the effects of different forms of leadership (viz. change, task, relational and passive) on different aspects of employee well-being (viz. psychological, hedonic, eudaimonic, negative and physical). They also categorize five pathways (social-cognitive, motivational, affective, relational and identification) through which any effects of leadership on employee well-being may manifest. Barling and Cloutier (2017) took a different perspective in their review, focusing primarily on leaders' own well-being. In doing so, they ask why leaders' own well-being has largely escaped attention, and raise questions about the emotional toll of enacting high-quality leadership on the leaders, and on possible interventions to enhance leaders' well-being.

Second, going beyond these qualitative reviews, Kaluza et al. (2020) recently published a review and meta-analysis of leadership behaviors and well-being. Their meta-analysis is significant for several reasons. (a) The fact that their analyses are based on 95 effects sizes and a total sample of 12,617 indicates just how much research already exists on the link between leadership behavior and well-being. (b) Their findings support Arnold's (2017) conclusions about the links between transformational leadership and employee well-being, and (c) extend Inceoglu et al.'s (2018) framework by showing that change and relational leadership (viz. transformational, participative) leadership are more closely tied to well-being than task-oriented (viz. transactional) leadership. (d) Extending our understanding of leadership and well-being, Kaluza et al. (2020) also showed that abusive supervision has a more negative effect on leaders' own well-being than does passive leadership.

Third, additional evidence of the robust interest in the topic of leadership and well-being comes from specialized small-group meetings special issues of journals. Ilke Inceoglu and the University of Exeter Business School hosted an EAWOP small group meeting on "Leadership and Health/Well-Being" in Exeter in June, 2019. At about the same time, *Work and Stress* published a special issue on the topic of leadership and well-being (Nielsen & Taris, 2019), while the *Journal of Occupational Health Psychology* will soon host a special issue on the same topic. Clearly, interest on the links between leadership and well-being is extensive and intensive, and likely to grow in the future.

The time is ripe, therefore, to consider how future research might broaden and intensify our understanding of leadership and well-being. At the outset, we acknowledge the substantial base of research that already exists, and will undoubtedly continue to grow. Our goal in this chapter is to offer ideas that expand existing research on leadership and well-being. Specifically, we first call for an understanding of the prevalence of leaders' well-being, and for a focus on leaders' well-being; not because it might be important in terms of its effects on others, but rather because leaders are important organizational members in and of themselves. We then look to other disciplines, primarily political science and psychiatry, for questions about leadership and well-being that are worth pursuing, and comment on ethical issues that might be important in any research on this topic. Last, we offer some ideas for research on how unique aspects of sex and sexual and gender identity might affect leader well-being.

"Testing, testing, testing!": prevalence of leaders' well-being

We wrote this section on the prevalence of leaders' well-being in the Spring of 2020, during the early stages of the global COVID-19 pandemic. One of the most salient lessons learned in being able to manage the virus was captured in the mantra heard so often, namely "testing, testing, testing!". What this referred to was the vital need to conduct the basic screening tests that would provide an understanding of the prevalence of virus, which is a precondition for the containment of the virus in the short term, and prevention of further outbreaks in the longer term.

Why is this instructive? We have learned much about employees' mental health in the past decade, and research conducted by Michael Frone in the United States exemplifies this. Based on a national probability sample of 2,805 employed people in the United States, Frone (2006a) provided estimates of the number of people who consume alcohol before arriving at work (1.83 percent, 2.3 million workers), or during the workday (7.06 percent, 8.9 million) at any point in the prior year. Going even further, Frone (2006a) used the same data to estimate the number of people who attend work under the influence of alcohol (1.68 percent, 2.1 million), or who work with a hangover (9.23 percent, 11.6 million). In a separate study (2006b), he provided prevalence data on the use of legal (e.g., over-the-counter medication) and illicit drug use (e.g., marijuana, cocaine, and psychotherapeutic drugs) and workplace violence (Schat et al., 2006).

Several broad lessons can be drawn for understanding workplace well-being from these studies, and from the data on workplace alcohol consumption in particular. First, the importance of establishing baselines of the particular phenomenon of interest is essential in (a) directing researchers to the critical issues that require research, and (b) enabling evidence-based management decision-making and practices within organizations. Second, the prevalence data on workplace alcohol use point specifically to the need for more data on leaders' well-being: managers reported higher rates of three of the four behaviors studied by Frone (2006b), namely consuming alcohol during the workday, being under the influence of alcohol while at work, and working with a hangover.

Yet, we simply have no comparable understanding of leaders' mental health, or mental illness. We would suggest that a first step in research on leadership and well-being should be to conduct research that enables an understanding of the prevalence of leaders' mental health/illness, and identifies risk factors that threaten leaders' well-being. Importantly, any such research should be based on large-scale representative samples. Doing so would be consistent with the influential national strategy proposed 30 years ago by the National Institute for Occupational Safety and Health (NIOSH; Sauter et al., 1990) that aimed to help prevent work-related psychological problems—a strategy that was primarily focused on employee well-being.

Leaders' well-being for the sake of leaders' well-being

As previously mentioned, both in the beginning of this chapter and by Barling and Cloutier (2017), the study of leaders' well-being and mental health/ illness should shift away from the focus of how leaders' well-being affects their employees, to simply focus on leaders' well-being for the sake of gaining knowledge on leaders' well-being. After all, leaders themselves are employees who just happen to be employed in a leadership position. More so, leaders are also people, whose unique work responsibilities may leave them vulnerable to mental illness or to diminished mental health. As scholars, we are not burdened with the responsibility to ensure ever-increasing levels of employee performance and productivity; instead, we have the liberty of focusing on the well-being of all people in organizations without such constraints.

While there is literature that highlights the advantages of being a leader (e.g. a higher salary and access to resources; Christie & Barling, 2009; Marmot, 2004), it is important to remember that being in such positions may carry additional stressors and pressures. For example, being a leader does not leave one immune to poor mental health and well-being. Due to the added stress of managing individuals, teams, and resources, and greater uncertainty inherent in the leadership role, leaders may also struggle with their well-being. Additionally, the emotional energy required to be a positive transformational and considerate leader may leave leaders vulnerable to burnout. As such, gaining an understanding of leaders' well-being simply for the sake of learning more about a group of individuals whose well-being is often ignored both in research and organizational interventions, is important and relevant to both theory and practice.

Finally, and as previously mentioned, leaders too are both people and employees. Opting not to study their well-being could have dire consequences for their mental health and well-being. Moreover, research could also be conducted to search for ways in which organizations can support the well-being of its leaders.

Having the well-being of the leader as the outcome of a research program rather than simply the antecedent or predictor of employee well-being can provide fruitful opportunities for research. In practice, doing so might identify the most beneficial supports and programs for these individuals.

Research ideas from different disciplines

As we noted in a comment in the opening of this chapter, the intersection of leadership and well-being has attracted considerable scholarly and empirical attention. However, the vast majority of that research falls within the fields of management, psychology and sociology. What we now do in this section of the chapter is visit some writings from disciplines such as medicine and political science, and extract ideas for future research that may not be readily apparent in the existing literatures. We view this as an important opportunity: all too often, we become stuck in our own silos, limiting the likelihood that we might learn from neighboring disciplines.

Physical well-being and leadership

One question that has been extensively considered outside of the disciplines of management, psychology and sociology is how physical illness might affect leadership and decision-making. Hugh L'Etang, a medical doctor, was perhaps the first to systematically raise this issue in his book, *The Pathology of Leadership*, which was published just over 50 years ago. Many of the questions L'Etang raised remain relevant to researchers and practitioners, and L'Etang has now been joined by other medical practitioners (e.g., Owen, 2008) asking similar questions, most of which focus on the multitude of medical conditions that have affected leaders' decision-making and behaviors throughout history. L'Etang's quote from noted US diplomat Dean Rusk, who observed that "the international list of those who have carried great responsibility while ill is a long one and there are fleeting glimpses of decisions which good health might have turned another way" (1969, p. 9), underscores just how important this topic is.

Relating to the current focus of leadership research, L'Etang explicitly questioned whether physical illnesses could explain the laissez-faire or passive leadership of otherwise engaged leaders. Given that our understanding of the antecedents of passive leadership remains in its infancy, this could be a topic worth pursuing. Elsewhere, it is intriguing to see that more than 50 years ago, L'Etang wondered about a possible link between sleep and leader behavior:

"Who knows how much turns on whether … the head of the Foreign Office has had sufficiency of sleep?" (p. 8), a topic that is now at the forefront of research (e.g., Barling et al., 2016; Barnes et al., 2015). While there is some research on the effects of major illnesses on employees' motivation (e.g., Westaby et al.'s [2005] study on the effects of ALS on work motivation), the link between physical illness and leadership behaviors remains a topic about which we know precious little, clearly limiting our understanding of the antecedents of positive and negative leadership behaviors.

Clinically diagnosed mental illness and leadership

When psychiatrist Nassir Ghaemi first published his controversially titled *A First Rate Madness* in 2011, it was predictably met with considerable interest, as well as disbelief: could he really be proposing that mental illness was a pre-requisite for leadership? A close reading of the book reveals unsurprisingly that his ideas were a lot more nuanced, and we suggest that his ideas carry considerable weight in guiding future research on leaders' well-being.

In essence, Ghaemi's argument is that any personal experience with mental illness would leave leaders better placed to successfully enact the interpersonal demands of leadership, an argument he supports with both empirical research and historical cases. As one empirical example, Ghaemi highlights Alloy and Abramson's (1979) well-known study showing that clinically depressed individuals have an accurate perception of how much control they have, but those who were not depressed overestimated their control. Ghaemi uses findings such as these to suggest that British Prime Minister Neville Chamberlain over-estimated the benevolence of Hitler in 1939 because he was mentally healthy. In contrast, Churchill was able to see the truth about Hitler's intentions because he lacked the same mental health.

Ghaemi also considers the effects of clinical depression on later leadership. Summarizing the effects of early mental and physical illness on leaders' later empathy and resilience, Ghaemi tells the story of Eleanor Roosevelt explaining how polio had affected FDR's politics: "He would certainly have been president", she remarked, "but a president of a different kind" (p. 146). This is important, because perhaps all existing empirical research focuses on sub-clinical levels of leaders' depression and other aspects of well-being. As one example, Byrne et al. (2014) studied the effects of depression and anxiety on transformational leadership and abusive supervision.

However, they emphasize that they were studying sub-clinical symptoms rather than clinically diagnosed levels of depression and anxiety. As a result, we suggest that future research focus on the effects of clinically diagnosed mental illness on leadership quality.

Positive effects of mental health and illness and leadership

Even if we extend our research focus to include physical illness and clinically diagnosed levels of mental illness, we need to be careful not to assume that they necessarily exert negative effects. Instead, we need to be open to the possibility that they might also exert beneficial effects. Ghaemi is not alone in pointing to the positive outcomes of early adversity for later leadership. Political scientist Rose McDermott's (2008) notes at the outset of her fascinating book *Presidential Leadership, Illness, and Decision Making* that illness, and death, are inevitable, even amongst the most powerful of leaders. Like Ghaemi, but focusing on the consequences of physical illness, McDermott dispels the simplistic notion that even the most significant physical illnesses would only exert negative effects. Instead, she concludes that experiencing physical illness or pain (e.g., President Kennedy was taking 26 different drugs each day in 1961) or facing what she terms a "foreshortened time horizon" (p. 11) due to a major illness brings with it a sense of urgency about creating a positive historical legacy. Also like Ghaemi, McDermott notes how early battles with significant hardship can affect later leadership positively, citing the tremendous influence of President Kennedy's experience with the death of his infant son Patrick on the subsequent development of the field of neonatology. Going further, McDermott notes, Roosevelt's experience with polio affected him for the rest of his life: "He would not accept failure, he denied the ability of illness to impact his behavior, he stayed positive and he kept working" (2008, p. 114).

Importantly, our understanding of the link between well-being and leadership quality will be expanded in the extent to which future research identifies the conditions under which the link is positive, or negative, and this is true both for physical and psychological well-being.

Hubris and leadership: person × situation interactions

Perhaps no one is better placed to offer credible insights into the link between well-being and leadership than David Owen. Trained as a neurologist and psychiatrist and a Fellow of the Royal College of Physicians in the UK, Owen also served as British Foreign Secretary and as the European Union Co-Chair of the International Conference on the former Yugoslavia between 1992 and 1995. His book, *In Sickness and in Power: Illnesses in Heads of Government During the Last 100 Years* was widely acclaimed when it was published in 2008.

Yet, the book that is more relevant in setting an agenda for research on leadership and well-being is Owen's *The Hubris Syndrome: Bush, Blair and the Intoxication of Power* (2012). Although Owen mentioned what he regarded as the hubristic syndrome, and hubristic incompetence in *In Sickness and in Power*, he develops the idea further in *The Hubris Syndrome*, as well as several academic articles in peer-reviewed journals (e.g., Owen & Davidson, 2009). Unlike the ideas of L'Etang, Ghaemi, McDermott and even Owen himself in his 2008 book, all of which focused on the effects of leaders' well-being on their own leadership behaviors and decisions, the hubris syndrome is offered as a problem of position and power—each of the 14 characteristics of the syndrome would only become manifest on the assumption of significant power. Thus, Owen assumes that the hubris syndrome is a property of the situation, suggests it is most likely to be manifest by political and military leaders, and proposes that a clinical diagnosis of hubris would be justified when four of the 14 symptoms are present (Owen, 2012).

The question that Owen raises implicitly, and one which should be explored further, is the effects of person x situation interactions in understanding leaders' well-being, and its effects on performance.

Ethical issues in researching leadership and mental illness

Moving away from ideas for research for a moment, L'Etang opens the book with an ethical dilemma that still today deserves serious thought: are doctors obliged, or allowed, to tell others if their patients have some form of illness? We would extend the challenge to include clinical psychologists and psychiatrists, or others in positions of power (e.g., members of the cabinet or congress in America). This is by no means an abstract issue for several reasons. First, serious questions were being raised about the mental fitness for office of President Donald J. Trump in his first few years in office (McAdams, 2020), and whether this posed a constitutional obligation on his cabinet members to remove him from office (Conway, 2019). Given that US presidents undergo regular medical examinations—a practice that existed in 1931 when then governor Franklin D. Roosevelt was trying show he was physically capable of discharging his duties, what responsibility does access to this knowledge pose for the medical staff involved, or for others with access to such knowledge (e.g., journalists, aides)?

Second, Dimoff and Kelloway (2019) reported a fascinating research study showing that managers and leaders could reliably identify when their employees were experiencing psychological difficulties. The clear extension of their findings is that management should monitor the psychological well-being of their employees, and intervene when they are struggling. In compassionate workplaces by extension, should or do employees have an equal responsibility to respond if they are aware that their leaders are suffering psychological difficulties? Would leaders manifest the same five signs of struggle (viz. psychological distress, withdrawal, reduced attendance, declines in performance, extreme behaviors) that employees do, or might their psychological struggles be manifest differently because of the fear of being stigmatized?

The ethical question about whether there is a responsibility to inform others is raised because involvement in research frequently gives researchers unusual access to sensitive knowledge, in this case about leaders' well-being, which could exert negative effects on organizations or their members. Researchers need to clearly define a priori who the research participants are, to whom they owe primary responsibility, and to be transparent in these decisions before embarking on their research.

Sex and discrimination

The discourse on gender and leadership has a long history, and has yet to exhaust the numerous issues attached to the topic. Our goal in this section is to provide a fresh lens on the topic of gender, sex and sexuality, and leadership, specifically as to how gender may play a role in leaders' well-being. We will begin this section by tackling topics unique to the experience of women leaders, followed by those unique to men, and finally discuss how being a member of the LGBTQ+ community can influence leaders' well-being.

Women and leadership

Important to this section are the experiences of people who menstruate or experience maternity in the workplace. In their review on the experiences of the working women, Grandey et al. (2020) introduce the concept of the three Ms (menstruation, maternity, and menopause), and discuss the literature on how those topics may influence the experience of those in the workplace who are directly affected. Menstruation refers to the hormonal and physical changes women experience during their menstrual cycle, where ovulation occurs, and the uterine lining thickens, and is eventually shed if an egg is not fertilized. Maternity refers to the time when a woman is either pregnant or breastfeeding, and menopause refers to the time period when women begin experiencing perimenopause and up until they reach eventual menopause.

Menstruation

Beginning at an early age, women may experience a variety of symptoms throughout their menstrual cycle, and these symptoms may vary in the amount of discomfort they cause, as well as in severity (Society of Obstetricians and Gynecologists of Canada [SOGC], 2020a). While the topic of menstruation is taboo in general, it may be more so when applied to women leaders. The experience of menstrual cramps may cause presenteeism in women workers (Hasselrot et al., 2018). Given the additional responsibilities of leadership, women leaders may be feel obliged to remain at work during times of discomfort, more so than women not holding leadership positions. Additionally, if women leaders are not able to take time away from work, work from home or work with flexible hours when experiencing negative menstrual symptoms, they may face further problems concerning not having access to appropriate menstrual supplies when at work.

With this come additional questions about the way in which menstruation may uniquely affect the well-being of leaders. As we just mentioned, women leaders may manifest more instances of presenteeism, which may prevent them from receiving the rest and recuperation required to manage their menstrual symptoms, potentially resulting in greater instances of burnout and decreased mental health. Second, especially in male-dominated industries, woman leaders may feel uncomfortable carrying a tampon or sanitary napkin to the bathroom. Additionally, given the stigma associated with menstruation (Grandey et al., 2020), these leaders may be ridiculed, or not taken seriously by their colleagues or followers. Not being taken seriously in one's role as leader may itself exert further negative effects on leaders' well-being.

Finally, the influence of contraceptives on the well-being of women, and women leaders specifically, should be addressed. The use of oral and intra-uterine devices carry with them a host of side-effects such as the onset of mental illness (i.e. anxiety and depression) as well as extra or irregular bleeding (SOGC, 2020b).

Maternity

In addition to the ways in which working during menstruation may affect leaders' well-being, many women also begin having and caring for children at some point in their careers. During the maternity phase of women's lives, they may become pregnant (some more than once), and may further take a maternity leave and breastfeed their child(ren).

First, pregnancy takes a toll on the body, which women leaders have to endure while continuing to bear the regular responsibilities and stresses of leadership. While some women may become pregnant and have children during the maternity phase, others may struggle to become pregnant, experience a loss of pregnancy in the form of miscarriage or abortion, and some may never have children—by choice or not. Not having children may affect women leaders' well-being in different ways. First, even among women, miscarriage is a taboo topic. Despite it being a common experience, with 15–20 percent of pregnancies resulting in a miscarriage (SOGC, 2020c), many women experience feelings of shame and guilt when miscarrying (Bardos et al., 2015). Relatedly, women may not feel comfortable discussing their experiences, and are burdened with emotionally healing without the support of others.

Further, women's discomfort with sharing their experience may negatively influence their well-being in the workplace by other means. While women may take "sick days" while physically going through a miscarriage, they may have no formal avenues for further paid time off to deal with the emotional repercussions of miscarrying, such as grief. As a result, they may return to work before being ready, and without the proper support (Burgess et al., 2008). One question for research would be how organizational leaders can support women and women leaders in such situations. Providing women who have miscarried with additional paid leave, and/or offering counselling services would involve recognizing that miscarriage is a legitimate issue that affects leadership behaviors, all of which could enhance women leaders' well-being in the workplace.

It is not just physically experiencing menstruation and maternity per se that affects women's leadership. Whether you plan to or not, with being a women, comes the expectation that you will become pregnant and have children. This is important in the workplace, as doing so may signal to some others that work is not a woman leader's greatest priority, which could hurt her career. As such, it may appear that women who chose not to have children may have an advantage when it comes to furthering their careers, and being treated with more respect in the workplace. However, this is not the case. Simply the expectation that a woman may become pregnant and take maternity leave is sufficient to negatively influence her treatment in the workplace (Gloor et al., 2015). This "maybe baby" effect may negatively affect the well-being of woman leaders specifically. The expectation that women leaders may soon become pregnant could result in their being given less organizational opportunities, irrespective of their abilities to execute them. Being passed over for opportunities for no legitimate reason could result in feelings of loss of control and diminish the leaders' well-being and mental health. Additionally, the thought of discussing this issue with supervisors may result in heightened feelings of anxiety for women leaders, which may be further exacerbated by the results of the conversation.

Finally, when mothers do return to work, they may need to take time during the workday to pump breastmilk (this is especially relevant in countries such as the United States where maternity leaves only span 12 weeks; Spitzmuller et al., 2016). Women leaders may be especially vulnerable to changes in their well-being during this time. Additionally, women may feel their careers are threatened taking a full maternity leave,[1] if they believe that their organizations perceive taking leave as a signal that family is more important than work (i.e. signaling theory; Spence, 1973). Mothers who are leaders on leave may thus return to work before they (and their infant) are psychologically or physically ready due to fears of being replaced, demoted or ignored. Add such stressors to the unique emotions women experience postpartum (i.e. baby blues or postpartum depression), and the importance of studying women leaders' well-being becomes more clear. Faced with an increase in both work and home stressors, pregnant or nursing leaders may be especially vulnerable to decreases in well-being and mental health.

Menopause

Finally, the time when most women are likely to be leaders is during their middle age, a time when they are more likely to begin experiencing perimenopause (Grandey et al., 2020). The perimenopause stage of a woman's life can last up to ten years. During this phase, women will experience a drop in estrogen, which could result in irregular menstrual cycles (length and flow). They may have trouble sleeping, and experience excessive bodily heat and perspiration (Grandey et al., 2020). Such physical experiences may have negative influences on women leaders' well-being at work.

Indeed, some perimenopausal women experience depression (Bromberger & Kravitz, 2011). Like any mental illness effects associated with pregnancy (i.e. postpartum depression), it is important to determine whether and which workplace characteristics exacerbate or diminish women leaders' well-being. As importantly, determining how workplace can enhance women leaders' well-being would be well worth future research.

The leadership experience of members of the LGBTQ+ community

A group of individuals whose well-being is disproportionately affected are the LGBTQ+ community. Even when not in leadership positions, people experience discrimination (e.g. Dixon & Dougherty, 2014), poor mental health and suicidal ideation (e.g. Sutter & Perrin, 2016). In one study, one individual spoke about a "don't ask don't tell" attitude that was prevalent in their work-place (Eliason et al., 2011). In a different study, many individuals expressed concerns about being "othered" at work, or being subject to various forms of discrimination including microaggressions. Some expressed an inability to talk about their families due to covert reinforcement of a traditional family structure at their workplace (Dixon & Dougherty, 2014). All such experiences have the potential to influence the well-being of members of the LGBTQ+ community. Further, it leaves open questions about well-being repercussions for employees unable or unwilling to share their identity when facing on-going discrimination at work.

All this begs the question of how holding a position of leadership may exacer-bate difficulties in the well-being of LGBTQ+ individuals. For one, the effects of leaders' feeling the need to hide their identity in the workplace needs to be understood. Such research should be designed to go beyond appropriate policies and provide insight into practices that can be implemented to create workplaces that are supportive. For example, the existence of policies that prevented discrimination against sexual identity in one company did little to positively influence the well-being of an employee. Management continuously attempted to make daily life for this individual more difficult in an effort to make them quit (Baker & Lucas, 2017).

Research needs to be conducted to determine what changes in the workplace might maximize the well-being of LGBTQ+ leaders. In one study, several indi-viduals spoke to the extra responsibilities they were assigned at work due to not conforming to the heteronormative family structure (Dixon & Dougherty, 2014). In an effort to keep their identity private, some individuals pretended to be single. Because of this, and of the assumption that they do not have respon-sibilities outside of work, they were asked to stay at work later, or take on responsibilities that they did not wish to, as they did not have children at home who required their time (Dixon & Dougherty, 2014). As holding a leadership role already has additional responsibilities, research could be conducted to determine how both regular leadership responsibilities and unique experiences of LGBTQ+ leaders influence well-being, and what factors might mitigate any effects of these stressors and experiences.

Finally, employees who are members of the LGBTQ+ community report experiencing autonomy violations (violations of privacy regarding their personal lives; Baker & Lucas, 2017). Unsolicited questions about private lives, such as those about their sexual lives, can negatively influence well-being. For leaders, such violations of autonomy may have additional negative implications for well-being. For example, if followers feel it is appropriate to ask leaders such personal questions, it may indicate that they do not legitimately see the individual as a leader, increasing difficulties in the leader's tasks and responsibilities, above and beyond those typical of a leadership role. As such, research might investigate how the relationship between leaders and followers influences the well-being of the leader specifically.

While research exists on the well-being of LGBTQ+ individuals in the workplace (e.g. Sutter & Perrin, 2016), specific research on the well-being of leaders is lacking. Conducting research on LGBTQ+ leaders could provide opportunities to change and improve practice as a means to improve the well-being of the LGBTQ+ community at work. However, it is important to note that peoples' experiences are unique, and that further, intersectionality should be considered in future research.

Prostate cancer

A full consideration of how sex might shape an agenda for research on leadership and well-being would be incomplete without some consideration of the possible effects of prostate cancer. The prevalence of prostate cancer suggests why it might be relevant to this discussion: while there are differences in prevalence across different countries[2] (Rawla, 2019), prostate cancer is the second most frequently diagnosed cancer amongst males across the world. Of particular significance to this chapter is the correlation of prostate cancer and age. Prostate cancer is extremely rare in younger males—9.1 percent of all cases occur in males aged 45–54 years of age, and 30.7 percent in males aged 55–64 (Brawley, 2012). Given that people now tend to retire later than the traditional retirement age of 65, it is noteworthy that most cases (35.3 percent) are diagnosed in males aged 65–74 years of age. These trends are important, because males aged 45 years and older are precisely those who might be expected to hold leadership positions of increasing importance and responsibility in organizations. As one example of this trend, about half of the CEOs of Fortune

500 and S&P 500 companies in 2019 were held by men aged 54–62 years old (Crist/Kolder Associates, 2020). As a result, prostate cancer is a disease that men in leadership positions might well encounter, and the question emerges whether their experience with prostate cancer might influence their leadership in any way needs to be confronted.

Not surprisingly, we could not find any research addressing whether having prostate cancer affects leadership. This is an important omission as there are several ways in which experiencing prostate cancer may affect diverse aspects of leadership. While much research has pointed to depressive symptoms experienced upon learning of the diagnosis and elevated anxiety whilst choosing a treatment method (De Sousa et al., 2012) that might well affect the quality of leadership behaviors (Byrne et al., 2014), this is true of perhaps all cancers, not just for men and not just for prostate cancer.

What makes prostate cancer especially challenging for men in this age group are the side-effects arising from the different treatment options. For example, radical prostatectomy or radiation can cause decreased sexual function, urinary incontinence or bowel function (Barocas et al., 2017), while hormonal treatments can result in hot flashes, emotional changes, voice (pitch) changes and weight gain, all of which could affect different aspects of leadership behaviors.

First, given the nature of these side effects, some men experience challenges to their identity, and specifically to their masculinity. As one interviewee stated "you know I've joined your club … I'm the hot flush boy" (Eziefula et al., 2013, p. 2825), which for many men results in a need to renegotiate their masculinity (Farrington et al., 2019), given the extent to which leadership remains stereotypically masculine (Koenig et al., 2011). In addition, returning to work following treatment raises issues of how they will be perceived by others, and the dilemma of whether, and how much to disclose, and to whom (Grunfeld et al., 2013). Taken together with any depression and anxiety, the quality of leadership behaviors might very well suffer. Second, as a result of the physical side effects and fears of being stigmatized, feelings of loneliness and social isolation are not uncommon (Ettridge et al., 2018), and business travel is often reduced (Grunfeld et al., 2013). This is potentially important, because the age at which many employed men will be diagnosed with prostate cancer coincides with a period of their work lives during which they may well seek opportunities for promotion to significant positions of responsibility. Negative perceptions about their involvement in work (such as withdrawal at work or a reluctance to engage in business travel) could be negatively perceived by those making leadership promotion decisions. Third, like comments made earlier that significant negative illnesses may have positive effects on leadership behaviors, the possibility that going through a diagnosis of and treatment for prostate cancer might have positive effects should not be dismissed. Farrington et al. (2019) found some men became "prostate champions", actively helping some people living with prostate cancer, and educating others who did not have the disease. In doing so, they would have an opportunity to exert positive effects on those around them at work.

Using technology in research on leadership and well-being

We would be remiss if we did not include some thoughts about the use of technology for research on leadership and well-being. We were first introduced to the idea of incorporating new technology in the study of well-being at a special session at the previously mentioned EAWOP small group meeting on *Leadership and Health/Well-being* in Exeter in June, 2019. There is a considerable amount and range of technology, such as Fitbits, Apple Watches, sleep actigraphs and ambulatory blood pressure monitors (Wong & Kelloway, 2016), that can be used to track physiological indicators of leaders' well-being. In conjunction with such technology, smart phones loaded with survey software can be used to contact leaders at random or systematic times of the workday to provide self-reports of leadership experiences and well-being. Insight from such technologies can used to guide experimental or field studies that establish causal relationships between certain workplace factors and leaders' well-being.

Conclusion

The many and diverse ideas offered in this chapter go beyond many of the questions currently researched on leadership and well-being, expanding the range of topics that could be considered as we move toward a more comprehensive understanding of this topic. Given the robust group of scholars already actively engaged in research aimed at understanding the intersection of leadership and well-being, we predict that much will be learned about leadership and well-being in the coming years.

Notes

1. Especially in countries such as Canada where they can take leave for up to 78 weeks (Government of Canada, 2018)
2. One substantive reason for these differences is the extent of PSA testing in different countries.

References

Alloy, L.B., & Abramson, L.Y. (1979). Judgment of contingency on depressed and nondepressed students: Sadder by wiser? *Journal of Experimental Psychology, 108*, 441–485.

Arnold, K.A. (2017). Transformational leadership and employee psychological well-being: A review and directions for future research. *Journal of Occupational Health Psychology, 22*, 381–393.

Baker, S.J., & Lucas, K. (2017). Is it safe to bring myself to work? Understanding LGBTQ experiences of workplace dignity. *Canadian Journal of Administrative Sciences/Revue Canadienne des Sciences de l'Administration, 34*(2), 133–148.

Bardos, J., Hercz, D., Friedenthal, J., Missmer, S.A., & Williams, Z. (2015). A national survey on public perceptions of miscarriage. *Obstetrics and Gynecology, 125*, 1313.

Barling, J., & Cloutier, A. (2017). Leaders' mental health at work: Empirical, methodological, and policy directions. *Journal of Occupational Health Psychology, 22*, 394–406.

Barling, J., Barnes, C.M., Carleton, E., & Wagner, D.T. (2016) (Eds.) *Sleep and Work: Research Insights for the Workplace*. NY: Oxford University Press.

Barnes, C., Lucianetti, L., Bhave, D., & Christian, M. (2015). You wouldn't like me when I'm sleepy: Leader sleep, daily abusive supervision, and work unit engagement. *Academy of Management Journal, 58*, 1419–1437.

Barocas, D.D. et al. (2017). Association between radiation therapy, surgery, or observation for localized prostate cancer and patient-reported outcomes after three years. *Journal of the American Medical Association, 317*, 1126–1140.

Brawley, O.W. (2012). Prostate cancer epidemiology in the United States. *World Journal of Urology, 30*, 195–200.

Bromberger, J.T., & Kravitz, H.M. (2011). Mood and menopause: Findings from the Study of Women's Health Across the Nation (SWAN) over 10 years. *Obstetrics and Gynecology Clinics, 38*(3), 609–625.

Burgess, S., Gregg, P., Propper, C., & Washbrook, E. (2008). Maternity rights and mothers' return to work. *Labour Economics, 15*, 168–201.

Byrne, A., Dionisi, A., Barling, J., Akers, A., Robertson, J., Lys, R., Wylie, J., & Dupré, K. (2014). The depleted leader: The influence of leaders' diminished psychological resources on leadership behaviors. *Leadership Quarterly, 25*, 344–357.

Christie, A.M., & Barling, J. 2009. Disentangling the indirect links between socioeconomic status and health: The dynamic roles of work stressors and personal control. *Journal of Applied Psychology, 94*(6), 1466–1478.

Conway, G.T. III. (October 3, 2019). Unfit for office. *The Atlantic*. https://www.theatlantic.com/ideas/archive/2019/10/george-conway-trump-unfit-office/599128/

Crist/Kolder Associates (2020). Volatility Report 2019. http://www.cristkolder.com/media/2438/volatility-report-2019-americas-leading-companies.pdf Accessed April 22, 2020

de Sousa, A., Sonavane, S., & Mehta J. (2012). Psychological aspects of prostate cancer: A clinical review. *Prostate Cancer and Prostatic Diseases, 15*, 120–127.

Dimoff, J.K, & Kelloway, E.K. (2019). Signs of struggle (SOS): The development and validation of a behavioural mental health checklist for the workplace. *Work and Stress, 33*, 295–313.

Dixon, J., & Dougherty, D. S. (2014). A language convergence/meaning divergence analysis exploring how LGBTQ and single employees manage traditional family expectations in the workplace. *Journal of Applied Communication Research, 42*, 1–19.

Eliason, M.J., DeJoseph, J., Dibble, S., Deevey, S., & Chinn, P. (2011). Lesbian, gay, bisexual, transgender, and queer/questioning nurses' experiences in the workplace. *Journal of Professional Nursing, 27*, 237–244.

Ettridge, K.A. et al. (2018). "Prostate cancer is far from hidden…": Perceptions of stigma, social isolation and help-seeking among men with prostate cancer. *European Journal of Cancer Care, 27*, e12790

Eziefula, C.U., Grunfeld, E.A., & Hunter, M.S. (2013). "You know I've joined your club … I'm the hot flush boy": A qualitative exploration of hot flushes and night sweats in men undergoing androgen deprivation therapy for prostate cancer. *Psycho-Oncology, 22*, 2823–2830.

Farrington, A.P., Wilson, G., Limbrick, H., & Swainston, K. (2019). The lived experience of adjustment to prostate cancer. *Psychology of Men and Masculinities.* http://dx.doi.org/10.1037/men0000237

Frone, M.R. (2006a). Prevalence and distribution of alcohol use and impairment in the workplace: A U.S. National Survey. *Journal of Studies on Alcohol, 67*, 147–156.

Frone, M.R. (2006b). Prevalence and distribution of illicit drug use in the workforce and in the workplace: Findings and implications from a U.S. National Survey. *Journal of Applied Psychology, 91*, 856–869.

Ghaemi, N. (2011). *A First-rate Madness: Uncovering the Links between Leadership and Mental Illness.* London, UK. Penguin Press.

Gloor, J. L., Okimoto, T. G., Feierabend, A., & Staffelbach, B. (2015). Young women are risky business? The "maybe baby" effect in employment decisions. In *Academy of Management Proceedings* (Vol. 2015, No. 1, p. 11858). Briarcliff Manor, NY 10510: Academy of Management.

Government of Canada: Parental leave – 808-IPG-014 (2019). Retrieved from https://www.canada.ca/en/employment-social-development/programs/laws-regulations/labour/interpretations-policies/parental-leave.html, Accessed July 21, 2021.

Grandey, A.A., Gabriel, A.S., & King, E.B. (2020). Tackling taboo topics: A review of the three Ms in working women's lives. *Journal of Management, 46*, 7–35.

Grunfeld, E.A., Drudge-Coates, L., Rixon, L., Eaton, E., & Cooper, A.F. (2013). "The only way I know how to live is to work": A qualitative study of work following treatment for prostate cancer. *Health Psychology, 32*, 75–82.

Hasselrot, K., Lindeberg, M., Konings, P., & Kopp Kallner, H. 2018. Investigating the loss of work productivity due to symptomatic leiomyoma. *PLoS One, 13*(6), e0197958.

Inceoglu, I., Thomas, G., Chu, C., Plans, D., & Gerbasi, A. (2018). Leadership and employee well-being: An integrated review and a future research agenda. *Leadership Quarterly, 29*, 179–202.

Kaluza, A.J., Boer, D., Buengeler, C., & van Dick, R. (2020). Leadership behavior and self-reported well-being: A review, integration and meta-analytic examination. *Work and Stress, 34*, 34–56.

Koenig, A.M., Eagly, A.H., Mitchell, A.A., & Ristikari, T. (2011). Are leader stereotypes masculine? A meta analysis of three research paradigms. *Psychological Bulletin, 137,* 616–642.

Kornhauser, A. (1965). *Mental Health of the Industrial Worker: A Detroit Study.* NY: Wiley.

Kornhauser, A.W., & Sharp, A.A. (1932). Employee attitudes: Suggestions from a study in a factory. *Personnel Journal,* 10, 393–404.

L'Etang, H. (1969). *The Pathology of Leadership: Old Diseases and New Treatments.* London: William Heinemann Medical Books

Leadership and Health/Well-Being (2019). http://www.eawop.org/news/small-group -meeting-on-leadership-and-health-well-being, Accessed July 21, 2021.

Marmot, M. (2004). *The Status Syndrome: How Social Standing Affects Our Health and Longevity.* London: Times Books/Henry Holt

McAdams, D.P. (2020). *The Strange Case of Donald J. Trump: A Psychological Reckoning.* NY: Oxford University Press.

McDermott, R. (2008). *Presidential Leadership, Illness, and Decision Making.* NY: Cambridge University Press.

Nielsen, K., & Taris, T.W. (2019). Leading well: Challenges to researching leadership in occupational health psychology – and some ways forward. *Work and Stress, 33,* 107–118.

Owen, D. (2008). *In Sickness and in Power: Illness in Heads of Government During the Last 100 Years.* CT: Praeger.

Owen, D. (2012). *The Hubris Syndrome: Bush, Blair and the Intoxication of Power.* North Yorkshire: Politico Publishing.

Owen, D., & Davidson, J. (2009). Hubris syndrome: An acquired personality disorder? A study of US Presidents and UK Prime Ministers over the last 100 years. *Brain, 132,* 1396–1406.

Rawla, P. (2019). Epidemiology of prostate cancer. *World Journal of Oncology, 10,* 63–89.

Sauter, S.L., Murphy, L.M., & Hurrell, J.J. (1990). Prevention of work-related psychological disorders: A national strategy proposed by the National Institute for Occupational Safety and Health (NIOSH). *American Psychologist, 45,* 1146–1158.

Schat, A.C.H., Frone, M.R., & Kelloway, E.K. (2006). Prevalence of workplace aggression in the U.S. workforce: Findings from a national study. In E.K. Kelloway, J. Barling, & J.J. Hurrell, Jr. (Eds.), *Handbook of Workplace Violence* (pp. 47–89). NY: Sage Publications.

Society of Obstetricians and Gynecologists of Canada (2020a). *Normal Periods: Menstrual Cycle Basics.* https://www.yourperiod.ca/normal-periods/menstrual-cycle -basics/, Accessed May 2020

Society of Obstetricians and Gynecologists of Canada (2020b). *Contraception: Hormonal Contraception.*   https://www.sexandu.ca/contraception/hormonal-contraception/, Accessed May 2020

Society of Obstetricians and Gynecologists of Canada (2020c). *Pregnancy: Special Considerations.*   https://www.pregnancyinfo.ca/your-pregnancy/special -consideration/miscarriage/, Accessed May 2020

Spence, M. (1973). Job market signalling. *Quarterly Journal of Economics, 87,* 355–374.

Spitzmueller, C., Wang, Z., Zhang, J., Thomas, C.L., Fisher, G.G., Matthews, R.A., & Strathearn, L. (2016). Got milk? Workplace factors related to breastfeeding among working mothers. *Journal of Organizational Behavior, 37,* 692–718.

Sutter, M., & Perrin, P.B. (2016). Discrimination, mental health, and suicidal ideation among LGBTQ people of color. *Journal of Counseling Psychology, 63,* 98–105.

Westaby, J.D., Versenyi, A., & Hausmann, R.C. (2005). Intentions to work during terminal illness: An exploratory study of antecedent conditions. *Journal of Applied Psychology, 90,* 1297–1305.

Wong, J.H.K., & Kelloway, E.K. (2016). What happens at work stays at work? Workplace supervisory social interactions and blood pressure outcomes. *Journal of Occupational Health Psychology, 21*(2), 133–141.

5. Observer interventions in workplace aggression: the state of the art and future directions

Ivana Vranjes, Zhanna Lyubykh and M. Sandy Hershcovis

When people work together in close proximity, frictions are bound to happen. The topic of workplace aggression has received considerable attention in recent years (Schilpzand et al., 2016). Research in this area spans across multiple disciplines and covers an array of aggression constructs, including incivility (e.g., Andersson & Pearson, 1999), bullying (e.g., Einarsen, 1999), violence (e.g., Rogers & Kelloway, 1997), antisocial behavior (e.g., O'Leary-Kelly et al., 2000), and harassment (e.g., Richman et al., 1999) (for a review, see Hershcovis, 2011). These phenomena fall under the umbrella term of aggression referring to negative behavior that targets are motivated to avoid (Baron & Neuman, 1996). While the prevalence rates of different types of aggressive behaviors vary widely (e.g., incivility *vs.* physical violence), studies consistently find that the majority of US and Canadian employees encounter some manifestations of workplace aggression throughout their career (Barling et al., 2009).

To date, research has examined both antecedents and consequences of aggressive behaviors. Contextual factors, such as perceived injustice and situational constraints, are especially powerful in predicting enacted aggression (Barling et al., 2009; Hershcovis et al., 2007). In addition, certain dispositional characteristics (e.g., trait anger and negative affectivity) relate to aggressive inclinations in individuals (Hershcovis et al., 2007). Dysfunctional cognitions and interaction patterns between the target and the perpetrator are also precipitating factors, as studies show that aggression can emerge from perceptions of provocation and hostile intent (Douglas & Martinko 2001; Martinko et al., 2002). From the target's perspective, aggression has devastating effects, resulting not only in

73

negative attitudes at work and reduced organizational commitment, but also in a general decline of well-being and life satisfaction (Bowling & Beehr, 2006).

Recently, researchers have started to focus on the role of observers – individuals indirectly involved in the aggression incident, either by seeing it or hearing about it (van Heugten, 2011). While there are a number of terms to describe individuals not directly involved in the incidents of aggression, such as witnesses (e.g., Lewis & Orford, 2005), third parties (e.g., Mitchell et al., 2015), and bystanders (e.g., D'Cruz & Noronha, 2011), throughout this chapter, we adopt the term 'observer'. Studies acknowledge that observers are not merely passive witnesses, but they can influence the dynamics of aggression (Bowes-Sperry & O'Leary-Kelly, 2005). Observers can display a range of responses, from challenging the perpetrator (Hershcovis et al., 2017) and comforting the target (Hershcovis & Bhatnagar, 2017; O'Reilly et al., 2016) to doing nothing at all (Latané & Darley, 1970). However, how they choose to respond can be of great importance. For instance, observers may be in a position to help targets, or alternatively, escalate the aggression by provoking the perpetrator or exacerbating its consequences by joining in. Consequently, researchers have acknowledged the importance of observer actions and consider observer interventions to be a promising avenue for mitigating or preventing aggression (e.g., Pouwelse et al., 2018).

In this chapter, we examine the current literature on the role of observers in the context of workplace aggression. We provide an overview of: (a) different typologies of observer roles ('What can they do?'), (b) the empirical evidence regarding observers' actual behavior ('What do they do?'), and (c) situational and personal constraints to observer interventions ('When do they do it?'). We conclude by exploring some future avenues for the further development of this promising research area and discussing practical implications of observer research on individuals confronted with aggression.

What can they do?

Researchers have proposed several typologies of observer roles, many of which draw on earlier work from the school literature (e.g., Twemlow et al., 2004). These different typologies vary in their complexity and scope. While some focus solely on the positive roles observers can have aimed at stopping or mitigating instances of aggression (Bowes-Sperry & O'Leary-Kelly, 2005; O'Reilly & Aquino, 2011), others map all possible observer reactions, including some that may worsen aggression episodes (Linstead, 2013; Paull et al., 2012).

Bowes-Sperry and O'Leary-Kelly (2005) distinguish between four categories of observer interventions, which can be classified alongside two dimensions: the level of immediacy of the intervention (high, low) and the level of involvement or immersion in the event (high, low). Low-immediacy and low-involvement interventions are reactions that occur after the aggression event has happened and require little risk on the part of the observer (e.g., approaching the target after the event and offering sympathy). Low-immediacy and high-involvement interventions occur after the event but require more investment from the observer (e.g., reporting the aggression to the management). High-immediacy and low-involvement interventions occur immediately but bear minimal risk for the observer (e.g., distracting the perpetrator of aggression). Finally, high-immediacy and high-involvement interventions happen both immediately and require a substantial investment from the observer (e.g., directly confronting the perpetrator).

O'Reilly and Aquino (2011) developed a model of observers' reaction to aggression in which they argue that observers display four types of behaviors: doing nothing, directly punishing the perpetrator (e.g., scold the perpetrator), indirectly punishing the perpetrator (e.g., report the mistreatment), or aiding the victim (e.g., provide a sympathetic ear). According to this model, observers are morally motivated to address the perceived injustice by intervening in the incidents of aggression. In this model, a number of factors influence observers' perceptions of justice, including the severity of harm, targets' deservingness of aggression, and attributions of blame. A specific observer intervention depends on the observer's power, belief in the disciplinary system, and perceptions of the target's power. For instance, when an observer thinks that organizational policies will punish aggressive acts, they are more likely to report the incident.

Paull et al. (2012) expanded on these perspectives by focusing not only on positive observer reactions (i.e., those that help the victim or stop the harassment), but also on mapping out negative ones (i.e., those that make harassment worse). Furthermore, they also added an active–passive continuum, resulting in 13 possible observer roles. They distinguished between four active–constructive roles (i.e., defending, sympathizing, defusing, and intervening) and one active–passive role (i.e., emphasizing). Furthermore, they identified four destructive–active roles (i.e., facilitating, manipulating, collaborating, and instigating) and four destructive–passive roles (i.e., submitting, succumbing, avoiding, and abdicating). While constructive–active roles require some kind of positive involvement of the observer, the constructive–passive roles assume a positive intent on the part of the observer but a lack of action. Alternatively, destructive–active roles involved actively contributing to the aggression by directly supporting the perpetrator, while destructive–passive roles provide indirect support to the perpetrator by abstaining from action.

Linstead (2013) criticized Paull et al.'s (2012) typology arguing that it does not entirely reflect the ambiguity of many workplace situations. Namely, he argued that people can have different perceptions regarding whether or not they deem certain behavior by the observer as constructive and that a typology should instead be based on the degree of moral challenge and responsibility implicit to the situation. He reduced the 13 roles identified by Paull et al. to eight, representing the moral position of observers in the destructive perpetrator–target relationship. The eight roles according to Linstead are: active accessory (e.g., assists bullying), bystander (e.g., does nothing), whistle-blower (e.g., takes action to halt bullying), mediator (e.g., prevents escalation), advocate (e.g., stands up for the victim), indexical victim (e.g., identifies with the victim), post hoc comforter (e.g., offers support in private), and the collateral victim (e.g., becomes fellow victim).

While these typologies are useful for furthering our understanding of different behaviors observers of aggression display, Pouwelse et al. (2018) called for the inclusion of dynamic observer roles as well, which account for individuals who switch positions from supporting the target to aiding the perpetrator (Bloch, 2012; Tye-Williams & Krone, 2015). According to them, the fact that this group of individuals is both largely prevalent and undecided in their blame attribution (Bloch, 2012), may make them particularly interesting with regard to implementation of observer interventions.

Overall, there are a number of typologies in the current literature. We concur with Linstead (2013) in arguing that there is inconsistency in the way the terms 'constructive' and 'destructive' are used to describe observer interventions. For instance, while Paull et al. (2012) assume that every observer strategy aimed at either addressing the aggression or comforting the target is constructive, Hershcovis and Bhatnagar (2017) suggested that perpetrator-directed retaliatory response is not a constructive observer intervention as it involves further aggression. The differences lie in whether constructiveness of an intervention is grounded in the observers' intention *or* consequences of their actions (or inaction).

Paull et al. (2012) define constructive *vs.* destructive interventions based on observers' intent, while other researchers (e.g., Hershcovis & Bhatnagar, 2017) argue that constructiveness of the intervention is contingent upon its consequences. In other words, while observers may intend to prevent aggression by directly confronting the perpetrator, this type of intervention may result in further escalation. That is, solving aggression with further aggression cannot be considered constructive. Furthermore, not immediately reacting to aggression (i.e., avoiding the incident), which Paull et al. classify as a passive–destructive reaction, can sometimes be a positive strategy aimed at avoiding further escalation (Stouten et al., 2019). Thus, we suggest integrating intervention intent and consequences when defining the constructiveness of observer interventions, and argue that a constructive intervention incorporates an observer's intent to mitigate or prevent aggression and, at least partially, achieves the stated intent. In contrast, a destructive intervention does not intend to prevent or mitigate aggression and/or results in negative consequences (e.g., escalation of aggression). In what follows, we review findings from empirical studies that have examined both constructive and destructive types of observer interventions.

What do they do?

While the previous section described several theoretically possible observer strategies for dealing with aggression, the reality of work life does not always correspond to the expectations of theory. When testing observer behavioral reactions, empirical studies rarely distinguish among numerous types of observer actions and instead focus on two broad categories of observer interventions: perpetrator-focused (e.g., Mitchell et al., 2015) and target-focused (e.g., Hershcovis & Bhatnagar, 2017).

Witnessing an unpleasant workplace interaction represents a negative work event, and employees feel emotionally drained as a result (Totterdell et al., 2012). Research demonstrates that witnessed aggression leads to a number of negative affective reactions for the observers (e.g., Zhou et al., 2017). Studies on observer reactions often draw on the deontic model of justice (Folger, 2001), which argues that when individuals witness mistreatment, they experience moral anger, which motivates them to intervene. According to the model, one way to restore justice is by punishing the perpetrator. However, perpetrator-directed retaliatory responses are not a constructive observer intervention as they may escalate the situation (Hershcovis & Bhatnagar, 2017). Providing an alternative view, Hershcovis and Bhatnagar suggested that observers can also experience an empathetic response that, in turn, results in target-aided observer intervention. Below, we discuss empirical findings regarding different observer reactions to witnessed aggression.

Several studies have looked at constructive observer reactions. Ryan and Wessel (2012) conducted two studies: a critical incident, in which they asked

participations about their interventions, and a vignette study, where participants indicated their intervention intentions. They found that, respectively,
57 percent and 67 percent of individuals reported that they either had, or
would have taken action. The intervention intentions mostly referred to
target-focused actions (e.g., supporting the target), rather than direct perpetrator confrontation. Consistent with this research, Hershcovis and Bhatnagar
(2017) found that when customers observed a fellow customer mistreat an
employee, only 11 percent intervened by confronting the perpetrator; however,
73 percent of witnesses engaged in supportive target-directed behaviors (e.g.,
being friendly to the target) and, on average, left higher tips.

While target-aided intervention may mitigate target negative consequences
of experienced aggression, this strategy is unlikely to prevent the perpetrator
from re-engaging in aggressive behaviors. In a study of aggressive incidents
in public spaces, Levine et al. (2011) found that observers were more likely to
engage in conciliatory behaviors aimed at preventing aggression from becoming violent (e.g., blocking contact between the target and the perpetrator)
than in escalation behaviors (e.g., hitting the perpetrator), and this tendency
increased with increased group size. Furthermore, conciliatory behaviors were
more effective when used by multiple observers.

When seeking to restore justice, observers may also engage in less constructive forms of intervention (e.g., retaliation). Research has demonstrated that
observers attempt to restore justice by punishing the perpetrator (O'Reilly et
al., 2016; Reich & Hershcovis, 2015), even at their own expense (Turillo et al.,
2002), and withholding resources from the perpetrator (Rupp & Bell, 2010).
While we know very little about the consequences of observer interventions,
retaliation is generally viewed as a destructive intervention due to its potential
to escalate (i.e., incivility spiral; Andersson & Pearson, 1999).

Furthermore, not all observers condemn witnessed aggression. In a study
based on a large sample of US employees (Namie & Lutgen-Sandvik, 2010),
60 percent of individuals who were mistreated by a solo harasser reported
that they felt that the perpetrator was supported or enabled by others within
the organization (e.g., managers, peers, HR), either actively (co-harassers) or
passively (accomplices). Empirical evidence suggests that not all observers
experience anger when witnessing aggression. In a two-wave survey, Mitchell
et al. (2015) found that some observers experienced contentment when they
perceived that the target was deserving of mistreatment. Additionally, Li et
al. (2019) theorized that some observers experience schadenfreude – pleasure
from observing another person's misfortune (Blader et al., 2010) – particularly
if they judged the target to be deserving of mistreatment. Subsequently, this

emotional reaction can lead to destructive observer actions such as mistreating the target or withdrawing help to the target (Mitchell et al., 2015). Thus, observers may not only direct destructive reactions towards the perpetrator in form of retaliation, but also towards the target in the form of condoning or joining in on mistreatment.

Finally, witnessing mistreatment can also elicit reactions that go beyond targets or perpetrators. For instance, observers may change their attitudes toward the organization. Miner-Rubino and Cortina (2007) showed that observing hostility towards women resulted in higher levels of job withdrawal. Some employees, who observe aggression, especially when it stems from the supervisor, may resort to organizational deviance as a means to restore their sense of justice (Greenbaum, Mawritz, Mayer, & Priesemuth, 2013). Even an observers' indirect knowledge of aggression within the group can result in observers' subsequent engagement in interpersonal deviant behaviors (Ferguson & Barry, 2011). Porath et al. (2010) demonstrated that witnessing incivility between employees can result in customers' negative generalizations about the company and other employees at the company.

In conclusion, while theory proposes a wide range of observer reactions to workplace aggression, empirical studies have examined only a few of those strategies. Some of those reactions have the potential to mitigate the negative effects of experienced aggression (e.g., supporting the target), while other forms of interventions can result in escalation (e.g., retaliation).

When do they intervene?

Most observers feel unable to act due to different internal and external factors (Paull et al., 2019). Although inaction is a common response (Latané & Darley, 1970), as described above, observers do sometimes intervene in the incidents of witnessed aggression. Certain dispositional and situational factors may influence whether and how observers react to aggression. In this section, we provide an overview of theories that predict observer actions and empirical studies that examined *when* observers are more or less likely to intervene.

Theoretical perspectives

Skarlicki and Kulik (2004) proposed a model of observer intervention arguing that observers' decision to act is a three-stage iterative process, where observers decide whether there is a negative impact to the target, attribute responsibility for the aggression, and judge to what extent the witnessed behavior is unfair. Actors' characteristics (e.g., target's attributes and behaviors), observers' characteristics (e.g., personality, moral identity), and the costs–benefits assessment (e.g., fear of retaliation, organizational climate) can all influence whether observers intervene.

Similarly, Bowes-Sperry and O'Leary-Kelly (2005) suggested that the decision to intervene is contingent upon cognitive processes. First, individuals determine whether an event requires action and whether observers perceive a responsibility to act. Next, observers determine whether it is better to act immediately or later (i.e., the urgency of the situation). Finally, observers assess the cost and the benefits of intervening for themselves in order to determine how involved they want to get. The result of these decision processes determines observer reaction, or lack thereof. Paull et al. (2019) extended this model adding that observers consider whether or not the intervention will result in positive outcomes for the target, as well as for themselves.

According to Goldberg et al. (2011), observers are more likely to intervene when: (a) their identification with the target outweighs the cost of being associated with a low-status member, (b) they prioritize positively changing target's circumstances over the cost of being perceived as a troublemaker, and (c) changing the work environment for the better is more important to them than going against the group. In this model, justice perceptions play a crucial role; observers' willingness to intervene depends on scope of justice (whether the target deserves just treatment) as well as the justice climate within the organization.

In all of these models, observer intervention is a deliberate decision resulting from complex cognitive processes in which individuals consider both organizational factors (e.g., justice perceptions) and their own or other actor's characteristics (e.g., responsibility perceptions). Furthermore, the cost–benefit analysis in which observers weigh the value of intervening against the intervention cost is salient in all models. However, another perspective on observer interventions highlights intuitive and reflexive reactions that happen in absence of complex cognitive processes.

O'Reilly and Aquino (2011) identified three factors that determine individual's responses to perceived injustice: their own moral identity, their perceptions of power, and their belief that the organization's justice system fairly and consistently punishes wrongdoers. They argue that the more someone considers being moral as central to their own self-concept, the more power they have, and the more they believe they can influence the situation, the more they will be inclined to respond to witnessed injustice. This model draws on the deontic perspective (Folger, 2001), according to which individuals do not always act out of self-interest, but are able to identify injustice committed towards others and feel morally motivated to act upon it. Thus, people act upon their moral intuition and experience an automatic reaction to restore wrongdoing even when it is unrelated to them. Unlike the previous models, this model does not consider the cost–benefit of their action.

Empirical evidence

Empirical studies so far have drawn on both the cost–benefit perspective (e.g., McDonald et al., 2016) and the deontic perspective (e.g., Hershcovis & Bhatnagar, 2017; Reich & Hershcovis, 2015) to investigate organizational, situational, and individual factors that may influence the likelihood of observer interventions.

The theoretical perspectives of Skarlicki and Kulik (2004) and O'Reilly and Aquino (2011) emphasize that there are organizational constraints to observer interventions. In support, empirical studies find that some organizational cultures tolerate and accept negative behaviors such as workplace mistreatment (Samnani & Singh, 2012), and such behavior can even become a norm (McDonald et al., 2016). In other contexts, there is not a unified vision on which behaviors constitute aggression (Omari & Sharma, 2016). Such factors can contribute to the emergence of institutionalized abuse (Liefooghe & Mackenzie Davey, 2001) and seriously impede both employees' recognition of aggression and their willingness to take actions against it. Furthermore, research demonstrates that employees are more likely to report unethical behavior of their co-workers or leaders when the behavior violates organizational norms (Mayer et al., 2013). Observer action is also restricted when organizations and their human resources department are not responsive to complaints (Paull et al., 2019) and when employees who report negative behavior fear potential negative consequences from it, such as reprisal or sanction from peers or superiors (McDonald et al., 2016). This ties in with both the cost–benefit perspective, and the moral perspective in that employees consider the risks of intervention, and also consider the overall justice climate in the workplace when deciding whether or not to act (Priesemuth & Schminke, 2019).

Empirical findings also support the importance of situational and dispositional factors in determining whether and how observers respond to aggression, as proposed by different theoretical perspectives. In line with the deontic perspective, studies show that powerful individuals (Hershcovis et al., 2017) and those high in moral identity (Skarlicki & Rupp, 2010) are generally more likely to react to mistreatment. The former relates to the fact that powerful individuals experience more responsibility to act and sometimes may even perceive aggression as a status challenge (Hershcovis et al., 2017). In line with the cost–benefit perspective, empirical studies identify several other factors that can influence observers' perceptions of responsibility to intervene. Identification with the target and proximity to the behavior are important triggers for observer action (McDonald et al., 2016). That is, the immediacy of the situation is more salient when the observer knows the target personally or empathizes with him or her. In addition, it is harder to ignore a behavior when one is directly involved in the situation or experiences it from very close proximity (McDonald et al., 2016). Observers are also more inclined to act when the negative behavior is unambiguously negative and directed at the target (Ryan & Wessel, 2012). Another situational factor that has a strong relationship with the likelihood of observer intervention is the number of observers. A smaller group elicits higher response likelihood (Ryan & Wessel, 2012), perhaps because observers feel directly responsible to intervene and there is therefore less diffusion of responsibility.

Finally, in line with the cost–benefit perspective, target characteristics can also influence observers' willingness to help as research shows that observers are less likely to support a target who is deemed deserving of mistreatment (Mitchell et al., 2015), or who responded to aggression in a tit-for-tat manner (Hershcovis & Bhatnagar, 2017). Van Heugten (2011) also found that observers were more likely to speak up after the target had declared the intention to leave the organization, probably because this further underlined the gravity of the situation.

In sum, organizational factors, such as culture, norms, fairness perceptions, and human resource practices are vital in creating trust and empowering employees to engage in constructive interventions. Additionally, individuals may feel more inclined to act when urgency is high, when they identify with the target, when they are high in moral identity and when they feel powerful enough to get involved.

Future directions

Despite recent advances in the field of observer interventions in the context of workplace aggression, we still lack a complete understanding of this phenomenon. Below, we discuss some of the most important gaps in the current literature and offer suggestions for future research.

Intervention effectiveness

Although theory and empirical research suggest that observers sometimes intervene in the incidents of aggression, we know very little about whether or not observer interventions can actually mitigate or prevent aggression. Researchers have already advocated for observer intervention as a means to deal with workplace aggression, assuming that observer interventions are effective. While we are not disputing the proposition that observer intervention can be an effective way to prevent or mitigate aggression, researchers need to investigate systematically whether and under what conditions such interventions are effective and safe. We suggest that some interventions may not only be ineffective, but also harmful to the target or the intervening observer.

An important underlying motive for workplace aggression is power protection (Porath et al., 2008). Power creates a social distance between the perpetrator and others (Magee & Smith, 2013) and reduces impulse control (Inesi et al., 2012). Evidence shows that people in power positions are more likely to engage in aggression, and that feeling powerful during a particular occasion leads to more abusive behavior (Foulk et al., 2018). Furthermore, a threat to someone's power position is often an instigating factor of aggression (Fast & Chen, 2009). Considering that power is a crucial motivator for aggression, perpetrator-targeted observer interventions are likely to threaten perpetrators' sense of power. This in turn can result in defensive reactions in perpetrators in the form of restricted and rigid information processing (de Wit et al., 2013). In other words, observer interventions may limit perpetrators' self-reflective tendencies and make them less likely to react constructively to the intervention. Following this reasoning, research needs to test whether observer interventions can evoke defensive reactions in perpetrators. Additionally, research should look at whether powerful observers – individuals whose behavior is consistent with their hierarchical role (Hershcovis et al., 2017) – stand a better chance of evoking positive change in perpetrators' behavior.

Consequences for intervening observers

When observers intervene, they may put themselves at risk. Research has not yet considered the long-term consequences of observer intervention for the observers themselves. Intervening observers may face backlash from other actors involved in the instance of aggression: the target, the perpetrator, or other observers. We propose that future research examine how all parties involved in the incident of aggression react to intervening observers.

As stated previously, perpetrators are motivated to preserve their sense of power and may feel threatened by an intervening observer. This may not only result in the perpetrator negatively perceiving the observer, but can also lead to retaliatory responses against the observer. Cortina and Magley (2003) found that targets who speak up against mistreatment face retaliation. Such retaliation could just as readily be targeted towards intervening observers, such that intervening may not only be ineffective, but also unsafe for the intervener.

Furthermore, targets may react negatively towards the intervening observer as they may not wish for others to get involved. Namely, receiving assistance may threaten targets' sense of self-esteem (Tessler & Schwartz, 1972) or induce feelings of inadequacy (Morris & Rosen, 1973). Targets may also be concerned about looking incompetent in the eyes of others (Wills, 1978) and worry about preserving their public image or status (Chan, 2013). Consequently, targets unwilling to accept assistance may in fact develop negative affect towards the intervening observer and avoid them in further interactions.

Finally, other observers who have not reacted to aggression themselves may feel threatened by the intervening observer. People strive for a positive moral self-image (Bandura, 1991) and tend to overestimate their own moral behavior (Peters et al., 2004). When confronted with another observer who acted when they themselves failed to do so, this may induce feelings of moral failure and defensive mechanisms. One way of restoring one's sense of moral self-worth is by derogating the source of moral threat (Monin et al., 2008). Thus, observers who have failed to act in the incident of aggression may feel threatened by the intervening observer and may respond negatively to this person, by, for instance, excluding the observer from future activities or even showing support to the perpetrator.

Following these arguments, future studies on observer interventions should consider the consequences of observer interventions for the observers themselves and investigate different factors that may influence how others react to intervening observers.

Consequences for non-intervening observers

Most observers are not indifferent to the witnessed incidents of aggression, and research suggests that observers experience a moral obligation to rectify the wrongdoing (Folger & Glerum, 2015). Yet, early research on the bystander effect demonstrated that observers' inaction, as opposed to intervention, is the most prevalent response (Latané & Darley, 1970). To date, researchers focused mostly on emotional consequences of witnessing aggression (e.g., Mitchell et al., 2015), and it remains unclear whether those negative emotions are driven by the witnessed aggression itself or represent observers' response to their failure to intervene.

When deciding whether to intervene, observers may fear embarrassment or potential retaliation from the perpetrator. Possible implications of these perceived immediate negative consequences may prevent observers from intervening even if they are morally motivated to correct the wrongdoing. Hence, observers can experience a discrepancy between the desired action (i.e., intervention) and their actual behavior (i.e., inaction), and perceive their failure to intervene as a signal of immoral behavior resulting in negative self-perceptions.

Furthermore, observer inaction can serve as a signal to perpetrators that aggression was justifiable. This can further result in perpetuating aggressive behaviors or even an escalation of aggression from relatively mild (e.g., incivility) to more severe forms (e.g., physical violence) (Dupré & Barling, 2006). Given that observer inaction is the most prevalent response among observers of workplace aggression, we propose that future research examine the consequences of observer failure to intervene in the incidents of aggression. Understanding this phenomenon from the perspectives of all parties involved – observers, targets, and perpetrator – is a fruitful avenue for future research.

Conclusion

In this chapter, we presented an overview of different typologies of observer interventions. Although theoretical frameworks theorize a variety of observer roles, empirical research mostly examines two types of observer responses: target- or perpetrator-focused. Given the growing interest in the role of observers in preventing workplace aggression, we suggest future research examines the effectiveness of observer interventions. Furthermore, we suggest that certain observer actions or lack of thereof, might have consequences for all parties involved in the aggression incident.

References

Andersson, L. M., & Pearson, C. M. (1999). Tit for tat? The spiraling effect of incivility in the workplace. *Academy of Management Review, 24*(3), 452–471.

Bandura, A. (1991). Social cognitive theory of self-regulation. *Organizational Behavior and Human Decision Processes, 50*(2), 248–287.

Barling, J., Dupré, K. E., & Kelloway, E. K. (2009). Predicting workplace aggression and violence. *Annual Review of Psychology, 60,* 671–692.

Baron, R. A., & Neuman, J. H. (1996). Workplace violence and workplace aggression: Evidence on their relative frequency and potential causes. *Aggressive Behavior: Official Journal of the International Society for Research on Aggression, 22*(3), 161–173.

Blader, S. L., Wiesenfeld, B., Rothman, R., & Wheeler-Smith, S. (2010). Social emotions and justice: How the emotional fabric of groups determines justice enactment and reactions. In E. A. Mannix, M. A. Neale (Series Eds.) & E. Mullen (Vol. Ed.), *Research on Managing Groups and Teams: Fairness & Groups* (pp. 29–62). Bingley, UK: Emerald.

Bloch, C. (2012). How witnesses contribute to bullying in the workplace. In N. Tehrani (Ed.), *Workplace Bullying* (pp. 81–96). London: Routledge.

Bowes-Sperry, L., & O'Leary-Kelly, A. M. (2005). To act or not to act: The dilemma faced by sexual harassment observers. *Academy of Management Review, 30*(2), 288–306.

Bowling, N. A., & Beehr, T. A. (2006). Workplace harassment from the victim's perspective: A theoretical model and meta-analysis. *Journal of Applied Psychology, 91*(5), 998–1012.

Chan, M. E. (2013). Antecedents of instrumental interpersonal help-seeking: An integrative review. *Applied Psychology, 62*(4), 571–596.

Cortina, L. M., & Magley, V. J. (2003). Raising voice, risking retaliation: Events following interpersonal mistreatment in the workplace. *Journal of Occupational Health Psychology, 8*(4), 247–265. https://doi.org/10.1037/1076-8998.8.4.247

D'Cruz, P., & Noronha, E. (2011). The limits to workplace friendship: Managerialist HRM and bystander behaviour in the context of workplace bullying. *Employee Relations, 33*(3), 269–288.

de Wit, F. R., Jehn, K. A., & Scheepers, D. (2013). Task conflict, information processing, and decision-making: The damaging effect of relationship conflict. *Organizational Behavior and Human Decision Processes, 122*(2), 177–189.

Douglas, S. C., & Martinko, M. J. (2001). Exploring the role of individual differences in the prediction of workplace aggression. *Journal of Applied Psychology, 86*(4), 547–559.

Dupré, K. E., & Barling, J. (2006). Predicting and preventing supervisory workplace aggression. *Journal of Occupational Health Psychology, 11,* 13–26.

Einarsen, S. (1999). The nature and causes of bullying at work. *International Journal of Manpower, 20*(1/2), 16–27.

Fast, N. J., & Chen, S. (2009). When the boss feels inadequate: Power, incompetence, and aggression. *Psychological Science, 20*(11), 1406–1413.

Ferguson, M., & Barry, B. (2011). I know what you did: The effects of interpersonal deviance on bystanders. *Journal of Occupational Health Psychology, 16*(1), 80–94.

Folger, R. (2001). Fairness as deonance. In S. Gilliland, D. D. Steiner, & D. P. Skarlicki (Eds.), *Research in Social Issues in Management* (pp. 3–31). Charlotte, NC: Information Age.

Folger, R., & Glerum, D. R. (2015). Justice and deonance: "You ought". In R. S. Cropanzano & M. L. Ambrose (Eds.), *Oxford Handbook of Justice in the Workplace* (pp. 331–350). Oxford: Oxford University Press.

Foulk, T. A., Lanaj, K., Tu, M. H., Erez, A., & Archambeau, L. (2018). Heavy is the head that wears the crown: An actor-centric approach to daily psychological power, abusive leader behavior, and perceived incivility. *Academy of Management Journal, 61*(2), 661–684.

Goldberg, C. B., Clark, M. A., & Henley, A. B. (2011). Speaking up: A conceptual model of voice responses following the unfair treatment of others in non-union settings. *Human Resource Management, 50*(1), 75–94.

Greenbaum, R. L., Mawritz, M. B., Mayer, D. M., & Priesemuth, M. (2013). To act out, to withdraw, or to constructively resist? Employee reactions to supervisor abuse of customers and the moderating role of employee moral identity. *Human Relations, 66*(7), 925–950.

Hershcovis, M. (2011). "Incivility, social undermining, bullying… oh my!": A call to reconcile constructs within workplace aggression research. *Journal of Organizational Behavior, 32*(3), 499–519.

Hershcovis, M. S., & Bhatnagar, N. (2017). When fellow customers behave badly: Witness reactions to employee mistreatment by customers. *Journal of Applied Psychology, 102*(11), 1528–1544.

Hershcovis, M. S., Neville, L., Reich, T. C., Christie, A. M., Cortina, L. M., & Shan, J. V. (2017). Witnessing wrongdoing: The effects of observer power on incivility intervention in the workplace. *Organizational Behavior and Human Decision Processes, 142*, 45–57.

Hershcovis, M. S., Turner, N., Barling, J., Arnold, K. A., Dupré, K. E., Inness, M., & Sivanathan, N. (2007). Predicting workplace aggression: a meta-analysis. *Journal of Applied Psychology, 92*(1), 228–238.

Hodgins, M., MacCurtain, S., & Mannix-McNamara, P. (2014). Workplace bullying and incivility: A systematic review of interventions. *International Journal of Workplace Health Management, 7*(1), 54–72.

Inesi, M. E., Gruenfeld, D. H., & Galinsky, A. D. (2012). How power corrupts relationships: Cynical attributions for others' generous acts. *Journal of Experimental Social Psychology, 48*(4), 795–803.

Latané, B., & Darley, J. M. (1970). *The Unresponsive Bystander: Why Doesn't He Help?* New York: Appleton-Century-Crofts.

Leiter, M. P., Laschinger, H. K. S., Day, A., & Oore, D. G. (2011). The impact of civility interventions on employee social behavior, distress, and attitudes. *Journal of Applied Psychology, 96*(6), 1258–1274.

Levine, M., Taylor, P., & Best, R. (2011). Third parties, violence, and conflict resolution: The role of group size and collective action in the microregulation of violence. *Psychological Science, 22*(3), 406–412.

Lewis, S. E., & Orford, J. (2005). Women's experiences of workplace bullying: Changes in social relationships. *Journal of Community & Applied Social Psychology, 15*(1), 29–47.

Li, X., McAllister, D. J., Ilies, R., & Gloor, J. L. (2019). Schadenfreude: A counternormative observer response to workplace mistreatment. *Academy of Management Review, 44*(2), 360–376.

Liefooghe, A. P., & Mackenzie Davey, K. (2001). Accounts of workplace bullying: The role of the organization. *European Journal of Work and Organizational Psychology*, *10*(4), 375–392.

Linstead, S. (2013). Organizational bystanding: Whistleblowing, watching the work go by or aiding and abetting? *M@n@gement*, *16*(5), 680–696.

Magee, J. C., & Smith, P. K. (2013). The social distance theory of power. *Personality and Social Psychology Review*, *17*(2), 158–186.

Martinko, M. J., Gundlach, M. J., & Douglas, S. C. (2002). Toward an integrative theory of counterproductive workplace behavior: A causal reasoning perspective. *International Journal of Selection and Assessment*, *10*(1–2), 36–50.

Mayer, D. M., Nurmohamed, S., Treviño, L. K., Shapiro, D. L., & Schminke, M. (2013). Encouraging employees to report unethical conduct internally: It takes a village. *Organizational Behavior and Human Decision Processes*, *121*(1), 89–103.

McDonald, P., Charlesworth, S., & Graham, T. (2016). Action or inaction: Bystander intervention in workplace sexual harassment. *The International Journal of Human Resource Management*, *27*(5), 548–566.

Miner-Rubino, K., & Cortina, L. M. (2007). Beyond targets: Consequences of vicarious exposure to misogyny at work. *Journal of Applied Psychology*, *92*(5), 1254–1269.

Mitchell, M. S., Vogel, R. M., & Folger, R. (2015). Third parties' reactions to the abusive supervision of coworkers. *Journal of Applied Psychology*, *100*(4), 1040–1055.

Monin, B., Sawyer, P. J., & Marquez, M. J. (2008). The rejection of moral rebels: Resenting those who do the right thing. *Journal of Personality and Social Psychology*, *95*(1), 76–93.

Morris, S. C., & Rosen, S. (1973). Effects of felt adequacy and opportunity to reciprocate on help seeking. *Journal of Experimental Social Psychology*, *9*(3), 265–276.

Namie, G., & Lutgen-Sandvik, P. E. (2010). Active and passive accomplices: The communal character of workplace bullying. *International Journal of Communication*, *4*, 343–373.

O'Leary-Kelly, A. M., Duffy, M. K., & Griffin, R. W. (2000). Construct confusion in the study of antisocial work behavior. *Research in Personnel and Human Resources Management*, *18*, 275–304.

Omari, M., & Sharma, M. (2016). In the eye of the beholder: Ethnic culture as a lens. In M. Omari & M. Paull (Eds.), *Workplace Abuse, Incivility and Bullying: Methodological and Cultural Perspectives* (pp. 39–54). London: Taylor and Francis/Routledge.

O'Reilly, J., & Aquino, K. (2011). A model of third parties' morally motivated responses to mistreatment in organizations. *Academy of Management Review*, *36*(3), 526–543.

O'Reilly, J., Aquino, K., & Skarlicki, D. (2016). The lives of others: Third parties' responses to others' injustice. *Journal of Applied Psychology*, *101*(2), 171–189.

Paull, M., Omari, M., D'Cruz, P., & Güneri Çangarli, B. (2019). Bystanders in workplace bullying: Working university students' perspectives on action versus inaction. *Asia Pacific Journal of Human Resources*, *58*(3), 313–334.

Paull, M., Omari, M., & Standen, P. (2012). When is a bystander not a bystander? A typology of the roles of bystanders in workplace bullying. *Asia Pacific Journal of Human Resources*, *50*(3), 351–366.

Peters, S. L., Van den Bos, K., & Bobocel, D. R. (2004). The moral superiority effect: Self versus other differences in satisfaction with being overpaid. *Social Justice Research*, *17*(3), 257–273.

Porath, C., MacInnis, D., & Folkes, V. (2010). Witnessing incivility among employees: Effects on consumer anger and negative inferences about companies. *Journal of Consumer Research*, 37(2), 292–303.

Porath, C. L., Overbeck, J. R., & Pearson, C. M. (2008). Picking up the gauntlet: How individuals respond to status challenges. *Journal of Applied Social Psychology*, 38(7), 1945–1980.

Pouwelse, M., Mulder, R., & Mikkelsen, E. G. (2018). The role of bystanders in workplace bullying: An overview of theories and empirical research. In P. D'Cruz et al. (Eds.), *Pathways of Job-related Negative Behaviour* (pp. 1–39). *Handbooks of Workplace Bullying, Emotional Abuse and Harassment*. Singapore: Springer Nature.

Priesemuth, M., & Schminke, M. (2019). Helping thy neighbor? Prosocial reactions to observed abusive supervision in the workplace. *Journal of Management*, 45(3), 1225–1251.

Reich, T. C., & Hershcovis, M. S. (2015). Observing workplace incivility. *Journal of Applied Psychology*, 100(1), 203–215.

Richman, J. A., Rospenda, K. M., Nawyn, S. J., Flaherty, J. A., Fendrich, M., Drum, M. L., & Johnson, T. P. (1999). Sexual harassment and generalized workplace abuse among university employees: Prevalence and mental health correlates. *American Journal of Public Health*, 89(3), 358–363.

Rogers, K. A., & Kelloway, E. K. (1997). Violence at work: Personal and organizational outcomes. *Journal of Occupational Health Psychology*, 2(1), 63–71.

Rupp, D. E., & Bell, C. M. (2010). Extending the deontic model of justice: Moral self-regulation in third-party responses to injustice. *Business Ethics Quarterly*, 20(1), 89–106.

Ryan, A. M., & Wessel, J. L. (2012). Sexual orientation harassment in the workplace: When do observers intervene? *Journal of Organizational Behavior*, 33(4), 488–509.

Samnani, A. K., & Singh, P. (2012). 20 years of workplace bullying research: A review of the antecedents and consequences of bullying in the workplace. *Aggression and Violent Behavior*, 17(6), 581–589.

Schilpzand, P., De Pater, I. E., & Erez, A. (2016). Workplace incivility: A review of the literature and agenda for future research. *Journal of Organizational Behavior*, 37, S57–S88.

Skarlicki, D. P., & Kulik, C. T. (2004). Third-party reactions to employee (mis)treatment: A justice perspective. *Research in Organizational Behavior*, 26, 183–229.

Skarlicki, D. P., & Rupp, D. E. (2010). Dual processing and organizational justice: The role of rational versus experiential processing in third-party reactions to workplace mistreatment. *Journal of Applied Psychology*, 95(5), 944–952.

Stouten, J., Tripp, T., Bies, R., & De Cremer, D. (2019). When something is not right: The value of silence. *Academy of Management Perspectives*, 33(3), 323–333.

Tessler, R. C., & Schwartz, S. H. (1972). Help seeking, self-esteem, and achievement motivation: An attributional analysis. *Journal of Personality and Social Psychology*, 21(3), 318–326.

Totterdell, P., Hershcovis, M. S., Niven, K., Reich, T. C., & Stride, C. (2012). Can employees be emotionally drained by witnessing unpleasant interactions between coworkers? A diary study of induced emotion regulation. *Work & Stress*, 26(2), 112–129. https://doi.org/10.1080/02678373.2012.681153

Twemlow, S. W., Fonagy, P., & Sacco, F. C. (2004). The role of the bystander in the social architecture of bullying and violence in schools and communities. *Annals of the New York Academy of Sciences*, 1036, 215–232.

Turillo, C. J., Folger, R., Lavelle, J. J., Umphress, E. E., & Gee, J. O. (2002). Is virtue its own reward? Self-sacrificial decisions for the sake of fairness. *Organizational Behavior and Human Decision Processes*, *89*(1), 839–865.

Tye-Williams, S., & Krone, K. J. (2015). Chaos, reports, and quests: Narrative agency and co-workers in stories of workplace bullying. *Management Communication Quarterly*, *29*(1), 3–27.

van Heugten, K. (2011). Theorizing active bystanders as change agents in workplace bullying of social workers. *Families in Society*, *92*(2), 219–224.

Wills, T. A. (1978). Perceptions of clients by professional helpers. *Psychological Bulletin*, *85*(5), 968–1000.

Zhou, B., Marchand, A., & Guay, S. (2017). I see so I feel: Coping with workplace violence among victims and witnesses. *Work*, *57*(1), 125–135.

6. Are your smart technologies 'killing it' or killing you? Developing a research agenda for workplace ICT and worker wellbeing

Arla Day, Ryan Cook, Rachael Jones-Chick and Vanessa Myers

Information and communication technology (ICT) such as smartphones, computers, tablets, and other devices, has become a fundamental component in our work and social lives. These technologies have allowed us to control how, when, and where we complete our work, help us keep connected with colleagues across geographic locations, improve access to information, and can improve our overall functioning and performance (Day et al., 2019). Advantages of ICT are more evident for jobs that are geographically distanced, or during emergency situations such as the COVID-19 pandemic. However, these technologies also have the potential to decrease our control over work, physically and psychologically distance us from our colleagues, and decrease overall performance (Day et al., 2019). Ultimately, ICT is not inherently good or bad, but we do not have a solid understanding of the work and nonwork factors that may affect ICT's influence on worker health.

This somewhat paradoxical effect of ICT on wellbeing has been implicitly or explicitly noted by many researchers (Day et al., 2010, 2012, 2019; Leonardi et al., 2010; Mazmanian et al., 2013; O'Driscoll et al., 2010; Rennecker & Godwin, 2005; Ter Hoeven et al., 2016), with several reviews identifying key aspects of ICT that are associated with worker wellbeing and ill-health. Based on these guiding models and frameworks, while acknowledging the major gaps in our knowledge, this chapter integrates and extends these works to create a practical research framework to identify the crucial research agendas in this area.

ICT and worker health

ICT is defined as any technological device that can gather and help disseminate information in some way (e.g., Steinmueller, 2000). The introduction of ICT can create massive improvements in how we do our work, when we do it, what we do, and where we do it (Cascio & Montealegre, 2016). Although ICT has been heralded as a solution to improve productivity and to improve workers' lives, many unintended effects such as decreased productivity and poor worker wellbeing have been noted (e.g., Day et al., 2012; Tarafdar et al., 2007).

ICT's effects on an individual's health may be primarily decided by how it is used or misused. According to the Transactional Model of Stress (Lazarus & Folkman, 1984), we can view aspects of ICT (e.g., being accessible outside of normal working hours) as potential stressors. Workers may view this potential stressor as a positive, negative, or neutral stimulus. This primary appraisal is influenced by one's personal evaluation of the importance and congruency of the stressor as it relates to their goals and motivation (Lazarus & Folkman, 1984). In general, stressors that are viewed negatively tend to lead to negative strain outcomes, unless workers perceive that they have the necessary resources to handle the stress (i.e., through secondary appraisal; Lazarus & Folkman, 1984), such as organizational support (see for example, Day et al., 2012). When ICT is used as a resource that improves communication, collegiality, and control, workers may view it positively and experience positive health outcomes. Conversely, when ICT creates hassles, miscommunication, and reduces control, workers may perceive it as being stressful and experience negative health outcomes.

We also can look to the job demands–resources (JD-R) model (Bakker & Demerouti, 2007; Demerouti et al., 2001) to help us understand the contextually complex relationship between ICT use and worker wellbeing. The JD-R model posits that workers are exposed to physical, psychological, social, and organizational aspects of the workplace that can be perceived as a demand (e.g., workload, time pressures, emotionally taxing work) or a resource (e.g., job control, social support, task variety; Bakker & Demerouti, 2007; Demerouti et al., 2001). Using this model, we would expect that when viewed as a demand, ICT would lead to strain responses. On the other hand, when viewed as a resource, it would lead to positive motivational and engagement outcomes (see for example, Day et al., 2010), and it also may buffer negative impacts of other work demands.

Additionally, Day et al. (2019) extended past ICT and health research by creating a model identifying the autonomy, social relatedness, and productivity paradoxes of ICT. They outlined the moderators and outcomes of these paradoxes and integrated the general work stress models as well as self-determination theory (SDT; Ryan & Deci, 2000). In the context of this 'iParadox Triad', ICT has the power both to enhance and hinder autonomy (i.e., the perception of control over one's work and life), relatedness (i.e., the extent of social connection with others at work and home), and productivity (i.e., the efficiency of task completion; Day et al., 2019). Day et al.'s model suggests that organizational moderators can influence both the primary and secondary appraisal processes determining whether ICT is experienced as a demand or resource and whether the individual has positive or negative responses. For example, potential moderators include resolving autonomy issues through job redesign and job crafting, exacerbating social issues through increased connectivity to the point of overload, and resolving or even hindering productivity through technology training (Day et al., 2019). However, even when ICT is perceived as a stressor, there is potential for the negative effects to be mitigated through additional resources, such as engaging in work behaviours that enhance autonomy, relatedness, and productivity.

ICT organizing framework

In order to advance a research agenda on workplace ICT and health, we developed an organizing framework based on these existing reviews and models. Research on how ICT is related to worker wellbeing can emanate from four theoretical perspectives: (1) the direct influence of *ICT characteristics on physical wellbeing,* (2) *ICT as a conduit for demands and resources* that influences wellbeing, (3) the *direct and indirect effects of psychosocial ICT demands and resources,* and (4) the *directionality of ICT–wellbeing relationships* (see Figure 6.1).

1.   ICT characteristics on physical wellbeing

Using this perspective, the most basic effect of ICT on wellbeing involves the actual physical usage of ICT, which comes with potential physical stressors/demands that negatively influence wellbeing.[1] There has been a lot of research on these potential negative effects, indicating that overusing any technology may place strains on the user. For example, occupational overuse syndrome – pertaining to the use, and excessive use, of ICT– is associated with diseases of the neck and shoulder, elbow, and wrist (Tiric-Campara et al., 2014), as well as

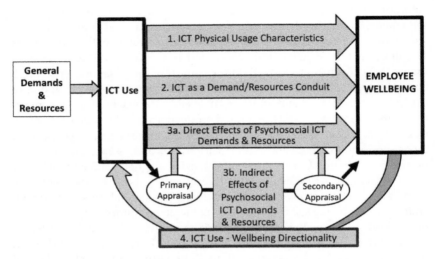

Figure 6.1   Mechanisms of the effects of ICT use on health

thumbs (e.g., 'tech thumb'; Epstein, 2020). Similarly, cumulative keyboard use has been linked with increased risk for carpal tunnel syndrome (Eleftheriou et al., 2012).

Moreover, simply spending a lot of time looking at screens may have negative consequences for worker health (see for example, Rosen et al., 2014). Although more research needs to be conducted with employee samples, existing data with youth suggest that large amounts of screen time have been linked with a list of adverse physical, psychological, social, and neurological outcomes, including poor sleep (Hale & Guan, 2015), impaired vision (Bener et al., 2010), depressive symptoms (Twenge et al., 2018), and addiction (Baer et al., 2011). However, the relationship between screen-time and depression applies to adults as well, and 'after-dark screen usage' for any age is a key cause of adverse physical outcomes, such as eye strain (see Lissak, 2018, for a comprehensive list of symptoms; see also Madhav et al., 2017). Given this potential for ICT to result in poor health outcomes, there are several questions that need to be addressed surrounding the development and extent of the effects, moderators of the ICT–health relationship, and the remediation of these symptoms.

- **_Research Question 1.1_**: What are the safe guidelines around ICT use and overuse? For example, how do we develop evidence-based standards for acceptable levels of screen time use for workers?

- **Research Question 1.2**: What are the individual and organizational factors that may mitigate any adverse physical outcomes from the physical aspects of ICT use?
- **Research Question 1.3**: How effective are organizational policies on safe ICT use in reducing the incidence of injury/disease due to ICT overuse?

2.   ICT as a conduit for demands and resources

Within this second perspective, the technology itself is not viewed as the primary stressor/demand or resource. Instead, ICT is merely a conduit or channel for other demands and resources. That is, technology allows people to engage in behaviours and activities that are perceived as negative and stress inducing (e.g., cyberbullying), or allows them a medium to engage in resource-enhancing behaviours (e.g., transformational leadership behaviours).

ICT as a demand conduit

There are several ways in which ICT can become a mechanism that increases stressors/demands on workers. One of the most predominant ways in which ICT can be seen as a negative indirect demand is when it is used for counter-productive behaviours that are directed toward other workers (e.g., cyber-bullying) or the organization (e.g., cybersmearing; Charlier et al., 2017). ICT also can increase the number of irrelevant tasks and functions that are either assigned by a supervisor or that are voluntary nonwork activities. That is, ICT provides opportunities for workers to engage in nonwork ICT activities that reduce their work productivity (i.e., cyberloafing), and for supervisors to increase the number of tasks and demands on one's time that are not directly relevant to one's job.

Counterproductive work behaviours via ICT

Within the range of counterproductive work behaviours (CWBs), there are various aggressive, deviant, bullying, and uncivil behaviours that can be enacted through ICT. In general, we have a solid understanding of the negative effects of CWBs on worker wellbeing (see Nielsen & Einarsen, 2012, for a review of bullying on worker wellbeing; see Schilpzand et al., 2016 for a review of incivility). However, having ICT as a medium for these types of disruptive behaviours may exacerbate any ill effects because it allows for direct distribution of aggressive and harmful messages to a large group, even across the entire organization (e.g., Day et al., 2010; Weatherbee & Kelloway, 2006).

Cyberaggression involves sending messages through ICT that are intended to harm others (e.g., threatening language, use of profanity, and unfair accusations; Schat & Kelloway, 2005). Some researchers also argue that less obvious messages (e.g., use of all capital letters) that are intentional also may be deemed as cyberaggression (Richard et al., 2020). Although cyberaggression acts may seem less intimidating than face-to-face aggression, they still have serious negative implications for workers. For example, researchers have found that cyberaggression was significantly related to decreased psychological health (Ford, 2013) and emotional energy (Giumetti et al., 2013), and to increased anxiety (Baruch, 2005) and psychological strain (Coyne et al., 2017; Weatherbee, 2007).

Incivility involves rude and discourteous behaviours with ambiguous intent to harm (Pearson et al., 2005), and *cyberincivility* involves the same category of behaviours that occur through ICT (Giumetti et al., 2012). Emails may be perceived as being rude if they violate norms for communication, such as being less polite, including poor spelling or grammar, or even missing a greeting, subject, or salutation (Francis et al., 2015). These perceived uncivil interactions can lead to negative health outcomes, such as higher affective and physical distress (Park et al., 2018).

Trolling is another form of cyberdeviance that typically involves harmful online messages targeting workers who work in more public positions (e.g., news reporters, politicians, actors; Golf-Papez & Veer, 2017; Hardaker, 2010). Despite the public nature of these attacks, the impact on one's health of receiving these types of derogatory communications (e.g., demeaning, misogynist, or racist comments) is not well studied or understood. These messages can range from relatively innocuous comments on the individual's appearance or performance, to threats of violence, rape, and death (Binns, 2012). Although there is a dearth of literature empirically exploring the influence of 'internet trolls' on workers who have these public jobs, there is some research that suggests that trolls are purposely trying to get under the skin of their target to elicit a response (Buckels et al., 2019). Therefore, engaging with them can spiral into more negative comments or a 'virtual shouting match' (Mackinnon & Zuckerman, 2012).

Given this varied literature on different CWBs enacted through ICT, the question is not whether CWBs conveyed through ICT can be harmful to workers, but how to examine their differential effects on workers, and the factors that may mitigate negative experiences.

- *Research Question 2.1*: Do CWBs enacted through ICT have more or less of a negative effect on wellbeing and functioning than direct, face-to-face CWBs?

- *Research Question 2.2*: What specific individual characteristics magnify or buffer the negative effects of harmful ICT content?
- *Research Question 2.3*: To what extent does the *source* of cyberaggression differentially affect wellbeing? For example, do negative messages from the public or community have more harmful effects than negative messages from supervisors or coworkers?

In contrast to using ICT to actively engage in cyberdeviant behaviour directed toward others, *cyberloafing* simply involves using ICT to engage in nonwork behaviours (e.g., accessing Facebook; playing games; Charlier et al., 2017). That is, technology can introduce 'new avenues and opportunities for individuals to misbehave' (Lim, 2002, p. 675). Cyberloafing is a form of production deviance and may result from perceived unfairness at work (Lim, 2002). Unlike cyberbullying, aggression, and trolling, the challenge in studying cyberloafing is that legitimate work and nonwork use of ICT must be differentiated from ICT tasks that do not help the worker or organization in any way. That is, nonwork ICT use during work time may be considered appropriate in some situations (e.g., checking in on a sick child). Lim's inclusion of the word 'misbehave' in cyberloafing's definition differentiates it from mere ICT usage, as it must be a form of reducing work and production deviance. However, where is the dividing line between when ICT use for nonwork activities is appropriate versus deviant? Can these behaviours negatively affect coworkers as well?

Conversely, we also know that microbreaks (doing nonwork activities during short breaks at work; Zacher et al., 2014) can help workers recover from job stress (Trougakos & Hideg, 2009). In fact, engaging in social microbreaks (including texting) is related to increased positive affect, which, in turn, is associated with increased sales performance (Kim et al. 2017, 2018). Therefore, even though cyberloafing is considered a bad thing, using ICT at work for nonwork purposes may be a form of distraction or microbreak to help workers deal with demands and foster their own wellbeing.

- *Research Question 2.4*: How common is nonwork ICT use and cyberloafing in organizations?
- *Research Question 2.5*: Under what conditions is nonwork use of ICT considered legitimate during work hours?
- *Research Question 2.6*: How can we differentiate cyberloafing from legitimate nonwork ICT use? Is cyberloafing defined by intent (e.g., retribution at the organization; Lim, 2002)?
- *Research Question 2.7*: Can nonwork ICT use at work have beneficial and therapeutic influences on worker health, because it provides opportunities for 'micro-breaks' for the worker as a form of recovery?

- **Research Question 2.8:** Is the relationship between nonwork ICT use and wellbeing nonlinear? For example, are ICT microbreaks therapeutic for workers and result in better health, whereas excessive nonwork ICT use is indicative of negative work outcomes, such as dissatisfaction and burnout?
- **Research Question 2.9:** To what extent do workers' cyberloafing behaviours influence the wellbeing of colleagues?
- **Research Question 2.10:** Do certain personality characteristics exacerbate or buffer the negative effects of trolling, cyberaggression, or cyberloafing?

Illegitimate tasks, ICT, and wellbeing

Illegitimate tasks in the workplace can be defined as unnecessary or unreasonable tasks that extend beyond the role boundaries of one's job, such that they violate norms related to aspects of wellbeing (Semmer et al., 2010). When these tasks are perceived as menial, unnecessary, redundant, or outside the scope of one's work, they may negatively affect worker health (Semmer et al., 2010). ICT provides a medium to easily introduce illegitimate tasks into one's work role. For example, new ICT systems may allow administrative tasks to be taken on by non-administrative people. In some cases, these changes are seen as efficient and streamlining work-related processes (e.g., using smart phones to conduct on-site payment transactions, instead of having the main office send bills to customers). However, any processes or systems that are seen to detract from the focal tasks of one's job have the potential for greater stress and strain outcomes.

For example, managers may have to spend more time completing administrative tasks due to new information technology in the workplace, such as employee surveillance and control (Arman et al., 2009; Mason et al., 2002). If these managers perceive these ICT-related responsibilities as 'busywork' or minor tasks that could be assigned to other workers, they are at risk for lower job satisfaction, lower motivation, and higher levels of burnout (Omansky et al., 2016; Semmer et al., 2015). As another example, physicians report that illegitimate tasks, such as ICT-based documentation and other administrative tasks, contribute to a significant proportion of their workdays which leads to presenteeism, lower motivation, and an inefficient distribution of organizational resources (Thun et al., 2018). However, thus far there is little empirical evidence which quantifies how much ICT increases presence of illegitimate tasks.

- **Research Question 2.11:** Are illegitimate tasks conducted via ICT associated with poorer health outcomes?

- **Research Question 2.12**: Is the perceived utility or legitimacy of an ICT-based task associated with worker wellbeing?

ICT as a resource conduit

Although the majority of ICT research has focused on negative outcomes, ICT also can be a conduit for positive work and nonwork resources, and as such, become a secondary resource in and of itself. One of the key ways in which ICT can be a channel for other resources is by using ICT to provide health information, tips, and training programs to workers. These communications may range from low-key educational pages and infographics, links to resources on their organizational website, to more sophisticated training programs and apps. These applications of ICT aim to increase physical health through various means including healthy behaviour education (e.g., SmartAPPetite; Gilliland et al., 2015), providing training to health care professionals (Wattanasoontorn et al., 2013), providing e-coaching to help set exercise and health goals, setting reminders and alarms to get up from one's desk and move around (e.g., Stand Up! The Work Break Timer; Herrmann & Kim, 2017), providing quick 'desk' workouts and stretches (e.g., Office YogaMD, Office-Fit; www.theactivetimes .com/train-office-your-smartphone), and helping workers relax and focus (e.g., Calm, Headspace; Mani et al., 2015). Overall, there is little research on the extent to which these ICT-based communications, programs, and apps have positive effects on worker health. However, Bostock et al. (2019) found that workers who used Headspace once a day had significant improvements in well-being and decreased systolic blood pressure compared to a control group of workers who did not use the app over a 16-week period. More research is needed to address questions about the prevalence and effectiveness of ICT being used as a positive conduit.

- **Research Question 2.13**: To what extent are organizations using technology to provide health education, awareness, and training programs?
- **Research Question 2.14**: How effective are these types of organizational ICT health communications and programs? Are certain types of ICT applications (e.g., skill training) more effective than other applications (e.g., education)?
- **Research Question 2.15**: To what extent is training and health information transmitted via ICT more beneficial than face-to-face training or non-ICT training?

In addition to conveying health information and programs, ICT can be used as a mechanism to increase worker wellbeing by communicating work-related factors, such as job control and organizational or supervisory support. That is, leaders can use ICT as a tool to demonstrate support to workers as well as use it to allow workers greater control over their work. Using ICT to recognize and support their workers may increase the immediacy of supportive communications, as well as the frequency and type of support. Although there has been little or no research examining ICT as a mechanism to increase support and control, there is a solid body of research demonstrating the effect of organizational and supervisory support (e.g., Rhoades & Eisenberger, 2002) and job control (Day et al., 2009, 2017; Fernet et al., 2004) on improved worker wellbeing and reduced burnout. Therefore, worker wellbeing may be influenced by the extent to which ICT is used to recognize and support workers and provide mechanisms to increase control. As one of the key components of self-determination theory, the extent to which one can meet needs for autonomy (control) over when, where, how they are working, on what projects, and for whom, is associated with better wellbeing (Deci & Ryan, 2002). Thus, it is also plausible that ICT may be able to increase control by functioning as a tool to provide opportunities for workers to adapt their work to fit their needs. Having ICT as a mechanism for demonstrating support and control may be especially important when workers are working remotely. However, the question remains as to what extent ICT can be used to demonstrate support for workers, and allow them greater control over aspects of their job, thus potentially increasing worker wellbeing.

- **Research Question 2.16**: To what extent is ICT an effective means through which workers can (a) receive social support from colleagues and supervisors; (b) increase control over their work schedule, the timing and location of work, and specific job tasks?
- **Research Question 2.17**: Are ICT-enabled indices of support more effective than traditional social support behaviours and communications?

3.   Direct and indirect effects of psychosocial ICT demands and resources

In addition to examining the health consequences of physical ICT characteristics, and ICT as a *conduit* for job demands and resources, we also integrate research that focuses on the direct and indirect influence of the psychosocial aspects of ICT use on wellbeing (e.g., Day et al., 2010; Diaz et al., 2012). That is, in addition to ICT being a mechanism to receive other work demands and resources, psychosocial characteristics of ICT use itself may be perceived as demands or resources, which can directly or indirectly influence worker wellbeing. This initial framework can be interpreted within the iParadox Triad, such that the extent to which these factors hinder or facilitate one's need for autonomy, relatedness, and productivity dictate whether they are classified as demands or resources, which then can affect health (Day et al., 2019).

Autonomy needs

In addition to using ICT to increase control over one's work, the degree to which workers have control over their actual ICT use (i.e., when, where, how they use it and for what purpose) also influences whether ICT is viewed as a demand or stressor. That is, worker wellbeing may be affected by the extent to which ICT provides them with the opportunity to work remotely (i.e., ICT as a conduit or means for increased control). Additionally, wellbeing may be affected by the extent to which they have autonomy over how, when, and where they use ICT. Based on the general autonomy literature, we know that greater autonomy over one's work tends to be associated with less strain and better wellbeing (Doef & Maes, 1999; Slemp et al., 2015; Thompson & Prottas, 2006), and that not having control of one's work–home boundaries increases the psychological distress experienced by workers (Kossek et al., 2012). Because the permeability of work and nonwork boundaries (i.e., doing work during nonwork time and vice versa) is increased substantially due to the use of ICTs, reducing control over ICTs (which results in less control over the boundary between work and nonwork roles) may decrease overall worker wellbeing. Interestingly, despite some organizations' attempts to reduce physical and cognitive workload by setting boundaries on when and where ICT can be used (e.g., workers aren't allowed to send or receive emails after 5:00pm), these good intentions may have the unintended effect of reducing workers' autonomy over when and how they choose to use ICT, and potentially reduce wellbeing (see Day et al., 2019, for a more in-depth discussion).

Features and settings of some ICT applications (e.g., focused inboxes, specified times to receive emails, turning off notifications) may allow workers to have more control over their experiences with ICT. However, the expectations around ICT use (from supervisor support and culture) may be more predictive of how ICT is used and any potential benefits of these technological features. That is, having settings that allow you to delay receipt or sending of messages is irrelevant if organizational culture and policies require you to respond as soon as possible.

- **Research Question 3.1**: Does having greater control over when, how, and where one uses ICT improve worker wellbeing?
- **Research Question 3.2**: What specific ICT settings and features provide greater control over one's ICT use?

- **Research Question 3.3**: Do organizational policies that limit ICT use after regular working hours have any effect on worker health? What factors of the policy would make it be perceived as being beneficial rather than paternalistic?

Relatedness needs

ICT can help workers meet their need for relatedness by allowing for greater interaction and improved communication with a variety of sources and access to colleagues around the globe. However, it also brings with it several challenges that could limit interactions with others, or make interactions with others more difficult due to miscommunication and perceived social pressures that challenge relatedness needs (Day et al., 2019). That is, in addition to being a *conduit* for negative or positive communication behaviours as discussed above (e.g., cyberbullying, support), actual ICT use can have negative outcomes (due to unintentional miscommunication or ineffective communication, increased potential for communication overload, and social pressure to respond) or positive outcomes from increased connectedness.

Because some types of ICT (e.g., email, text messages) may provide minimal information in terms of the tone and intent of the message (Day et al., 2010; Rainey, 2000), workers may misinterpret received messages, which can result in increased conflict and frustration with colleagues. In one study, 72 per cent of individuals were angered by emails that resulted in miscommunication and 36 per cent of individuals misinterpreted emails (Markus, 1994). That is, despite the intended tone of the message, messages that are perceived as being negative may result in interpersonal conflict, stress, and negative wellbeing (Markus 1994; Ramirez et al., 2002).

Beyond miscommunication via ICT, reliance on ICT for work-related communication can result in a constant connection to work (Diaz et al., 2012). With the ability to be constantly connected to work, workers also may feel an increased pressure to respond quickly to messages from clients, coworkers, and supervisors. This increased pressure to respond in a timely manner, known as 'telepressure', can lead to the prioritization of ICT communication throughout the workday and negatively influence the completion of work tasks (Barber & Santuzzi, 2015). Telepressure tends to be negatively associated with employee outcomes including burnout, absenteeism, and sleep quality (Barber & Santuzzi, 2015; Hu et al., 2019; Santuzzi & Barber, 2018).

Due to the (real or perceived) expectation of having to do time-sensitive tasks at a moment's notice, telepressure can cause some workers to feel more restricted in what they can do in their time away from the workplace (Barber & Santuzzi, 2015). That is, being on call 24/7 can directly reduce the number of hours that one is able to socialize outside of work, and it can indirectly reduce socialization because workers are hesitant to do things that may limit their ability to respond promptly to work matters.

Although ICT communications can increase connectedness with one's colleagues (Ninaus et al., 2015), the seemingly never-ending influx of ICT messages may result in communication overload (Day et al., 2010) and a lack of perceived goal progress (Rosen et al., 2014), especially for workers who report that ICT is less critical to their job. For example, Brown et al. (2014) found that email quantity was associated with increased emotional exhaustion and stress.

- **Research Question 3.4**: To what extent can ICT create information or social overload and ultimately stress? What organizational factors could help reduce the excess of information coming from ICT?
- **Research Question 3.5**: To what degree does ICT use increase miscommunication? Conversely, are there situations in which ICT can improve communication (e.g., by decreasing response time or dissipating face-to-face conflict)?
- **Research Question 3.6**: Is the relationship among ICT use, miscommunication, and wellbeing consistent for everyone, or does ICT only increase miscommunication in those who currently have poor work relationships (e.g., poor communication and lower levels of trust and respect)?
- **Research Question 3.7**: To what extent can telepressure decrease both time spent on recovery activities and wellbeing by (a) increasing one's workload and (b) by increasing anxiety about failing to respond in a timely manner?
- **Research Question 3.8**: How can organizations maximize workers' social and communication needs when using ICT, without creating information overload?
- **Research Question 3.9**: To what extent do personal preferences for work-related social interactions affect how workers perceive ICT?

Productivity needs

Ideally, ICT use is intended to have positive effects on work productivity. Yet, ICT use can negatively affect worker productivity by creating ICT-related hassles, requiring workers to learn new ICT, and creating ICT overload (Day et al., 2010). Based on the conservation of resources model (Hobfoll, 1989), high quantities of hassles experienced by an employee can deplete their resources, resulting in increased stress (Day et al., 2010). ICT hassles, such as technological malfunctions, can reduce functioning, performance, and perceived competence (Shu et al., 2011), and may also increase employee frustration and stress (Day et al., 2010; Hudiburg, 1995; Wood, 2001). Similarly, there may be unintended consequences for the individuals who have to learn how to use new ICT systems. If the learning curve is too steep without adequate organizational supports to aid learning, the technology is more likely to be viewed as a demand, which may result in increased stress (Day et al., 2010). These hassles of learning ICT may be why workers generally report wanting to learn new ICT informally, as quickly as possible, and without much effort (Korpelainen & Kira, 2010).

These negative factors are contrasted by the positive ways in which ICT may support productivity. In line with self-determination theory (SDT), when workers perceive that their organization is supportive, they may be more likely to experience autonomous motivation to use new ICT because they believe that their leaders respect them and care about their wellbeing (Mitchell et al., 2012). Perceived organizational support has been associated with greater enjoyment and acceptance in using new ICT systems (Mitchell et al., 2012). In line with the JD-R model, having high levels of resources in terms of organizational support (e.g., supervisor; expert ICT assistance) to facilitate the learning process for new ICT should be associated with better wellbeing outcomes, and ultimately performance. Having an environment that is supportive of learning and problem solving, and having specific training for learning new ICT may be associated with more positive outcomes (Day et al., 2012; Marler et al., 2006). Similarly, based on SDT (Gagné & Deci, 2005), experiencing intrinsic motivation to use new ICT, experiencing competency from accepting the new system, and feeling supported by the organization all contribute to workers having their needs met, which may result in higher wellbeing and lower stress.

- *Research Question 3.10*: To what degree are ICT breakdowns or hassles related to worker wellbeing?
- *Research Question 3.11*: Do frequent ICT updates and changes result in greater worker stress?
- *Research Question 3.12*: What personal and industry characteristics help individuals adapt to new ICT easier, such that it is viewed more positively?
- *Research Question 3.13*: What organizationally supportive behaviours and policies around ICT use have a positive influence on worker mental health?

ICT use wellbeing moderators

Given the main effects of ICT demands and resources on worker wellbeing, it is important to consider the potential indirect relationship between ICT use and worker health through individual and organizational mediators and moderators. That is, based on Lazarus and Folkman's (1984) transactional model of stress, having ICT resources may help during both the primary and secondary appraisal process. For example, knowing one has an effective ICT support team may have a positive influence on wellbeing directly (i.e., discussed in Research Area #2), and also buffer the ICT use–wellbeing relationship by reducing the perceived stress of technological problems and minimizing work disruptions, which may improve employee engagement and wellbeing (Day et al., 2010; O'Driscoll et al., 2010; Ragu-Nathan et al., 2008). Some research has shown that general work support can buffer the negative outcomes of job demands on worker health (Bakker et al., 2005; Kirmeyer & Dougherty, 1988). This support may be beneficial when looking at ICT demands (e.g., Day et al., 2010). Day et al. (2012) tested this hypothesis and found that ICT training and support mitigated the negative aspects of ICT demands on wellbeing and enhanced workers' self-efficacy in using new ICT. Korunka and Vitouch (1999) found that workers who were adequately trained to use ICT experienced less dissatisfaction, stress, and strain.

Similarly, providing high quality training when new ICT is adopted by the organization may mitigate negative effects of ICT use and increase the willingness of workers to practise using the ICT (Beas & Salanova, 2006; Marler et al., 2006). In addition to training, providing further resources during the ICT implementation process and ensuring that workers are aware of the resources available to support their learning experience can increase intentions to use the new systems (Marler et al., 2006). Access to resources for new ICT is also related to higher quality training reactions from workers, which may improve the transfer of training process, making the new ICT more successful and useful to the organization (Marler et al., 2006).

Therefore, although there is some evidence that ICT usage and organizational supports can be helpful in mitigating ICT demands, we need to have a better understanding of the specific types of supports and mechanisms by which support can buffer the relationship between ICT work demands and wellbeing.

- **Research Question 3.14**: What types of organizational supports (ICT training, supportive ICT leadership behaviours) buffer the negative relationship between ICT psychosocial demands and worker health?
- **Research Question 3.15**: Does greater control over one's ICT use buffer the negative effects of work and ICT demands on wellbeing?

Moreover, certain ICT characteristics may buffer the negative relationship between demands and worker health. For example, in the event of a conflict between colleagues, the asynchronous timing of communication may provide the means (time, distance) for the recipient to reflect upon the incident, time to acquire resources (e.g., support from colleagues), and more time to craft a response. Similarly, because ICT communication is not 'in person', it may allow a sense of distance away from the deviant behaviour and/or allow time for issues to de-escalate.

- **Research Question 3.16**: What characteristics of ICT can be leveraged to help reduce the negative effect of both general and ICT-related work demands on worker health? For example, could ICT be used to help to improve poor relationships between coworkers?

In addition to these organizational moderators, individual worker characteristics may moderate the relationship between ICT usage and worker wellbeing as well. For example, boundary/integration preference is the extent to which workers want their work and nonwork lives integrated or kept separated (Allen et al.; Bulger et al., 2007). As mentioned earlier, workers experience higher psychological distress when feel they are not in control of these boundaries (Kossek et al., 2012). However, when workers do have control, some prefer to enact strict boundaries whereas others prefer a high degree of integration. People with high integration preferences prefer to have flexible work and home boundaries. These workers may prefer using ICT because these technologies allow them to work during the hours that are most convenient for them whether that be at work or at home (Derks et al., 2016). Conversely, workers who have low integration preferences prefer to have strict and impermeable boundaries between their work and home domains. For these workers, ICT may create more stress if the organization expects them to use their work devices during home hours. For example, Gadeyne et al. (2018) found that work-related computer use outside of work hours was positively related to work–home conflict for those workers who have low integration preferences. Additionally, this relationship was buffered for those workers who preferred to integrate their home and work domains. Other personality factors, such as openness to experience, may allow individuals to adapt more easily to new technologies, thus minimizing the negative effects of learning new technologies or dealing with ICT breakdowns (see for example, Day et al., 2010).

Another route for ICT to influence worker health is via the worker's family. Given the potential for ICT to create stress for workers, it isn't surprising that this effect can continue after work hours, especially for workers who prefer to have strong work–home boundaries (Kinnunen et al., 2016; Park et al., 2011).

However, the effect of ICT on one's spouse and family (and the mediating effect on worker wellbeing) hasn't been considered to any great extent. Carlson et al. (2018) found that mobile device use for work at home led to work–family conflict, which resulted in a crossover effect where relationship tension occurred for both spouses. The experience of relationship tension initiated by the ICT-user resulted in family–work conflict for the other spouse, and ultimately was related to lower spousal job satisfaction and job performance.

ICT also may affect wellbeing via the degree to which workers can recover from work demands. Recovery is typically characterized as the process of increasing one's individual resources (Sonnentag, 2001) as opposed to the resource-depleting strain process (Meijman & Mulder, 1998). Recovery can help to mitigate the negative outcomes experienced by stressful working conditions. However, the cognitive demands of ICT use, such as increased workload and accessibility of work, can affect workers' recovery experiences. For example, work-related ICT use during nonwork hours has been associated with decreased psychological detachment (i.e., abstaining from work activities and mentally disengaging from work during nonwork hours; Barber & Jenkins, 2014; Park et al., 2011). Therefore, ICT use during nonwork hours not only increases demands, such as workload, but also decreases the ability for workers to detach from stressful work environments, which then can result in negative wellbeing outcomes.

- **Research Question 3.17**: What worker characteristics (e.g., integration preference; openness to experience; resilience) influence the relationship between ICT use and wellbeing?
- **Research Question 3.18**: Do interpersonal functioning factors (e.g., trust, respect, conflict) moderate the relationships between ICT use and wellbeing via the mediator or communication effectiveness?
- **Research Question 3.19**: Can nonwork factors moderate and/or mediate the relationship between worker ICT use and wellbeing? For example, does spousal conflict or satisfaction mediate the relationship between worker ICT use and worker wellbeing?

Given the potential for these direct and indirect relationships between individual factors on wellbeing, taking a person-centred approach may be one way to better understand ICT experiences. Person-centred analyses consider the complete experience of each individual and determine the most common patterns of scores on the variables of interest (Wang et al., 2013). The patterns of scores themselves are of interest, and researchers are also able to test for significant differences between these statistically determined groups of individuals sharing common experiences. Person-centred approaches are also superior for implementing interventions as they can be differentiated to suit the unique problems faced by each individual (Leiter & Maslach, 2016).

Some research has used person-centred approaches to create profiles of ICT usage, which illustrate the most common 'experiences' that workers have with ICT. Kinnunen et al. (2016) used work–nonwork interruptions and nonwork–work interruptions as grouping variables and found five unique profiles highlighting differences in how workers experience these two types of interruptions. They found that 'work guardians' (high work–nonwork interruptions and low nonwork–work interruptions) reported the worst outcomes including having the lowest levels of relaxation, control, and psychological detachment, along with the highest levels of exhaustion. Additionally, Vayre and Vonthron (2019) grouped CEOs and senior executives into four unique clusters based on their degree of ICT usage and where they typically used ICT (work versus home). For example, CEOs and executives who were most dedicated to their work used ICT at a low intensity outside of work hours. Vayre and Vonthron suggested that there are individual differences in the extent and place of ICT usage that work for some people, but extreme ICT usage appears to be harmful in all cases. Person-centred research could be beneficial to further help us understand how workers experience ICT, why some workers consider it helpful whereas others consider it a hindrance, and to understand how personality factors relate to experiences of ICT. Similarly, future research may address whether profiles based on ICT preferences (segmentation, boundary control, work-nonwork, nonwork-work) are related to ICT usage (frequency, place of use, and outcomes).

- *Research Question 3.20*: Are worker profiles based on ICT usage and perceptions related to worker wellbeing?
- *Research Question 3.21*: Are worker profiles based on job and personal characteristics related to worker wellbeing?
- *Research Question 3.22*: Is it more valuable to study profiles based on ICT usage, or is there more to learn by determining how ICT usage differs among clusters based on other variables (e.g., segmentation preferences, personality)?

As with all discussions of worker wellbeing, one of the implicit questions revolves around the target of change. That is, do we focus our research, and any programs or interventions, on internal (i.e., individual) factors or on external factors? Although most of the ICT literature focused on individual factors and change, we argue for the continued expansion of the work to include not only the individual, but also the group, leaders, and overall organization (see Nielsen et al., 2013, for an overview of the four level IGLO approach to participatory intervention) as mechanisms both to understand and address the relationship between ICT and wellness.

- **Research Question 3.23**: To what extent is stress/wellness a function of organizational culture in terms of ICT policy, use, expectations, group norms, leadership behaviours (which support or detract from worker health), or individual characteristics?
- **Research Question 3.24**: What organizational, group, and leader factors affect the relationship between these potential stressors/demands/resources and worker health?

4.   Directionality of ICT-wellbeing relationships

The above mechanisms look at how ICT may create increased stress or improve wellbeing in workers through various mechanisms. It is also possible that this relationship is reciprocal such that wellbeing predicts ICT use. For example, workers with high levels of physical and psychological health may feel more confident to try new technology and use it more, whereas stressed individuals may avoid ICT. Alternatively, stressed workers may use ICT more to help as a mechanism to cope (e.g., problem- or emotion-focused coping). It may be used in a work-related manner (i.e., to increase productivity), in a work (stressor) avoidance manner, or as a way to help minimize anxiety and feelings of stress (e.g., ICT as emotion-focused coping).

For example, Tonet (2019) examined the relationship among supervisor use of ICT after hours (e.g., emailing workers after regular work hours), expectations of workers responding to ICT requests, and wellbeing outcomes. Workers' reports of supervisors' ICT use and expectations for them to respond was not related to workers' own level of burnout. In contrast, supervisors tended to report higher levels of burnout when they used ICT and expected prompt responses from their workers. Given the cross-sectional nature of the study, it is possible that supervisors who were more stressed may have used ICT as a problem-focused coping tool to help complete tasks and reduce workload. This mechanism has the potential for positive outcomes (e.g., task completion, anxiety reduction) as well as negative outcomes (e.g., worker stress, overload).

Conversely, workers who are stressed may turn to ICT functions (e.g., social media) as a way to cope or provide recovery (e.g., detaching from work), thus creating a cyclical relationship. We know that on one hand, cyberloafing is a potential response to mistreatment at work, but if ICT can also be used as a form of microbreak to help workers recover lost resources (Park et al., 2011; Trougakos & Hideg, 2009; see section 2), can it also become a response to a stressful environment? To date, no research has examined using micro-breaks as a reaction to stress. Similarly, although there are no known studies examining the ritualistic use of ICT as a way to reduce stress, Karl and Fischer (2018) found that stress increased participant engagement in repetitive behaviour, which subsequently reduced participant stress responses. It is possible workers' response to job stress is to use ICT as a form of repetitive behaviour, and as such, potentially reduce their stress. Alternatively, ICT may be used to reduce anxiety by increasing control over tasks. That is, using ICT to respond to email after work hours may increase the worker's perceived control over a task, and thus reduce anxiety.

- **Research Question 4.1**: How does psychological wellbeing influence (either positively or negatively) the frequency and type of work-related ICT use?
- **Research Question 4.2**: To what extent may ICT help individuals cope with work stress? That is can ICT use be a method of problem- or emotion-focused coping with work stress and/or provide time for recovery (e.g., detaching from work)?
- **Research Question 4.3**: Is non-work ICT use during work hours (or 'cyber-loafing') a symptom of stress? That is, is it reactionary to a stressful work situation such that it acts as a form of recovery and it is used in order to disengage from work in order to help them relax, distract themselves, and reduce anxiety at work?

The issue of reciprocity highlights a key concern in much of the current ICT literature in that part of our inability to answer these questions is the lack of longitudinal research on ICT and well-being, despite repeated calls for doing so (see for example, Day et al., 2010). Longitudinal research is needed to understand the dynamics of ICT demands and resources, their effects on well-being, and potential moderators over time. Without this work, our understanding of how one may adapt to ICT use over time is rather limited. Therefore, as a more general research goal that applies to all of the previous sections, it is necessary to implement longitudinal designs in order to better understand directionality of all of these relationships, as well as how these relationships change over time.

Summary: moving forward with ICT use and wellbeing research

The ubiquity of ICT across organizational, industry, and job tasks has cemented itself as key factor in the workplace. The varied effects of ICT on worker functioning demonstrates its potential to either improve work and worker outcomes or detract from one's functioning and increase stress. However, blaming technology for negative worker outcomes is akin to blaming a pen for writing lies: ICT is simply a tool for communicating, working, and staying connected with others. How we use ICT dictates its impact on our health and wellbeing. Therefore, based on several related models (e.g., iParadox Model, Day et al., 2019; JD-R Model, Demerouti et al., 2001), we created a framework to better understand these conflicting effects, and to help develop future ICT research. This framework integrates the four perspectives of direct physical effects, ICT as a conduit, direct and indirect effects of psychosocial ICT demands and resources, and directionality of the ICT-wellbeing relationship. It is an important step in guiding researchers and practitioners to understand *under what conditions* ICT use is good or bad for worker health and functioning and how we leverage ICT to create these positive outcomes.

Notes

1. We could find no studies suggesting that the simple physical use of ICT can benefit health. That is, most beneficial outcomes come as a result of increasing resources through ICT use, or using ICT as a conduit for positive outcomes (see the following sections).

References

Allen, T. D., Cho, E., & Meier, L. L. (2014). Work–family boundary dynamics. *Annual Review of Organizational Psychology and Organizational Behavior, 1*, 99–121. doi: 10.1146/annurev-orgpsych-031413-091330

Arman, R., Dellve, L., Wikström, E., & Törnström, L. R. (2009). What health care managers do: Applying Mintzberg's structured observation method. *Journal of Nursing Management, 17*(6), 718–729.

Baer, S., Bogusz, E., Green, D. A. (2011). Stuck on screens: Patterns of computer and gaming station use in youth seen in a psychiatric clinic. *Journal of the Canadian Academy of Child and Adolescent Psychiatry, 20*(2), 86–94.

Bakker, A. B., & Demerouti, E. (2007). The job demands–resources model: State of the art. *Journal of Managerial Psychology, 22*(3), 309–328. doi: 10.1108/02683940710733115

Bakker, A. B., Demerouti, E., & Euwema, M. C. (2005). Job resources buffer the impact of job demands on burnout. *Journal of Occupational Health Psychology, 10*(2), 170–180. doi: 10.1037/1076-8998.10.2.170

Barber, L. K., & Jenkins, J. S. (2014). Creating technological boundaries to protect bedtime: Examining work home boundary management, psychological detachment and sleep. *Stress and Health, 30*, 259–264. doi: 10.1002/smi.2536

Barber, L. K., & Santuzzi, A. M. (2015). Please respond ASAP: Workplace telepressure and employee recovery. *Journal of Occupational Health Psychology, 20*(2), 172–189. doi: 10.1037/a0038278

Baruch, Y. (2005). Bullying on the net: Adverse behavior on e-mail and its impact. *Information & Management, 42*(2), 361–371. https://doi.org/10.1016/j.im.2004.02.001

Beas, M. I. & Salanova, M. (2006). Self-efficacy beliefs, computer training and psychological well-being among information and communication technology workers. *Computers in Human Behavior, 22*(6), 1043–1058. doi: 10.1016/j.chb.2004.03.027

Bener, A., Al Mahdi, H. S., Vachhani, P. J., Al Nufal, M., & Ali, A. I. (2010). Do excessive internet use, television viewing and poor lifestyle habits affect low vision in school children? *Journal of Child Health Care, 14*(4), 375–385. doi: 10.1177/1367493510380081

Binns, A. (2012). Don't feed the trolls: Managing troublemakers in magazines' online communities. *Journalism Practice, 6*, 547–562. doi: 10.1080/17512786.2011.648988

Bostock, S., Crosswell, A. D., Prather, A. A., & Steptoe, A. (2019). Mindfulness on-the-go: Effects of a mindfulness meditation app on work stress and well-being. *Journal of Occupational Health Psychology, 24*(1), 127–138. doi: 10.1037/ocp0000118

Brown, R., Duck, J., & Jimmieson, N. R. (2014). E-mail in the workplace: The role of stress appraisals and normative response pressure in the relationship between e-mail stressors and employee strain. *International Journal of Stress Management, 21*(4), 325–347. http://dx.doi.org/10.1037/a0037464

Buckels, E. E., Trapnell, P. D., Andjelovic, T., & Paulhus, D. L. (2019). Internet trolling and everyday sadism: Parallel effects on pain perception and moral judgment. *Journal of Personality, 87*, 328–340. doi:10.1111/jopy.12393

Bulger, C. A., Matthews, R. A., & Hoffman, M. E. (2007). Work and personal life boundary management: Boundary strength, work/personal life balance, and the segmentation integration continuum. *Journal of Occupational Health Psychology, 12*(4), 365. doi: 10.1037/1076-8998.12.4.365

Carlson, D. S., Thompson, M. J., Crawford, W. S., Boswell, W. R., & Whitten, D. (2018). Your job is messing with mine! The impact of mobile device use for work during family time on the spouse's work life. *Journal of Occupational Health Psychology, 23*(4), 471–482. doi: 10.1037/ocp0000103

Cascio, W. F. & Montealegre, R. (2016). How technology is changing work and organizations. *Annual Review of Organizational Psychology and Organizational Behavior, 3*, 349–375. doi: 10.1146/annurev-orgpsych-041015-062352

Charlier, S. D., Giumetti, G. W., Reeves, C. J., & Greco, L. M. (2017). Workplace cyberdeviance. In G. Hertel, D. L. Stone, R. D. Johnson, & J. Passmore (Eds.), *The Wiley Blackwell Handbook of the Psychology of the Internet at Work* (pp. 131–156). Wiley Blackwell Handbooks in Organizational Psychology. https://doi.org/10.1002/9781119256151.ch7

Coyne, I., Farley, S., Axtell, C., Sprigg, C., Best, L., & Kwok, O. (2017). Understanding the relationship between experiencing workplace cyberbullying, employee mental strain and job satisfaction: A dysempowerment approach. *The International Journal of Human Resource Management, 28*(7), 945–972.

Day, A., Barber, L., & Tonet, J. (2019). Information technology and employee well-being: Understanding the iParadox Triad at work. In R. Landers (Ed.), *Cambridge Handbook of Technology and Employee Behavior*. Cambridge University Press, pp. 580–607.

Day, A., Crown, S. N., & Ivany, M. (2017). Organisational change and employee burnout: The moderating effects of support and job control. *Safety Science, 100,* 4–12.

Day, A., Paquet, S., Scott, N., & Hambley, L. (2012). Perceived information and communication technology (ICT) demands on employee outcomes: The moderating effect of organizational ICT support. *Journal of Occupational Health Psychology, 17*(4), 473–491. doi: 10.1037/a0029837

Day, A., Scott, N., & Kelloway, E. K. (2010). Information and communication technology: Implications for job stress and employee well-being. In P. L. Perrewé & D. C. Ganster (Eds.), *New Developments in Theoretical and Conceptual Approaches to Job Stress, Volume 8* (pp. 317–350). Bingley, UK: Emerald Group Publishing Limited. doi: 10.1108/S1479-3555(2010)0000008011

Day, A. L., Sibley, A., Scott, N., Tallon, J. M., & Ackroyd-Stolarz, S. (2009). Workplace risks and stressors as predictors of burnout: The moderating impact of job control and team efficacy. *Canadian Journal of Administrative Sciences/Revue Canadienne des Sciences de l'Administration, 26*(1), 7–22.

Deci, E. L., & Ryan, R. M. (2002). Overview of self-determination theory: An organismic dialectical perspective. *Handbook of Self-determination Research* (pp. 3–33). Rochester, NY: University Rochester Press.

Demerouti, E., Bakker, A. B., Nachreiner, F., & Schaufeli, W. B. (2001). The job demands–resources model of burnout. *Journal of Applied Psychology, 86,* 499–512. doi: 10.1037/0021-9010.86.3.499

Derks, D., Bakker, A. B., Peters, P., & Van Wingerden, P. (2016). Work-related smartphone use, work–family conflict and family role performance: the role of segmentation preference. *Human Relations: Studies Towards the Integration of the Social Sciences, 69*(5), 1045–1068. doi: 10.1177/0018726715601890

Diaz, I., Chiaburu, D. S., Zimmerman, R. D., & Boswell, W. R. (2012). Communication technology: Pros and cons of constant connection to work. *Journal of Vocational Behavior, 80*(2), 500–508. doi:10.1016/j.jvb.2011.08.007

Doef, M. van der, & Maes, S. (1999). The job demand–control (–support) model and psychological well-being: A review of 20 years of empirical research. *Work & Stress, 13*(2), 87–114. https://doi-org.library.smu.ca/10.1080/026783799296084

Eleftheriou, A., Rachiotis, G., Varitimidis, S. E., Koutis, C., Malizos, K. N., & Hadjichristodouloul, C. (2012). Cumulative keyboard strokes: A possible risk factor for carpal tunnel syndrome. *Journal of Occupational Medicine and Toxicology, 7,* 16. doi: 10.1186/1745-6673-7-16

Epstein, H. B. (2020). Texting thumb. *Journal of Hospital Librarianship, 20*(1), 82–86. doi: 10.1080/15323269.2020.1702846

Fernet, C., Guay, F., & Senécal, C. (2004). Adjusting to job demands: The role of work self-determination and job control in predicting burnout. *Journal of Vocational Behavior, 65*(1), 39–56. https://doi.org/10.1016/S0001-8791(03)00098-8

Ford, D. P. (2013). Virtual harassment: Media characteristics' role in psychological health. *Journal of Managerial Psychology, 28,* 408–428. doi: 10.1108/JMP-12-2012-0398

Francis, L., Holmvall, C. M., & O'Brien, L. E. (2015). The influence of workload and civility of treatment on the perpetration of email incivility. *Computers in Human Behavior, 46,* 191–201. https://doi.org/10.1016/j.chb.2014.12.044

Gadeyne, N., Verbruggen, M., Delanoeije, J., & De Cooman, R. (2018). All wired, all tired? Work-related ICT-use outside work hours and work-to-home conflict: The role of integration preference, integration norms and work demands. *Journal of Vocational Behavior, 107,* 86–99. doi: 10.1016/j.jvb.2018.03.008

Gagné, M., & Deci, E. L. (2005). Self-determination theory and work motivation. *Journal of Organizational Behavior, 26*(4), 331–362. doi: 10.1002/job.322

Gilliland, J., Sadler, R., Clark, A., O'Connor, C., Milczarek, M., & Doherty, S. (2015). Using a smartphone application to promote healthy dietary behaviours and local food consumption. *BioMed Research International, 2015*, 1–11. doi :10.1155/2015/841368

Giumetti, G. W., Hatfield, A. L., Scisco, J. L., Schroeder, A. N., Muth, E. R., & Kowalski, G. W. (2013). What a rude e-mail! Examining the differential effects of incivility versus support on mood, energy, engagement, and performance in an online context. *Journal of Occupational Health Psychology, 18*, 297–309. doi: 10.1037/a0032851.

Giumetti, G. W., McKibben, E. S., Hatfield, A. L., Schroeder, A. N., & Kowalski, R. M. (2012). Cyber-incivility @ work: The new age of interpersonal deviance. *Cyberpsychology, Behavior & Social Networking, 15*, 148–154.

Golf-Papez, M., & Veer, E. (2017). Don't feed the trolling: Rethinking how online trolling is being defined and combated. *Journal of Marketing Management, 33*, 1336–1354. doi: 10.1080/0267257X.2017.1383298

Hale, L. & Guan, S. (2015). Screen time and sleep among school-aged children and adolescents: A systematic literature review. *Sleep Medicine Reviews, 21*, 50–58. https://doi.org/10.1016/j.smrv.2014.07.007

Hardaker, C. (2010). Trolling in asynchronous computer-mediated communication: From user discussions to academic definitions. *Journal of Politeness Research, 6*(2), 215–242. https://doi-org.library.smu.ca/10.1515/jplr.2010.011

Herrmann, K. L. & Kim, J. (2017). The fitness of apps: A theory-based examination of mobile fitness app usage over 5 months. *Mhealth, 3*, 1–9. doi: 10.21037/mhealth.2017.01.03

Hobfoll, S. E. (1989). Conservation of resources: A new attempt at conceptualizing stress. *American Psychologist, 44*, 513–524. doi:10.1037/ 0003-066X.44.3.513

Hudiburg, R. A. (1995). Psychology of computer use: XXXIV. The computer hassles scale: Subscales, norms, and reliability. *Psychological Reports, 77*(3), 779–782.

Hu, X., Santuzzi, A. M., & Barber, L. K. (2019). Disconnecting to detach: The role of impaired recovery in negative consequences of workplace telepressure. *Journal of Work and Organizational Psychology, 35*(1), 9–15. doi:http://dx.doi.org.library.smu.ca:2048/10.5093/jwop2019a2

Karl, J. A. & Fischer, R. (2018). Rituals, repetitiveness and cognitive load: A competitive test of ritual benefits for stress. *Human Nature, 29*, 418–441. doi: 10.1007/s12110-018-9325-3

Kim, S., Park, Y., & Headrick, L. (2018). Daily micro-breaks and job performance: General work engagement as a cross-level moderator. *Journal of Applied Psychology, 103*(7), 772.

Kim, S., Park, Y., & Niu, Q. (2017). Micro-break activities at work to recover from daily work demands. *Journal of Organizational Behavior, 38*, 28–44.

Kinnunen, U., Rantanen, J., Bloom, J. D., Mauno, S., Feldt, T., & Korpela, K. (2016). The role of work-nonwork boundary management in work stress recovery. *International Journal of Stress Management, 23*(2), 99–123. doi:10.1037/a0039730

Kirmeyer, S. L. & Dougherty, T. W. (1988). Work load, tension, and coping: Moderating effects of supervisor support. *Personnel Psychology, 41*(1), 125–139. doi: 10.1111/j.1744-6570.1988.tb00635.x

Korpelainen, E., & Kira, M. E. (2010). Employees' choices in learning how to use information and communication technology systems at work: Strategies and approaches. *International Journal of Training and Development, 14*(1), 32–53.

Korunka, C., & Vitouch, O. (1999). Effects of the implementation of information technology on employees' strain and job satisfaction: A context-dependent approach. *Work & Stress, 13*(4), 341–363. doi: 10.1080/02678379950019798

Kossek, E. E., Ruderman, M. N., Braddy, P. W., & Hannum, K. M. (2012). Work–nonwork boundary management profiles: A person-centered approach. *Journal of Vocational Behavior, 81*(1), 112–128. doi: 10.1016/j.jvb.2012.04.003

Lazarus, R. S., & Folkman, S. (1984). *Stress, Appraisal, and Coping.* New York: Springer Publishing Company.

Leiter, M. P., & Maslach, M. P. (2016). Latent burnout profiles: A new approach to understanding the burnout experience. *Burnout Research, 3*(4), 89–100. https://doi.org/10.1016/j.burn.2016.09.001

Leonardi, P. M., Treem, J. W., & Jackson, M. H. (2010). The connectivity paradox: Using technology to both decrease and increase perceptions of distance in distributed work arrangements. *Journal of Applied Communication Research, 38*(1), 85–105. doi: 10.1080/00909880903483599

Lim, V. K. G. (2002). The IT way of loafing on the job: Cyberloafing, neutralizing and organizational justice. *Journal of Organizational Behavior, 23*(5), 675–694. doi: 10.1002/job.161

Lissak, G. (2018). Adverse physiological and psychological effects of screen time on children and adolescents: Literature review and case study. *Environmental Research, 164,* 149–157. https://doi.org/10.1016/j.envres.2018.01.015

Mackinnon, R., & Zuckerman, E. (2012). Don't feed the trolls. *Index on Censorship, 41,* 14–24. doi: 10.1177/0306422012467413

Madhav, K. C., Sherchand, S. P., & Sherchan, S. (2017). Association between screen time and depression among US adults. *Preventive Medicine Reports, 8,* 67–71. doi: 10.1016/j.pmedr.2017.08.005

Mani, M., Kavanagh, D., Hides, L., & Stoyanov, S. (2015). Review and evaluation of mindfulness-based iPhone apps. *JMIR MHealth and UHealth, 3,* 1–11. doi: 10.2196/mhealth.4328

Markus, M. L. (1994). Electronic mail as the medium of managerial choice. *Organization Science, 5*(4), 502–527. doi: 10.1287/orsc.5.4.502

Marler, J. H., Liang, X., & Dulebohn, J. H. (2006). Training and effective employee information technology use. *Journal of Management, 32*(5), 721–743. doi: 10.1177/0149206306292388

Mason, D., Button, G., Lankshear, G., Coates, S., & Sharrock, W. (2002). On the poverty of apriorism: Technology, surveillance in the workplace and employee responses. *Information, Communication & Society, 5*(4), 555–572. doi: 10.1080/13691180208538806

Mazmanian, M., Orlikowski, W. J., & Yates, J. (2013). The autonomy paradox: The implications of mobile email devices for knowledge professionals. *Organization Science, 24,* 1337–1357. doi: 10.1287/orsc.1120.0806

Meijman, T. F., & Mulder, G. (1998). Psychological aspects of workload. In P. J. D. Drenth & H. Thierry (Eds.), *Handbook of Work and Organizational Psychology, Volume 2* (pp. 5–33). Hove, UK: Psychology Press.

Mitchell, J. I., Gagné, M., Beaudry, A., & Dyer, L. (2012). The role of perceived organizational support, distributive justice and motivation in reactions to new information technology. *Computers in Human Behavior, 28*(2), 729–738. doi: 10.1016/j.chb.2011.11.021

Nielsen, K., Stage, M., Abildgaard, J. S., & Brauer, C. V. (2013). Participatory intervention from an organizational perspective: Employees as active agents in creating a healthy work environment. In G. F. Bauer & G. J. Jenny (Eds.), *Salutogenic Organizations and Change: The Concepts Behind Organizational Heath Intervention Research* (pp. 327–350). Dordrecht: Springer.

Nielsen, M. B., & Einarsen, S. (2012). Outcomes of exposure to workplace bullying: A meta-analytic review. *Work & Stress, 26*, 309–332. doi:10.1080/02678373.2012.734709

Ninaus, K., Diehl, S., Terlutter, R., Chan, K., & Huang, A. (2015). Benefits and stressors – Perceived effects of ICT use on employee health and work stress: An exploratory study from Austria and Hong Kong. *International Journal of Qualitative Studies on Health and Well-being, 10*, 1–15. doi: 10.3402/qhw.v10.28838

O'Driscoll, M. P., Brough, P., Timms, C., & Sawang, S. (2010). Engagement with information and communication technology and psychological well-being. In P. L. Perrewé & D. C. Ganster (Eds.), *New Developments in Theoretical and Conceptual Approaches to Job Stress, Volume 8* (pp. 269–316). Emerald Group Publishing Limited.

Omansky, R., Eatough, E. M., & Fila, M. J. (2016). Illegitimate tasks as an impediment to job satisfaction and intrinsic motivation: Moderated mediation effects of gender and effort-reward imbalance. *Frontiers in Psychology, 7*, 1818. doi: 10.3389/fpsyg.2016.01818

Park, Y., Fritz, C., & Jex, S. M. (2011). Relationships between work–home segmentation and psychological detachment from work: The role of communication technology use at home. *Journal of Occupational Health Psychology, 16*, 457–467. doi:10.1037/a0023594

Park, Y., Fritz, C., & Jex, S. M. (2018). Daily cyber incivility and distress: The moderating roles of resources at work and home. *Journal of Management, 44*, 2535–2557. doi: 10.1177/0149206315576796

Pearson, C. M., Andersson, L. M., & Porath, C. L. (2005). Workplace incivility. In S. Fox & P. E. Spector (Eds.), *Counterproductive Work Behavior: Investigations of Actors and Targets* (p. 177–200). Washignton, D.C.: American Psychological Association. https://doi.org/10.1037/10893-008

Ragu-Nathan, T. S., Tarafdar, M., & Ragu-Nathan, B. S. (2008). The consequences of technostress for end users in organizations: Conceptual development and empirical validation. *Information Systems Research, 19*, 417–433. doi:10.1287/isre.1070.0165

Rainey, V. P. (2000). The potential for miscommunication using e-mail as a source of communication. *Journal of Integrated Design and Process Science, 4*(4), 21–43.

Ramirez, A., Walther, J. B., Burgoon, J. K., & Sunnafrank, M. (2002). Information-seeking strategies, uncertainty, and computer-mediated communication. *Human Communication Research, 28*, 213–228. doi: 10.1111/j.1468-2958.2002.tb00804.x

Rennecker, J., & Godwin, L. (2005). Delays and interruptions: A self-perpetuating paradox of communication technology use. *Information and Organization, 15*(3), 247–266. doi: 10.1016/j.infoandorg.2005.02.004

Rhoades, L. & Eisenberger, R. (2002). Perceived organizational support: A review of the literature. *Journal of Applied Psychology, 87*(4), 698–714. doi: 10.1037//0021-9010.87.4.698

Richard, E. M., Young, S. F., Walsh, J. J., & Giumetti, G. W. (2020). Cyberaggression in work-related email: Nomological network and links to victims' counterproductive work behavior. *Occupational Health Science*. https://doi.org/10.1007/s41542-020-00056-3

Rosen, L. D., Lim, A. F., Felt, J., Carrier, L. M., Cheever, N. A., Lara-Ruiz, J. M., Mandoza, J. S. & Rokkum, J. (2014). Media and technology use predicts ill-being among children, preteens and teenagers independent of the negative health impacts of exercise and eating habits. *Computers in Human Behavior, 35*, 364–375. Doi: 10.1016/j.chb.2014.01.036

Ryan, R. M., & Deci, E. L. (2000). Self-determination theory and the facilitation of intrinsic motivation, social development, and well-being. *American Psychologist, 55*(1), 68–78. doi: 10.1037110003-066X.55.1.68

Santuzzi, A. M., & Barber, A. M. (2018). Workplace telepressure and worker well-being: The intervening role of psychological detachment. *Occupational Health Science, 2*(4), 337–363.

Schat, A. C., & Kelloway, E. K. (2005). Workplace aggression. In J. Barling, E. K. Kelloway & M. R. Frone (Eds.), *Handbook of Workplace Stress* (pp. 189–218). Thousand Oaks, CA: Sage.

Schilpzand, P., De Pater, I. E., & Erez, A. (2016). Workplace incivility: A review of the literature and agenda for future research. *Journal of Organizational Behavior, 37*, S57–S88. doi:10.1002/job.1976

Semmer, N. K., Jacobshagen, N., Meier, L. L., Elfering, A., Beehr, T. A., Kälin, W., & Tschan, F. (2015). Illegitimate tasks as a source of work stress. *Work & Stress, 29*(1), 32–56. doi: 10.1080/02678373.2014.1003996

Semmer, N. K., Tschan, F., Meier, L. L., Facchin, S., & Jacobshagen, N. (2010). Illegitimate tasks and counterproductive work behavior. *Applied Psychology: An International Review, 59*(1), 70–96. https://doi-org.library.smu.ca/10.1111/j.1464 -0597.2009.00416.x

Shu, Q., Tu, Q., & Wang, K. (2011). The impact of computer self-efficacy and technology dependence on computer-related technostress: A social cognitive theory perspective. *International Journal of Human–Computer Interaction, 27*(10), 923–939. doi: 10.1080/10447318.2011.555313

Slemp, G. R., Kern, M. L. & Vella-Brodrick, D. A. (2015). Workplace well-being: The role of job crafting and autonomy support. *Psychology of Well-Being, 5*, 7. https://doi .org/10.1186/s13612-015-0034-y

Sonnentag, S. (2001). Work, recovery activities, and individual well-being: A diary study. *Journal of Occupational Health Psychology, 6*(3), 196–210.

Steinmueller, W. E. (2000). Will new information and communication technologies improve the 'codification' of knowledge? *Industrial and Corporate Change, 9*(2), 361–376. doi:10.1093/icc/9.2.361

Tarafdar, M., Tu, Q., Ragu-Nathan, B. S., & Ragu-Nathan, T. S. (2007). The impact of technostress on role stress and productivity. *Journal of Management Information Systems, 24*(1), 301–328. doi: 10.2753/MIS0742-1222240109

Ter Hoeven, C. L., van Zoonen, W., & Fonner, K. L. (2016). The practical paradox of technology: The influence of communication technology use on employee burnout and engagement. *Communication Monographs, 83*(2), 239–263. doi: 10.1080/03637751.2015.1133920

Thompson, C. A., & Prottas, D. J. (2006). Relationships among organizational family support, job autonomy, perceived control, and employee well-being. *Journal of Occupational Health Psychology, 11*(1), 100–118.

Thun, S., Halsteinli, V., & Løvseth, L. (2018). A study of unreasonable illegitimate tasks, administrative tasks, and sickness presenteeism amongst Norwegian physicians: An everyday struggle? *BMC Health Services Research, 18*(1), 407. doi: 10.1186/ s12913-018-3229-0

Tiric-Campara, M., Krupic, F., Biscevic, M., Spahic, E., Maglajlija, K., Masic, Z., Zunic, L. & Masic, I. (2014). Occupational overuse syndrome (technological diseases): Carpal tunnel syndrome, a mouse shoulder, cervical pain syndrome. *Acta Informatica Medica*, 22(5), 333–340. doi: 10.5455/aim.2014.22.333-340

Tonet, J. (2019). Worker well-being and digital boundaries: Exploring the effect of leader ICT expectations and behaviours [Unpublished master's thesis]. Saint Mary's University.

Trougakos, J. P. and Hideg, I. (2009), Momentary work recovery: The role of within-day work breaks. In S. Sonnentag, P. L. Perrewé, & D. C. Ganster (Eds.), *Current Perspectives on Job-Stress Recovery (Research in Occupational Stress and Well Being, Vol. 7)* (pp. 37–84), Bingley, UK: Emerald Group Publishing Limited. https://doi-org.library.smu.ca/10.1108/S1479-3555(2009)0000007005

Twenge, J. M., Joiner, T. E., Rogers, M. L., & Martin, G. N. (2018). Increases in depressive symptoms, suicide-related outcomes, and suicide rates among U.S. adolescents after 2010 and links to increased new media screen time. *Clinical Psychological Science*, 6(1), 3–17. https://doi.org/10.1177/2167702617723376

Vayre, E., & Vonthron, A. M. (2019). Identifying work-related internet's uses – at work and outside usual workplaces and hours – and their relationships with work–home interface, work engagement, and problematic internet behavior. *Frontiers in Psychology*, 10, 2118. https://doi.org/10.3389/fpsyg.2019.02118

Wang, M., Sinclair, R. R., Zhou, L., & Sears, L. E. (2013). Person-centered analysis: Methods, applications, and implications for occupational health psychology. In R. R. Sinclair, M. Wang, & L. E. Tetrick (Eds.), *Research Methods in Occupational Health Psychology: Measurement, Design, and Data Analysis* (pp. 349–373). New York: Routledge, Taylor & Francis Group.

Wattanasoontorn, V., Boada, I., García, R., & Sbert, M. (2013). Serious games for health. *Entertainment Computing*, 4(4), 231–247.

Weatherbee, T. G. (2007). Cyberaggression in the workplace: Construct development, operationalization, and measurement. Dissertations International.

Weatherbee, T., & Kelloway, E. K. (2006). A case of cyberdeviancy: Cyberaggression in the workplace. In E. K. Kelloway, J. Barling, & J. J. Hurrell (Eds.), *Handbook of Workplace Violence* (pp. 445–487). Thousand Oaks, CA: Sage Publications, Inc.

Wood, C. (2001). Dealing with tech rage. *MacLean's*, 114(12), 41–42.

Zacher, H., Brailsford, H. A., & Parker, S. L., (2014). Micro-breaks matter: A diary study on the effects of energy management strategies on occupational well-being. *Journal of Vocational Behavior*, 85(3), 287–297. https://doi.org/10.1016/j.jvb.2014.08.005

7. Work–family research: questioning assumptions and looking forward for true impact

Winny Shen and Kristen M. Shockley

Research on work–family issues is thriving, fueled in large part by growing awareness that such matters are related to key societal priorities, including career equity and workforce participation for women (e.g., Kossek et al., 2017; Hegewisch & Gornick, 2011) and population growth or decline (i.e., fertility; e.g., Thévenon & Gauthier, 2011). Furthermore, work–family issues have strong organizational implications, affecting workers' performance and organizational functioning (e.g., Hoobler et al., 2010), employee retention or turnover (e.g., Shockley et al., 2017b), and the health and well-being of workers and their families (e.g., Amstad et al., 2011; Wheeler et al., 2018), Thus, it is not surprising that since the inception of the field in the 1970s (French & Johnson, 2016), work–family research has increasingly shifted over time from a topic that was viewed by some to be peripheral or niche in several disciplines to a mainstream, interdisciplinary, and highly regarded and oft-cited domain with associated journals (e.g., *Community, Work & Family*), conferences (e.g., International Conference of Work and Family), and professional associations (e.g., Work–Family Researchers Network).

Based on the exponential growth and legitimization of work–family research over the past five decades, we view work–family research to be at a crossroads. Given the large body of literature that has amassed, the value of and knowledge gained from doing the "same old, same old" is becoming increasingly limited. Does the literature really benefit from another cross-sectional study linking variables such as work–family conflict or enrichment to indicators of strain or satisfaction? We ask this especially since a meta-analysis of panel studies compellingly revealed that work–family conflict and strain are reciprocally related (Nohe et al., 2015). Although there was a time and place for such studies, we argue that the time has passed. Rather, in order to ensure work–

family research continues to prosper, we argue that researchers need to both question fundamental assumptions as well as expand the direction and nature of their investigations. To this end, in this chapter we articulate our perspective regarding some of the most pressing and likely generative areas of inquiry for future work–family research.

Specifically, we raise three questions regarding implicit assumptions in the work–family literature that we believe should be revisited. First, we question whether we truly understand the underlying construct(s) being assessed by common work–family measures (e.g. work–family conflict). Second, we ask whether existing interventions have honed in on the most effective point of intervention. Third, we problematize whether it is reasonable to expect changes in work–family conflict and whether we should even seek to change people's work–family experiences.

We then turn to the future and raise three questions regarding the future of work–family research and how it should be expanded to ensure its continuing relevance and impact. First, we question whether the field has sufficiently embraced its interdisciplinary nature, highlighting some domains where greater integration across disciplinary approaches would be beneficial. Second, we ask whether we sufficiently understand the rich variety of differences at the work–family interface reflecting the experiences of different groups or at particular, critical periods of time. We emphasize the need to drill down rather than rely simply on global and relatively crude measures of "interference," as the different ways in which work may interfere with or enrich family (and vice versa) may be challenging or non-equivalent in important ways. Finally, we highlight the need for an infusion of new theoretical perspectives in order for work–family research to avoid stagnation.

Questioning assumptions

What are we measuring?

Arguably, the most frequently assessed work–family construct is work–family conflict (WFC), whereby participation in one role, work or family, is made more difficult due to participation in the other role (Greenhaus & Beutell, 1985). Typically, researchers distinguish between the two directions of conflict, assessing work interference with family (WIF) and family interference with work (FIW) separately. Commonly used measures of WFC ask respondents to what extent they agree or disagree with certain statements (e.g., "The time

I spend with my family often causes me not to spend time in activities at work that could be helpful to my career"; Carlson et al., 2000) or to report how frequently these inter-role conflict events or experiences occur. Studies using these types of measures form the basis of the vast majority of the work–family literature, and consequently, our knowledge base on these issues.

In some respects, these WFC measures have been validated extensively; researchers have replicated their factor structures repeatedly and have established evidence of convergent, discriminant, and criterion-related validity. Despite this, we contend that we continue to have a poor understanding of the relationship between individuals' standing on the underlying latent construct of WFC and the response processes that give rise to their ratings on WFC measures, which is increasingly viewed as a key component of validation (Borsboom et al., 2004). MacDermid (2005) breaks down how this seemingly simple rating task actually masks a complex cognitive process involving: (1) reading and understanding the question, (2) recalling relevant WFC episodes and attributing the cause of conflict to either work or family, (3) estimating aggregate severity or frequency, and (4) mapping one's choice onto and choosing the best response option.

Each of these steps may be error-prone both in systematic and non-systematic ways that are critical for work–family scholars to understand, especially as these inaccuracies likely affect our ability to make inferences about the underlying construct. As an example, it is currently unclear whether and how social comparison processes may affect participants' responses to WFC measures (Shockley et al., 2017a). What referents are people using when responding to items? Are men comparing themselves to other men or to their spouses in evaluating the severity of WFC?

Additionally, recent work by Min et al. (2021) found that various measures of WFC, although typically assumed to be interchangeable in the extant literature, seem to be measuring somewhat different things. It is unclear whether this is due to varied item content, item wording unrelated to content, scale lengths, response formats, or some other characteristics of the scales. Using differential item functioning (DIF) techniques, Min and colleagues also found that various scales performed better or worse at different locations of the latent trait continuum (i.e., Netemeyer et al.'s [1996] scale provides less test information than Carlson et al.'s [2000] measure for people on the low and high extremes of latent WFC). Thus, many questions remain regarding what is being assessed by common WFC measures.

One way forward to better understand what is happening cognitively when people respond to various WFC measures may be to use cognitive task analysis methods, which ask respondents to "talk-aloud" and verbalize their thought process while they are responding to items (for an example of this approach in a different domain, see Robie et al., 2007). This could elucidate, for example, specific wording in items that drive participants' responses and/or cause them to interpret items in a particular way. As an exercise, we consider a single item from the frequently used Netemeyer et al. (1996) scale: "The time I must devote to my job keeps me from participating equally in household responsibilities and activities." A person who does 75 percent of the household labor might respond "strongly disagree" to the item because she does more of the house-work, although she still struggles with work interfering with her family life. It is just simply that her spouse struggles more and is unable to contribute as much at home, but this should theoretically not alter her own level of WIF, although it does here based on this particular item wording. Conversely, a person who does 75 percent of the household labor might interpret this item less literally and think, yes, work does hinder me from doing a better job on what I need to do at home, even though I do more than my fair share and respond "agree." We mention this not as a critique of the measure per se; rather, we point out that we ultimately have just assumed people respond in a given way without actually asking them or otherwise ensuring that is the case.

Further, given our lack of insight into respondents' cognitive process as they are completing these assessments, it seems possible that we could be wrong about how people are making these ratings entirely. For example, rather than the process outlined by MacDermid (2005), perhaps most participants do not make any effort to recall relevant WFC episodes, but rather rely on affective cues (i.e., how generally overwhelmed one feels) or their general sense of control (or lack thereof) over their work–family management to determine their WFC ratings. This seems plausible given that recent research focused on discrete episodes of WFC (e.g., Shockley & Allen, 2015; Shockley et al., 2016) finds that although there are no differences in aggregate or "levels-based" chronic WFC reported (echoing meta-analytic findings; Shockley et al., 2017a), there are gender differences in discrete episodes, such that women report more episodes. Both studies also found a similar number of WIF versus FIW episodes reported, although levels-based studies continually find greater WIF prevalence (Bellavia & Frone, 2005). Thus, part of our measurement concerns could be addressed by reconciling episodic and level-based results in work–family research (Maertz & Boyar, 2011) and pinpointing the source and boundary conditions of discrepancies.

Why are solutions to a multi-actor problem focused on a single actor?

The work–family literature has focused, to some extent, on identifying practical solutions to reducing people's WFC. The majority of these intervention-based solutions have focused on changing the organizational environment, such as through offering alternative work arrangements (e.g., self-scheduling, flexible work hours, telework, and compressed work week), enhancing family-supportive supervisor behaviors (Hammer et al., 2016), or engaging in self-regulation practices (e.g., mindfulness, Kiburz et al., 2017). Surprisingly, we know of no intervention to date that has focused on the couple or family level as a point of intervention. This is particularly important given the relatively small effect sizes – and often for only particular subgroups – found for the typical, individual- or organizational-focused interventions.

Although not all workers experiencing WFC are partnered (e.g., Casper et al., 2016), the number of dual-career couples has risen substantially over the past decades. Furthermore, both shorter-term (e.g., who will pick up the sick child from daycare?) and longer-term (e.g., will the family relocate for mom's promotion?) decisions are likely to be jointly made or negotiated between partners and impact both partners' WFC. Supporting these arguments, Wilson et al. (2007) found that knowledge-based training sessions to reduce WFC among shift workers were only efficacious when partners also attended the training. Thus, perhaps one problem with these prior interventions is that by only impacting one individual within a family system, effects are generally constrained. We encourage future research that seeks to create work–family interventions that explicitly targets both partners or the family as a whole, with hopes that such interventions may be more efficacious. We speculate that perhaps couples counselling could even act as a work–family intervention by providing couples with a safe space where they could discuss and process important work–family issues, such as division of labor and career compromise, with feedback and guidance from a trained therapist.

Should we expect (or even try) to alter people's work–family conflict?

As an alternative explanation to the small effect sizes for work–family interventions noted above, it could be that perceptions of WFC are highly resistant to change and that researchers need to re-evaluate the magnitude of changes that they can reasonably expect or engender with regard to these variables. In fact, Cho et al. (2013) find evidence for a dispositional tendency to experience work–family spillover that is distinct from other dispositional characteristics, such as the Big Five traits. This dispositional tendency to experience spillover, which was found to be stable over a ten-year period, also raises other potential concerns for work–family intervention work. For example, might there be unintended consequences of extant work–family interventions, such that these interventions are not only reducing WFC but also inadvertently reducing positive spillover between work and family domains (e.g., work–family enrichment or facilitation)? As these positive outcomes have generally not been assessed in prior work–family intervention research, this possibility remains largely untested. Another possibility, based on the measurement concerns we articulated above, is that although WFC *perceptions* may be difficult to change, other methods of assessing work–family management may reveal that existing interventions are actually more effective than they currently appear; for example, perhaps they reduce the number of WFC episodes or result in quicker or more satisfying resolutions of these events.

Moreover, we raise the question of whether we should even attempt to reduce WFC. Matthews et al. (2014) demonstrate that the longitudinal relationship between WFC and subjective well-being reveals evidence of adaptation, such that after controlling for concurrent WFC, prior levels of WFC are actually *positively* related to subjective well-being. Thus, this research indicates that most workers naturally adapt to WFC over time, begging the question of whether work–family interventions are necessary, and even raises the possibility that exposure to this type of stressor may be beneficial in the development of resilience. A more generous interpretation may be that although this research highlights that successful adaptation is possible or even likely, future research is still needed to uncover what gives rise to this pattern of results (e.g., does this reflect changes in problem- or emotion-focused coping, is this part of a natural maturation process, etc.) in order to facilitate speedier or more effective adaptation among workers faced with this stressor.

Moving the field forward

Are we sufficiently and truly interdisciplinary?

Work–family scholarship prides itself in being interdisciplinary in nature, with researchers from a variety of disciplines, including but not limited to economics, family studies, labor relations, life course studies, psychology, management, and sociology. However, despite our common interest in unpacking work–family issues, there still appear to be key disciplinary divides within the work–family literature. Thus, one important direction for work–family research to expand and develop in the future would be to break down some of these siloes and to truly embrace an interdisciplinary approach.

An example of this type of disciplinary divide is the constructs of focus within different fields appear to vary, and there is little integration in terms of how these constructs intersect each other, leaving our knowledge base fragmented. For example, division of labor within households, both paid and unpaid, has been a longstanding focus in many disciplines that address work–family issues (e.g., sociology, economics, demography, and women's studies). Division of labor is typically measured by examining the relative amount of time spent on different tasks (e.g., paid work, housework, and childcare) between partners, often using time-use diaries (Shockley & Shen, 2016). In contrast, work–family researchers in psychology and management tend to focus on perceptual varia-bles, such as WFC. However, to our knowledge, there are less than a handful of studies that have assessed both constructs (e.g., Zhao, Settles, & Sheng, 2011), despite both variables being seen as central to understanding work–family issues.

As a result, key gaps are present in the literature. As an example, gender is the most predictive variable that we know of in determining division of labor, such that men tend to perform more paid labor and women tend to perform more family labor (e.g., U.S. Bureau of Labor Statistics, 2015). In contrast, gender differences in WFC are generally quite small (Shockley et al., 2017a). Thus, it would be extremely fruitful for the field to understand the processes via which objective differences in time-based divisions of labor do or do not translate into personal perceptions of conflict or facilitation between work and family domains.

Additionally, we see far-reaching implications for the broader work–family literature based on exciting new developments in division of labor from a sociological perspective. In a recent article, Daminger (2019) compellingly articulated that existing research on family labor, and therefore also division of labor, has been deficient because it has ignored the cognitive dimension of labor (i.e., the "mental work" involved in running a household, including plan-ning and decision-making). Her qualitative research revealed that cognitive labor consists of four components: (1) anticipation: recognition of an upcom-ing need; (2) identification: discovery and research of potential solutions; (3) decision: choice amongst potential solutions, and (4) monitoring: ensuring that the decision was carried out and the solution was (or remains) effective. Additionally, her work highlighted that cognitive labor appeared to be highly gendered, such that women tended to engage in more cognitive labor than their spouses (particularly in anticipation and monitoring) and in virtually all domains (e.g., logistics/scheduling, child care, social relationships, travel/ leisure) except for finances.

An important extension of Daminger's (2019) work will be to determine methods of quantitatively assessing the division of cognitive labor for ease of comparison across studies and subpopulations. However, Daminger notes that such assessments are likely to be challenging in that cognitive labor is largely invisible, may often be done simultaneous to other activities (e.g., researching flight options while waiting for water to boil), and is frequently done in short bursts of time that are hard to mentally sum. As such, work–family researchers may need to expand their toolkit and be creative in their efforts; for example, an indirect way to assess anticipation or identification behaviors may be to examine the Google search histories of individuals to quantify their research efforts related to household management.

Additionally, although Daminger (2019) found gender differences in cognitive labor in many domains, including child care, it is important to note that Daminger interviewed primarily couples from upper-middle class households. However, issues surrounding work–family experiences and concerns are likely to be shaped by income and socio-economic status in complex ways. For example, beliefs around the need for intensive mothering tends to be more prevalent among upper-middle-class women (e.g., Romagnoli & Wall, 2012). Thus, we echo prior research that work–family research needs to move beyond the study of primarily white-collar workers to include workers and their families from a wider range of financial and economic circumstances (Casper et al., 2007). Finally, we posit that gender differences in division of cognitive labor may also have implications for processes such as psychological detachment from work and recovery. Overall, we call for future work–family research that explores these possibilities as well as other innovative work that connects constructs from different traditions of studying work–family concerns.

Do we understand the varied, lived experiences at the work–family interface?

One of the benefits of common WFC measures (and similarly with measures of work–family enrichment and balance) is that they are non-specific and can be applied to many different situations. For example, when responding to the item, "The time I spend with my family often causes me not to spend time in activities at work that could be helpful to my career" (Carlson et al., 2000), some participants may be spending time caring for children, others may be responsible for the care of elderly parents, and yet others may be thinking about the time spent traveling to be with a spouse with whom they live apart from. Similarly, the activities they are sacrificing at work could be very different, ranging from high-profile projects, to networking lunches with well-connected colleagues, to the ability to travel to see clients. However, the nature of the item wording makes it so that the nature or severity of the work and family components is not taken into account, and the same "score" may nevertheless reflect vastly different situations. This could also be contributing to the inefficiency of our work–family interventions to date, as the diversity of difficulties workers are attempting to address may require very different types of resources or interventions. In other words, by using measures that cover a wide range of circumstances, perhaps we fail to appreciate the uniqueness inherent in work–family issues.

One way forward to better capture the lived experiences of workers is to pursue more research using experience sampling methods (ESM), whereby multiple daily measures are obtained across a timespan of a week or two. We argue that ESM coupled with an episodic approach is particularly informative. That is, if we look at discrete WFC events and cognition and behaviors that follow them we can better disentangle what is actually happening in people's lives as they deal with conflict (e.g., French & Allen, 2019). The current work–family literature is lacking in that its over-reliance on cross-sectional work makes directionality very difficult to disentangle. For example, Shockley and Singla (2011) note stronger correlations between WIF and work satisfaction than with family satisfaction and argue that this supports the notion of source attribution (i.e., people blame the origin of the conflict and then have a resulting decrease in satisfaction with that domain). This could indeed be the case, but it could also be that people who are less satisfied with work in the first place are more likely to perceive WFC and blame it on work (i.e., satisfaction causes perceptions of conflict versus conflict affecting satisfaction).

Although an episodic ESM approach cannot fully overcome limitations of causal assertion, it can get us closer to understanding how processes unfold. To better address the aforementioned research question, job satisfaction could be measured at several points throughout the day along with the timing of any WFC episodes. Using sophisticated technology within Qualtrics or other survey software, researchers can design a survey so that once a WFC episode is reported, participants are then asked questions about experiences *before* the WFC event occurred (i.e., How satisfied were you at work before the event at 1:00pm?) and then *after* the event occurred (How satisfied were you at work after 1:00pm?). This design can take us one step closer to understanding the complex nature of WFC in relation to attitudes. Furthermore, the episodic ESM approach is very well suited to studying discrete emotional reactions to WFC, which have been discussed often as theoretically meaningful in the work–family context (e.g., Greenhaus et al., 2006), but are rarely studied. Episodic approaches could allow researchers to understand the specific type of conflict events that are the most emotionally damaging (e.g., having to miss a child's recital due to an impending work deadline versus missing family dinner because of a client dinner), and then in turn, how those emotional reactions impact subsequent behaviors (e.g., feelings of guilt following WIF may cause one to engage in compensatory behaviors at home). In summary, moving past cross-sectional designs to capture short-term experiences shortly after they occur overcomes numerous measurement limitations and allows for better isolation of how WFC processing actually occurs.

As another way to capture and understand lived experiences, we urge researchers to further explore the unique work–family experiences of specific populations. A small body of work has begun to develop on this topic. Sawyer et al. (2017) investigated how some LGBT workers experience a unique type of WFC due to heteronormative assumptions about what constitutes a "family." As a result, these workers experience additional pressures and strains in navigating when and with whom they can share basic details about their family composition in order to avoid prejudice and discrimination. Gabriel et al. (2020) explored the experiences of breastfeeding mothers at work. Their work highlights how pumping at work creates a blended work–family experience that can have both positive and negative consequences for meeting both work and family goals.

Other populations that may face unique work–family challenges include workers who suffer a miscarriage or pregnancy loss or those who are dealing with fertility issues (Petriglieri & Maitlis, 2019). Both groups of workers may be experiencing high levels of emotional distress and navigating unclear work environments, both in terms of social norms and legal protections. Another key transition point that we believe has been understudied is when parents return to work after parental leave, as this often coincides with other important changes such as placing children into a new childcare arrangement (e.g., daycare). The transition to daycare is often accompanied by frequent sickness as the child's immune system adjusts, requiring a parent to miss work (assuming an alternative arrangement is not available). The typical transition back to work does not include any type of additional sick leave to care for children, and frequent absence from work after returning from a long leave may send a signal to employers that the employee's priorities and commitments have changed (whether or not this is true). We suspect that this may be a critical period of time where gendered division of labor becomes codified and where women who previously always planned on returning to work fulltime after having a child start questioning their ability to do so, especially if work colleagues react negatively to their absences due to caring for a sick child. Generally speaking, we know relatively little about factors that predict successful, or unsuccessful, return to work from parental leaves.

We have new (and old) theory! What can we do with it?

Work–family research has historically been dominated by only a few theoretical approaches (e.g., Conservations of Resources Theory, Job Demands–Resources Theory, Role Theory), and these theoretical approaches tend to neglect important aspects of contemporary work–family dynamics. In their call for a special issue on work–life theory for the *Academy of Management Review*, guest editors Gary Powell et al. (2019) point out the following areas that were particularly deficient in existing work–family theorizing: a focus on broader issues of work–*life*, taking into account multiple levels of analyses (e.g., individuals and couples, workers and organizations, organizations and countries), an understanding of decision-making processes, incorporating temporal perspectives, and considering diversity (e.g., gender and socioeconomic status). The call resulted in six exciting new theoretical papers that address many of these issues.

Unfortunately, the vast majority of theoretical arguments that are published in the *Academy of Management Review* are never tested (Edwards et al., 2014). We urge work–family researchers to buck this trend and put the numerous propositions put forth in this special issue to the test. As an example, we will focus on one paper that an author of this chapter also co-authored – Hirschi et al. (2019). The paper describes a theoretical model of how changes in demands, resources, and barriers across time can impact the use of different action strategies to better achieve work and family goals and, ultimately, work–family balance. The authors proposed four different action strategies that people might engage in (i.e., allocating, changing, sequencing, and revising) based on different combinations of demands, resources, and barriers. It would be quite useful to both academics and practitioners alike if these strategies were actually tested, ideally over time. We could then offer concrete advice to individuals at various life stages on how best to achieve work–family balance.

Additionally, other seemingly basic but so far unanswered questions could stem from testing and extending this theoretical model. For example: Which goal revision strategies are most effective? How does the effectiveness of different strategies change at various points in one's career? Are strategies differentially effective for different segments of the population (e.g., men vs. women, blue vs. white collar)? What unique combination of demands, resources, and barriers contributes to people abandoning goals altogether (i.e., exiting the workforce to care for family, deciding not to have children to focus on career)? How do couples jointly negotiate and revise their work and family goals across time? We bring up this specific example to illustrate the plethora of research ideas that can stem from just one theoretical paper, including specific propositions related to testing the theory itself as well as other, related ideas.

Beyond testing "new" theory, there is still much refinement needed regarding our understanding of existing work-family theory. Indeed, as Cucina and McDaniel (2016) note, "a good theory is one that has survived the challenge of competing hypotheses" (p. 1119). Shockley et al. (2017a) is a rare illustrative example of work that aims to comprehensively test competing work–family theories. The authors conducted a narrative review of the gender and WFC literature and found that researchers used numerous different theoretical ideas to predict gender differences in WFC and that these ideas were sometimes in direct contradiction to one another (i.e., the rationale view of gender differences argues that men should have more WIF than women whereas the sensitization perspective argues the exact opposite). Using meta-analytic path analysis, they were able to determine which theoretical perspectives received the most empirical support. This study was recognized as a monograph by the *Journal of Applied Psychology*, reinforcing that the field truly needs and values this type of work (i.e., methodologically strong tests of contrasting theoretical predictions). Ultimately, we would likely have a much better understanding of some of the puzzling and counterintuitive findings in the work-family literature (e.g., Why are there no gender differences in WFC? Why is the relationship between flexible work arrangements and WFC not stronger?) if we actually rigorously tested existing theories, cast aside those that are continually not supported, and refine those with some support by examining important boundary conditions.

Conclusion

The study of the intersection of employees' work and family (or more broadly, non-work) lives is of pivotal importance to both organization and employee well-being. From its inception in the 1970s, the field has grown tremendously and the knowledge base is now quite large. However, we believe the time is ripe to stop and explore more deeply some basic assumptions upon which this literature is built, including measurement issues and approaches to intervention. By doing so, we may be able to conduct better science that maps on more clearly to employees' actual experiences and needs. Beyond revisiting past work and premises, we also outline several avenues that we see as particularly important to allowing the work–family literature to continue to flourish, including a greater interdisciplinary focus on employees' varied, "lived experiences" and a more nuanced consideration and rigorous testing of new and existing theories.

References

Amstad, F. T., Meier, L. L., Fasel, U., Elfering, A., & Semmer, N. K. (2011). A meta-analysis of work–family conflict and various outcomes with a special emphasis on cross-domain versus matching-domain relations. *Journal of Occupational Health Psychology, 16,* 151–169.

Bellavia, G. M., & Frone, M. R. (2005). Work family conflict. In J. Barling, K. E. Kelloway, & M. R. Frone (Eds.), *Handbook of Work Stress* (pp. 113–148). Thousand Oaks, CA: Sage.

Borsboom, D., Mellenbergh, G. J., & van Heerden, J. (2004). The concept of validity. *Psychological Review, 111,* 1061–1071.

Carlson, D. S., Kacmar, K. M., & Williams, L. J. (2000). Construction and initial validation of a multidimensional measure of work–family conflict. *Journal of Vocational Behavior, 56,* 249–276.

Casper, W. J., Eby, L. T., Bordeaux, C., Lockwood, A., & Lambert, D. (2007). A review of research methods in IO/OB work–family research. *Journal of Applied Psychology, 92,* 28–43.

Casper, W. J., Marquardt, D. J., Roberto, K. J., & Buss, C. (2016). The hidden family lives of single adults without dependent children. In T. D. Allen & L. T. Eby (Eds.), *The Oxford Handbook of Work and Family* (pp. 182–198). New York: Oxford University Press.

Cho, E., Tay, L., Allen, T. D., & Stark, S. (2013). Identification of a dispositional tendency to experience work–family spillover. *Journal of Vocational Behavior, 82,* 188–198.

Cucina, J. M., & McDaniel, M. A. (2016). Pseudotheory proliferation is damaging the organizational sciences. *Journal of Organizational Behavior, 37,* 1116–1125.

Daminger, A. (2019). The cognitive dimension of household labor. *American Sociological Review, 84,* 609–633.

Edwards, J. R., Berry, J., & Kay, V. S. (2014). Bridging the great divide between theoretical and empirical management research. *Academy of Management Proceedings, 2014*(1), 17696.

French, K. A., & Allen, T. D. (2019). Episodic work–family conflict and strain: A dynamic perspective. *Journal of Applied Psychology, 105*(8), 863–888.

French, K. A., & Johnson, R. C. (2016). A retrospective timeline of the evolution of work–family research. In T. D. Allen & L. T. Eby (Eds.), *The Oxford Handbook of Work and Family* (pp. 9–22). New York: Oxford University Press.

Gabriel, A. S., Volpone, S., MacGowan, R. L., Butts, M. M., & Moran, C. M. (2020). Examining the daily experiences of breastfeeding mothers at work. Academy of Management Journal, 63, 1337–1369.

Greenhaus, J. H., & Beutell, N. J. (1985). Sources of conflict between work and family roles. *Academy of Management Review, 10,* 76–88.

Greenhaus, J. H., Allen, T. D., & Spector, P. E. (2006). Health consequences of work–family conflict: The dark side of the work–family interface. In P. L. Perrewé & D. C. Ganster (Eds.), *Research in Occupational Stress and Well-Being*, Vol. 5 (pp. 61–98). Greenwich, CT: JAI.

Hammer, L. B., Demsky, C. A., Kossek, E. E., & Bray, J. W. (2016). Work–family intervention research. In T. D. Allen & L. T. Eby (Eds.), *The Oxford Handbook of Work and Family* (pp. 271–294). New York: Oxford University Press.

Hegewisch, A., & Gornick, J. C. (2011). The impact of work–family policies on women's employment: A review of research from OECD countries. *Community, Work & Family, 14*, 119–138.

Hirschi, A., Shockley, K. S., & Zacher, H. (2019). Achieving work–family balance: An action regulation model. *Academy of Management Review, 44*(1), 150–171. https://doi.org/10.5465/amr.2016.0409

Hoobler, J. M., Hu, J., & Wilson, M. (2010). Do workers who experience conflict between the work and family domains hit a "glass ceiling?": A meta-analytic examination. *Journal of Vocational Behavior, 77*, 481–494.

Kiburz, K. M., Allen, T. D., & French, K. A. (2017). Work–family conflict and mindfulness: Investigating the effectiveness of a brief training intervention. *Journal of Organizational Behavior, 38*, 1016–1037.

Kossek, E. E., Su, R., & Wu, L. (2017). "Opting out" or "pushed out"? Integrating perspectives on women's career equality for gender inclusion and interventions. *Journal of Management, 43*, 228–254.

MacDermid, S. M. (2005). (Re) considering conflict between work and family. In E. E. Kossek & S. J. Lambert (Eds.), *Work and Life Integration: Organizational, Cultural, and Individual Perspectives* (pp. 19–40). Mahwah, NJ: Erlbaum.

Maertz Jr., C. P., & Boyar, S. L. (2011). Work–family conflict, enrichment, and balance under "levels" and "episodes" approaches. *Journal of Management, 37*, 68–98.

Matthews, R. A., Wayne, J. H., & Ford, M. T. (2014). A work–family conflict/subjective well-being process model: A test of competing theories of longitudinal effects. *Journal of Applied Psychology, 99*, 1173–1187.

Min, H., Matthews, R.A., Wayne, J.H., Parsons, R.E., & Barnes-Farrell, J. (2021). Psychometric evaluation of work–family conflict measures using classic test and item response theories. Journal of Business and Psychology, 36, 117–138.

Netemeyer, R. G., Boles, J. S., & McMurrian, R. (1996). Development and validation of work–family conflict and family–work conflict scales. *Journal of Applied Psychology, 81*, 400–410.

Nohe, C., Meier, L. L., Sonntag, K., & Michel, A. (2015). The chicken or the egg? A meta-analysis of panel studies of the relationship between work–family conflict and strain. *Journal of Applied Psychology, 100*, 522–536.

Petriglieri, G., & Maitlis, S. (2019). When a colleague is grieving. *Harvard Business Review*, July–August Issue, 116–123.

Powell, G. N., Greenhaus, J. H., Allen, T. D., & Johnson, R. E. (2019). Advancing and expanding work–life theory from multiple perspectives. *Academy of Management Review, 44*, 54–71.

Romagnoli, A., & Wall, G. (2012). "I know I'm a good mom": Young, low-income mothers' experiences with risk perception, intensive parenting ideology and parenting education programmes. *Health, Risk & Society, 14*, 273–289.

Robie, C., Brown, D. J., & Beatty, J. C. (2007). Do people fake on personality inventories? A verbal protocol analysis. *Journal of Business & Psychology, 21*, 489–509.

Sawyer, K. B., Thoroughgood, C., & Ladge, J. (2017). Invisible families, invisible conflicts: Examining the added layer of work-family conflict for employees with LGB families. *Journal of Vocational Behavior, 103*, 23–39.

Shockley, K. M., & Allen, T. D. (2015). Deciding between work and family: An episodic approach. *Personnel Psychology, 68*, 283–318.

Shockley, K. M., & Shen, W. (2016). Couple dynamics: Division of labor. In T. D. Allen & L. Eby (Eds.), *The Oxford Handbook on Work and Family* (pp. 125–139). New York: Oxford University Press.

Shockley, K. M., & Singla, N. (2011). Reconsidering work–family interactions and satisfaction: A meta-analysis. *Journal of Management, 37*, 861–886.

Shockley, K. M., Boyd, E., & Yuan, Z. (2016). Discrete episodes of work–family conflict and associated attributions. In K. M. Shockley (Chair), *Research Incubator: (Truly!) Novel Methods to Advance Work–Family Research*. Society for Industrial and Organizational Psychology Annual Conference, Anaheim, CA.

Shockley, K. M., Shen, W., DeNunzio, M. M., Arvan, M. L., & Knudsen, E. A. (2017a). Disentangling the relationship between gender and work–family conflict: An integration of theoretical perspectives using meta-analytic methods. *Journal of Applied Psychology, 102*, 1601–1635.

Shockley, K. M., Smith, C. R., & Knudsen, E. (2017b). The impact of work–life balance on employee retention. In H. Goldstein, E. Pulakos, J. Passmore, & C. Semedo (Eds.), *The Wiley-Blackwell Handbook of the Psychology of Recruitment, Selection, and Employee Retention* (pp. 513–543). West-Sussex, UK: Wiley–Blackwell.

Thévenon, O., & Gauthier, A. H. (2011). Family policies in developed countries: a "fertility-booster" with side-effects. *Community, Work & Family, 14*, 197–216.

U.S. Bureau of Labor Statistics (2015). Time spent in primary activities by married mothers and fathers by employment status of self and spouse, average for the combined years 2011–15, own household child under age 18. Retrieved from https://www.bls.gov/tus/tables/a7_1115.pdf. Last accessed June 29 2021.

Wheeler, L. A., Lee, B., & Svoboda, E. (2018). Implications of work–family connections for children's well-being across the globe. In K. S. Shockley, W. Shen, & R. C. Johnson (Eds.), *The Cambridge Handbook of the Global Work–Family Interface* (pp. 681–698). Cambridge, UK: Cambridge University Press.

Wilson, M. G., Polzer-Debruyne, A., Chen, S., & Fernandes, S. (2007). Shift work interventions for reduced work–family conflict. *Employee Relations, 29*, 162–177.

Zhao, J., Settles, B. H., & Sheng, X. (2011). Family-to-work conflict: gender, equity and workplace policies. *Journal of Comparative Family Studies, 42*, 723–738.

PART III

INTERVENTIONS

8. Mental health in the workplace: where we've been and where we're going

Jennifer K. Dimoff, Whitney E.S. Vogel and Olivia Yoder

Mental illness directly affects more than 450 million people around the world (World Health Organization [WHO], 2004). Estimates suggest that at least one in five people will experience a significant mental health problem each year (National Alliance on Mental Illness [NAMI], 2019; WHO, 2002; 2004). The stigma surrounding mental illness limits disclosure and treatment seeking – leading many people to go undiagnosed or misdiagnosed for years (Corrigan, 2004). Not only are mental illnesses remarkably common and stigmatized, but they are also costly. For instance, mental illnesses cost the U.S. economy over $300 billion each year, with many losses attributable to absenteeism and reduced productivity (American Institute of Stress, 2005; NAMI, 2019; Rosch, 2001; Sauter et al., 1990). Similarly, in Canada, over $52 billion is lost each year due to productivity declines, and in the U.K., 94 billion British pounds are lost annually. Mental illnesses are also among the primary drivers of disability among working adults (WHO, 2019; Mental Health Commission of Canada [MHCC], 2012). These losses do not begin to capture the full economic impact of mental illness, such as healthcare and pharmaceutical expenditures (Canadian Mental Health Association, 2013; WHO, 2004).

As a result of the prevalence and associated costs of mental illness, many organizations have begun to take notice of the impact of mental health, and mental ill health, on workplace outcomes. To help propel research and practice related to workplace mental health, we provide: (a) a summary of the relationship between mental health and the workplace; (b) some examples of recent progress and current practices that organizations are undertaking to protect employee mental health; and (c) a call to action for future research and practice on employee mental health and mental illness in the workplace.

The relationship between mental health and work

According to WHO (2004), mental health is a state of wellbeing in which the individual realizes his or her own abilities, can cope with the normal stresses of life, can work productively and fruitfully, and is able to make a contribution to his or her community. When mental health is compromised, mental health problems (i.e., short-term abnormal psychological patterns, such as stress, that affect how individuals feel, think and behave) can arise (WHO, 2004). If left untreated, some mental health problems have the potential to evolve into diagnosable mental illnesses, such as depression (WHO, 2019). Through various psychosocial factors, the workplace can either exacerbate or protect against the negative progression of mental health problems to mental illnesses.

Under the right circumstances, the workplace can be an incredibly supportive environment for employees. Work itself (i.e., being employed) can protect employee mental health. Through work and the workplace, employees can develop social networks and support systems, a sense of meaning, and accomplishment, and time structure (see Jahoda, 1982). Through these functions, work can help fulfill critical human needs, such as the needs for competence, connection/belonging, and autonomy (Ryan & Deci, 2000). Employers can help employees meet these needs by fostering psychologically healthy workplaces that, according to the American Psychological Association (APA, 2020), are built on the hallmarks of work–life balance, health and safety, employee involvement, employee growth and development, recognition, and communication. By providing employees with opportunities for growth and development through training, mentorship, and supportive work environments, employers can play an active role in protecting the mental health of their employees.

Job characteristic theory specifies that skill variety, task identity, task significance, autonomy, and feedback are all integral to enriching jobs and supporting employee health and wellbeing (see Fried & Ferris, 1987). These five core job characteristics affect work-related outcomes, such as motivation, job satisfaction, performance, absenteeism, and turnover by helping employees find meaning in the work that they do, responsibility for the work that they do, and knowledge of the impact that their work has on important outcomes (Fried & Ferris, 1987). Therefore, employers seeking to improve both employee-level outcomes, such as mental health, as well as organizational outcomes, such as productivity and performance, should aim to incorporate each of these five characteristics into the design of each job.

However, work can also be an extraordinary stressor for many employees. In fact, 60 percent of employees report that work is one of the most significant sources of stress in their lives (APA, 2007; 2012). Moreover, 83 percent of employees report feeling stressed almost all of the time and recent estimates suggest that 26 percent of employees are burned out (i.e., in a state of emotional, physical, and mental exhaustion caused by excessive and prolonged stress; Center for Disease Control [CDC], 2014; Everest College, 2013). Thus, need-fulfillment alone may not be enough to fully protect against mental health problems or work-specific stressors (e.g., job insecurity, inadequate wages, poor leadership). Although most work-specific stressors, on their own, are unlikely to cause an employee to develop a mental illness, they may certainly contribute to or exacerbate the deterioration of employee mental health (Hobfoll, 1989, 2001; Wells et al., 1999). For instance, work can negatively influence employee mental health through an imbalance between job demands and job resources.

According to the job demands–resources (JD-R) theory, job demands are any physical, psychological, social, or organizational aspect of a job that requires employees to exert effort or skills toward; job resources are any physical, psychological, social, or organizational aspect of a job that helps employees reduce job demands, achieve work goals, or stimulate personal growth and development (Demerouti et al., 2001). Imbalances between job demands and job resources can create the circumstances under which an employee's mental health may become negatively affected. Job resources, such as autonomy, emotional support, and feedback, have the potential to buffer against the depleting effects of job demands or stressors (Bakker & Demerouti, 2007). Resources can provide employees with the tools required to perform their job tasks well and maintain a positive foundation of health and wellbeing (Demerouti et al., 2001; Hobfoll, 2011).

Workplace resources designed to support employees, such as Employee Assistance Programs (EAP), can help employees cope with work-related and non-work-related demands. Mental health supportive resources, such as mental health counseling and mental health self-help apps, are effective in improving health outcomes (e.g., reducing strain; Chandrashekar, 2018; Hunsely et al., 2013). Free counseling services, as well as access to mobile app-enabled mental health support are commonly offered by benefits groups and EAPs (Conference Board of Canada, 2016) and are associated with lower levels of presenteeism and a significant return on investment (Hargrave et al., 2008). Telemedicine, prescription drug coverage, and paid time off (PTO) can also improve treatment-seeking, which is associated with improved mental health prognosis (Craig et al., 2004; Ekeland et al., 2010; Frank et al., 2005).

As a result, such resources have the potential to reduce strain (i.e., negative response to long-term, frequent, or intense stressors) and burnout among employees. Given the "epidemic" surrounding stress and the reality that burnout has recently been categorized as an "occupational phenomenon" (WHO, 2019), these resources have never been more critical.

Impact of poor employee mental health on the workplace

If resources are not available or under-utilized, employee mental health may deteriorate and leave an impact that reaches far beyond the individual employee level (Dimoff & Kelloway, 2017). Employees with poor mental health may experience symptoms, such as poor concentration, reduced attention, social withdrawal, and fatigue, that lead to negative work outcomes, such as poor performance, presenteeism, and absenteeism (Dimoff & Kelloway, 2018a, 2018b). These outcomes can have cascading effects on the workplace's ability to protect employees from mental health problems. For instance, although work can serve as a protectant against loneliness by providing social interaction and a sense of belonging (Jahoda, 1982), this protection is no longer available if an employee is withdrawing from social interactions due to deteriorated mental health (Dimoff & Kelloway, 2018b).

The impact of poor employee mental health can also impact others in the workplace, such as managers and coworkers (MHCC, 2012; WHO, 2004). The stigma (i.e., negative attitudes, beliefs, and stereotypes about mental illness and people with mental illness) surrounding mental illness can impact the way others in the workplace perceive employees with mental health problems (Cooper et al., 2003; Dimoff et al., 2016). Coworkers may feel that they need to contribute more to team-based work if their coworker is experiencing a mental illness that affects their work quality or quantity. Similarly, coworkers may express concerns about workload distributions if one of their coworkers must be accommodated or go on disability leave due to a mental illness. Accommodation and disability leave for mental illness are often stigmatized and poorly communicated when compared to those associated with physical illness or injury (Saint-Arnaud et al., 2007). The length of disability leave and the risk of disability recurrence for mental illnesses are often substantially longer than for physical illnesses (Attridge & Wallace, 2010). This prolonged period of disability, coupled with the stigma surrounding mental illness, can breed an environment of resentment among coworkers who must absorb the workload of their peer who is on leave. It can also lead to other stressors, such as job insecurity or role ambiguity, for temporary workers who may fill in for the role of the employee who is on leave (Haukka et al., 2015). When there is no observable illness or injury, as is often the case with mental illness, coworkers have the potential to harbor feelings of resentment toward the employee who is on leave, questioning the validity of their absence and the impact that it has on those left behind at the workplace (see Follmer & Jones, 2018).

Like coworkers, managers are not immune to potential feelings of frustration related to the impact of an employee's ill health on the workplace (Oakie et al., 2018). Managers may become frustrated if an employee experiencing an untreated mental illness exhibits performance issues or other behavioral concerns (e.g., crying at work; frequent absenteeism; social withdrawal; Dimoff & Kelloway, 2018b). As a result, managers may not provide adequate support to employees with mental illnesses, especially if they hold stigmatizing attitudes or do not feel confident in their abilities to accommodate these employees (Dimoff et al., 2016; Smith et al., 2019). Accommodation requires managers to understand and enact workplace policies and manage logistic requirements with their teams and with Human Resources – all things that are part of a manager's job duties, but may also be daunting at times (Dimoff & Kelloway, 2013).

Both managers and coworkers can benefit from mental health awareness training designed to increase mental health literacy, self-efficacy, and supportive behaviors related to employee mental health (Dimoff et al., 2016; Dimoff & Kelloway, 2019; Oakie et al., 2018), while also decreasing the stigma surrounding mental illness. Similarly, clear workplace policies and guidelines surrounding employee mental health, accommodation, support, disability leave, and return to work can improve the experiences of employees with mental illnesses and reduce ambiguity and uncertainty for coworkers and managers (Dimoff & Kelloway, 2013).

Finally, the cascading effect of poor employee mental health is also observed at the organizational level (Stephens & Joubert, 2001). Disability leave related to mental illness is among the costliest forms of disability leave for organizations, in part due to the longer nature of such leaves (Attridge & Wallace, 2010). On average, disability leave duration for mental illness is nearly 100 days and 40 percent of long-term disability claims are attributable to mental illness (Attridge & Wallace, 2010; Dewa et al., 2002; Watson Wyatt Worldwide, 2010). While only 30 percent of disability claims are related to mental illness, they account for more than 60–70 percent of disability costs in most organizations (Attridge & Wallace, 2010; Dewa et al., 2002; MHCC, 2012; National Joint Council, 2008). Still, disability claim data is only one organizational metric by which the consequences of poor employee mental health may be observed. Other data, such as pharmaceutical drug medication costs, turnover, reduced performance, and union grievances (if applicable) can provide further insight into the impact of poor employee mental health on organizational outcomes.

With hundreds of billions of monetary losses each year due to reductions in productivity and increases in absenteeism attributable to mental illness (Lim et al., 2008; MHCC, 2013), employers have both a psychosocial and financial stake in protecting and improving employee mental health.

Protecting employee mental health: current practices

The high level of stigma surrounding mental illness poses a unique challenge for organizations attempting to improve employee mental health and employees' usage of mental health resources (Smith et al., 2019). In fact, as many as two in three people do not seek or receive treatment for mental health problems due to the fear of being stigmatized or discriminated against (Canadian Medical Association [CMA], 2013; Clement et al., 2015). This concern is particularly relevant to workplace situations, where employees' livelihoods are on the line. Many people with mental illnesses report feeling afraid that they will not be taken seriously by those they disclose to and/or that they will not be able to access the services that they need (Clement et al., 2015). With concerns such as these, it is unsurprising that so few people seek help for their mental health concerns.

However, employers can play a critical role in destigmatizing mental illness by: (a) creating, implementing, and enforcing inclusive, non-stigmatizing policies and procedures related to mental health and mental illness; (b) raising mental health literacy and providing managers with clear, actionable guidelines on how to be supportive of employees managing a mental health problem; and (c) providing accessible resources and benefits that help protect employees' existing mental health, prevent the escalation of mental ill health, and help employees recover when their mental health has deteriorated.

Policies, procedures, and benefits

Although people with mental illnesses have been protected from discrimination under the Americans with Disability Act in the United States since 1991, and under similar legislation in other countries (e.g., Employment Equity Act in Canada) the stigma surrounding mental illness is still high, particularly within work domains (see Follmer & Jones, 2018). Today, stigma is regarded as one of the central reasons for low utilization of available mental health resources, such as Employee Assistance Programs (EAPs; Corrigan, 2004). Although 98 percent of large organizations offer EAPs to employees, utilization rates are remarkably low, with some estimates suggesting fewer than 5 percent of employees use EAP resources on an annual basis (Attridge et al., 2013). Yet, with 1/3 of workers reporting that they encounter significant stressors and work–life challenges daily (American Institute of Stress, 2005), it seems that at least 33 percent of employees could benefit from free and accessible support.

A commonly held misconception is that EAPs only offer psychological counseling; in reality, many EAPs now offer a wide variety of counseling (e.g., legal counsel; financial counsel) that can help employees cope with other, less stigmatized life stressors (Conference Board of Canada, 2016). By communicating the breadth of services offered by EAPs, as well as their effectiveness (e.g., Hargrave et al., 2008), the stigma surrounding EAPs may decline. As a result, employees may receive help sooner for a wide variety of stressors that could negatively impact their mental health, if left unaddressed. As utilization improves, normalization of such services might ensue – leading to greater uptake of both general EAP services as well as mental health-specific counseling services.

The World Health Organization (2002) also recommends that organizations introduce mental health programs and interventions as part of broader health and wellness initiatives. Such a strategy reminds employees that mental health is an important piece of overall health and wellbeing. The National Standard of Canada for Psychological Health and Safety in the Workplace (i.e., "the Standard") also suggests that policies and practices include guidelines on minimizing or eliminating psychologically unsafe practices, reducing potential sources of distress, and recognizing and rewarding employee contributions (MHCC, 2013). The Standard provides organizations with guidelines on 13 psychosocial risk factors to take into consideration when building a workplace that supports employee mental health (MHCC, 2013). Eliminating or reducing psychosocial risks and hazards in the workplace is critical in creating a healthy, inclusive work environment.

A key piece of any strategy begins with awareness – not simply of mental health, but of the sources of support that are available to employees. Thus, WHO (2004, 2019) also recommends that organizations not "reinvent the wheel" by understanding what programs are already out there, what the best practices are, and following other organizations who have taken successful action toward better supporting employee mental health. In 2015, American Express was awarded the American Psychiatric Association's (APA) inaugural Organizational Excellence Award for its commitment to mental health and applying behavioral science to health and safety practices. Recognizing the need for improved mental health and reduced stress levels among employees, American Express asked employees what services might be most beneficial. In response to employee feedback, American Express extended their EAP services by adding onsite professionals who offered free, face-to-face counseling. They simultaneously rebranded their EAP service to be part of an overall "Healthy Living" program that covered lifestyle, safety, resource utilization, and more – helping to reduce the stigma surrounding the service.

In addition to these efforts, American Express partnered with well-known celebrities to help with a joint effort with the National Alliance on Mental Illness to promote mental health awareness and bring a sense of normalcy to mental illness. Their Time to Talk campaign in the U.K., where employees were invited to take five minutes to talk about mental health in a meeting or a one-on-one conversation resulted in over 24 hours of "talk time" throughout the campaign. Through awareness campaigns, educational resources, and robust EAP offerings, American Express has demonstrated a strong commitment to providing employees and their families with resources that help both protect and foster positive mental health and wellbeing (see American Psychiatric Association, 2016).

The role of managers and manager training

Sound policies and procedures are insufficient if they are not consistently enforced (Dimoff & Kelloway, 2019). Decades of research suggest that the success or failure of strategies and interventions, especially related to employee health and safety, depends upon front-line managers and supervisors. Leadership training is critical when trying to realize outcomes related to health and wellbeing (Dimoff & Kelloway, 2019; Hammer et al., 2019; Kelloway & Barling, 2010; Nielsen & Randall, 2009). Recent workplace mental health interventions focus on training leaders to identify and support employees who may be struggling with mental health challenges. The most widely researched of these interventions are Mental Health First Aid Training (MHFA; Kitchener & Jorm, 2002, 2004, 2008) and Mental Health Awareness Training (MHAT; Dimoff & Kelloway, 2018; Dimoff et al., 2016). MHFA was developed to teach the public how to assist a person who is in crisis due to a mental health problem. The training has been evaluated in public, government, and organizational contexts and has been shown to increase mental health literacy and confidence in providing assistance to others (Kitchener & Jorm, 2002, 2004, 2008).

The training was not, however, developed specifically for the workplace context, nor was it focused on supervisors or managers. Therefore, the MHAT was developed specifically for the workplace to help leaders identify and support employee mental health in the workplace (Dimoff & Kelloway,

2018; Dimoff et al., 2016). The three-hour training focuses on support and resource mobilization for employees who may be struggling with mental health issues. Results show improved supervisor knowledge and attitudes about mental health and intent to promote mental health at work (Dimoff et al., 2016). Employees reported that their supervisors are more supportive of mental health issues and that they were more likely to use available mental health resources (Dimoff & Kelloway, 2018a). When it comes to employee mental health, supervisors may serve as an important resource in improving employee mental health and wellbeing. Supervisors are in a unique position to establish strong, supportive relationships (Hammer et al., 2019; Nielsen & Randall, 2009; Odle-Dusseau, Hammer, Crain, & Bodner, 2016), identify signs that indicate employees may be struggling (Dimoff & Kelloway, 2018), and intervene to help employees cope with job demands (Hammer et al., 2019; Nielsen & Randall, 2009).

Within the manufacturing sector, Caterpillar has been a leader within the area of workplace mental health and supervisor training. Caterpillar takes an integrated approach to health and safety promotion, offering a variety of complementary human resources, such as an EAP and internal disability management arrangement. Like American Express, Caterpillar also uses behavioral science and data-driven techniques to tailor their programs to the needs of their employees. For instance, they have developed and manage their own health risk appraisal system to better understand their employees and what interventions might be most helpful. Although they incorporate tertiary, reactive programs to help employees who are already struggling, many of their efforts are also concentrated on health promotion – ideally designed to prevent illness or the escalation of illness in much the same way that physical safety promotion programs protect workers from injuries on the job. Additionally, supervisors are also trained to look for patterns of behavioral changes or performance deteriorations as opportunities to provide additional support to employees – either directly or through available resources, such as the EAP (see American Psychiatric Association, 2010).

Thus, supervisors are in a good position to provide social support (i.e., psychological or material resources provided by family, friends, and/or coworkers; House, 1981) to employees who may be struggling. According to House (1981), there are four forms of social support: emotional, informational, instrumental, and appraisal. Emotional support involves conveying empathy and compassion for the individual, such as expressing empathetic concern for someone struggling with a mental health problem or illness. Information support involves providing information, guidance, and advice, such as advertising mental health resources or making suggestions about workplace accommodations that might be helpful. Instrumental support occurs when tangible resources are provided, such as workplace accommodation or disability leave. Finally, appraisal support involves affirming one's self-evaluation, such as assuring an employee that they are a valuable member of the team. Social support can have a direct, moderating, or mediating effect on stressors and strain, according to social support theory (House, 1981). Supervisors, as part of an employee's workplace social support network, can help provide emotional, informational, instrumental, and appraisal support to employees (Dimoff & Kelloway, 2013).

Each of these types of support is likely necessary for employees experiencing mental health problems or mental illnesses (Holdsworth & Cartwright, 2003). These employees are already experiencing demands and need resources. Social support, when provided to people experiencing strain, can be associated with positive outcomes, such as improved psychological wellbeing, positive affect, and more adaptive coping behaviors (Langford et al., 1997). Dimoff & Kelloway (2017) propose that supervisor support may help employees cope more adaptively by accessing mental health resources. Specifically, managers can de-stigmatize mental health resources, promote mental health resources, and provide assistance to employees trying to access or use resources.

To have greatest impact, as observed at Caterpillar and American Express, mental health interventions should be focused on taking a three-pronged approach of prevention, early recognition, and support (Dimoff & Kelloway, 2019). Such interventions have the potential to result in significant returns-on-investment; some findings suggest that for every $1 invested into providing improved mental health support, a $4 return is achieved through improved health and productivity (Chisholm et al., 2016).

Protecting employee mental health: future research and practice

While it is invigorating to see so much attention paid to mental illness, both from research and applied perspectives, there is still a great deal of information needed in order to improve the health of employees and workplaces. We propose future research initiatives that: (a) use an identity-based perspective to measure and understand the stigma surrounding mental illness and specific mental illnesses in the workplace; (b) understand the experiences of employees with mental illnesses at various organizational levels (e.g., part-time employees, full-time employees, front-line supervisors, managers, executives); and (c) explore how different contextual factors in the workplace can help and hinder the success of mental health policies, practices, and interventions.

Mental illness identity and stigma in the workplace

While efforts to de-stigmatize mental illness in the workplace are promising, considerable work is still needed (see Follmer & Jones, 2018). With only a few exceptions (e.g., Smith et al., 2019), little workplace research has sought to measure the stigma surrounding the most common mental illnesses, such as depression, anxiety, and addiction. In general, most workplace research on mental health has grouped all mental health problems and illnesses together, claiming that the details of each illness are not relevant to the workplace (e.g., Dimoff et al., 2016). However, it is arguable that, while these details may not be important for managers or coworkers to understand, it is still important to understand how the differences between these illness may impact the way others view them or the types of accommodations that might be most appropriate for different illnesses (Follmer & Jones, 2018; Smith et al., 2019).

For employees to seek or receive resources or treatment when their mental health has become compromised, they must first recognize and admit that they are experiencing a mental health problem or illness. Oftentimes, this recognition and admittance depends on some form of self-identification (Goetzel et al., 2002; Hepburn et al., 2010). According to researchers from a more traditional diversity lens focused on race and gender (e.g., Follmer & Jones, 2018; Smith et al., 2019), individuals with mental illness may conceptualize their mental illness as part of their social identity (i.e., "the aspects of an individual's self-image that derive from the social categories to which he perceives himself as belonging"; Tajfel & Turner, 1986, p. 16).

As such, people with mental illnesses have a unique perspective from which they interact with the workplace – a perspective that can impact how they interact with others, how they view the workplace, and how they view themselves as contributors to the workplace (Smith et al., 2019). Similarly, if mental illness status is viewed as a social identity, it may be possible to shift the narrative surrounding mental illness in the workplace – a shift that could reduce stigma (Onken & Slaten, 2000). For instance, rather than experiencing feelings of shame or guilt associated with having a mental illness, it is possible for individuals with mental illnesses to experience a shift toward positive identity formation related to their mental health status – a shift that could result in feelings of pride (Onken & Slaten, 2000) or even gratitude. In treating mental illness as an "affliction" or as a "disorder" that one should be ashamed of or that should go undisclosed or undiscussed, stigma surrounding mental illness perpetuates (see Lyons et al., 2018; Nittrouer et al., 2014).

As a result, future research should aim to better explore: (a) how mental illness is viewed as a component of social identity; (b) how the narrative surrounding mental illness, as an identity, may be shifted towards a more positive orientation; (c) how this shift can be encouraged in workplaces; and ultimately (d) how this shift can positively impact individuals with mental illnesses, their coworkers and managers, and the organizations that they work for, more broadly.

Experiences of employees with mental illness

While considerable work has been dedicated to better understanding the role that managers can play in recognizing and responding to mental health problems in the workplace (for review see Dimoff & Kelloway, 2019), there is still much research needed on best practices surrounding (a) disclosure of mental health status, (b) accommodations and resources that managers/employers should be offering, (c) disability leave, and (d) how return-to-work practices can improve mental health prognosis and return-to-work success among employees who have had to be away from the workplace due to poor mental health.

In order to gain access to resources and sources of support, employees must disclose their mental illness status at work. Sometimes, this disclosure can be handled confidentiality through a Human Resources department; however, many times, there must be some form of disclosure provided to the employee's manager and coworkers if accommodations or disability leave are required (see Dimoff & Kelloway, 2017). In situations where the disclosure is kept vague or when managers are only provided with information about the required accommodations (and not the reasons for the accommodations), mental illness status is implied.

Disclosure may come from the employee directly or can come from HR or some other party internal to the organization – typically a party that the employee has confided in and has authorized to provide the disclosure on their behalf. While research related to the disclosure of other identities (e.g., LGBT+) or diagnoses (e.g., cancer) have been explored in the literature (e.g., Day & Schoenrade, 1997; Martinez et al., 2016; Ragins et al., 2007), little information is available surrounding employee experiences related to disclosure and/or best practices.

Given what is known from other areas of the disclosure literature, the handling of the disclosure process – both on the part of the discloser and the person to whom the information is disclosed – can be critical to the success of the future working relationship (Jones, 2017). Disclosure is a critical requirement, in many cases, for employees to be able to access and receive resources or support that they need in order to cope, recover/heal, and continue to perform well in their workplace roles (Ragins, 2008). Thus, it is rarely a question of if or why an employee must disclose a mental illness in the workplace, but how this disclosure can be done best for all involved. Therefore, we argue that more research is needed to better understand: (a) how employees can disclose their mental illness status in order to gain the most efficient access to available resources and support; (b) the circumstances under which disclosure results in the most positive outcomes for the employee and the workplace; and (c) whether or not, or the extent to which, the reasons for disclosure impact employee and workplace outcomes, both in the short and long term.

Of course, disclosure is only part of the overall experience for employees with mental illnesses. Post-disclosure, employees may need to cope with the realities of accessing resources, creating or enacting a new social identity, being accommodated in the workplace or taking leave, and potentially returning to the workplace. These scenarios may unfold differently for each individual employee and within each workplace, depending on policies and procedures. However, despite growing evidence that workplaces are aiming to develop strong frameworks and best practices surrounding mental health resources, accommodation, disability leave, and return to work, very little empirical research has been published in these areas specific to mental health and mental illness. Therefore, we argue that future research must take a more process-focused approach to understand how mental illness disclosure unfolds beyond the initial stages of disclosure. Such research will provide insight into how employers can better support employees in accessing resources and staying in the workplace as high-performing, contributing members of the organization – something that is of vested interest to both employees and their leaders.

Policies, practices, and interventions

While attention has been paid to improving mental health literacy among leaders through training programs and other interventions (e.g., Kitchener & Jorm, 2002, 2004, 2008), little attention has been paid to understanding the contextual factors that may help or hinder a leader's ability to provide support to employees disclosing a mental illness and/or seeking resources and accommodation. The majority of recent workplace mental health research has been focused on tertiary intervention strategies targeted at the employee level and at the leader level. At the employee level, the focus has been on stress management, healthy workplace initiatives (e.g., weight loss competitions; walking challenges; ergonomically sound work areas) and offering resources, such as benefits and EAP services (Gayed et al., 2019). At the manager level, the focus has been on providing training that aims to lower stigma and improve managers' confidence with regard to recognizing and responding to warning signs that an employee needs additional support (Dimoff & Kelloway, 2018a; Dimoff et al., 2016; Gayed et al., 2019). In turn, much of the burden is placed on managers to recognize when employees need resources and on employees to use these resources – perhaps during a time when they are already feeling too overwhelmed.

As a consequence, more information is needed about how employers can better support leaders who are managing an employee with a mental illness. For instance, in a manager-focused intervention study by Vogel et al. (2018), a mental health training was rolled out to all supervisors in a call center organization. The organization had an EAP as well as other health and wellness programs and resources. Results of pre-training surveys suggested training readiness was high – managers reported wanting training; following the training, managers were highly motivated to promote mental health and employees observed behavior changes. Yet, the training did not have an impact on specific employee outcomes related to resources (e.g., willingness to use resources, perceived changes in leaders' promotion of resources). When researchers presented results and asked for insight regarding the high rate of attrition, it became clear that there were a number of significant systematic failures that explained the lack of training transfer.

Specifically, managers reported not knowing about certain resources, not knowing policies related to accommodation or disability leave, feeling as though some of the policies that existed were punitive in nature (e.g., prioritizing performance management over employee health and wellbeing), not having the time to speak with employees about mental health concerns due to priorities being placed on call production, and feeling concerned that the resources were designed to act as "Band-Aids" rather than solutions. Similarly, employees reported feeling frustrated or disillusioned after reaching out to resources that were available, but not accessible – (e.g., an EAP program that was not available 24/7 in a shift-work climate), not being able to access sources of support or treatment in a timely basis (e.g., not being able to see a counselor or psychologist for six to eight weeks or a psychiatrist for six or more months), or experiencing fear that certain disclosures or diagnoses could jeopardize certain aspects of their lives (e.g., their ability to gain life insurance).

Many of these reports from managers and employees are emblematic of contextual inconsistencies that prohibit successful disclosure, accommodation, as well as leave and return to work, if applicable. While employees and managers are being asked to promote mental health and use resources, their ability to do so is remarkably compromised – not because they don't want to access them, but because they can't – or they can't do so efficiently and in a timely manner. Therefore, in order for mental health promotion and protection programs, interventions, and policies to be effective, future research should aim to take an operational lens to better understand how system-based failures and contextual factors may be preventing early prognosis and treatment of mental health problems, let alone how these failures may be exacerbating them.

Conclusion

With at least one in five people experiencing a significant mental health problem each year, and with productivity losses in the hundreds of billions annually, employers cannot afford to ignore the mental health of employees. Fortunately, many organizations have recognized the financial and psychosocial burdens of a depleted workforce. In turn, companies such as American Express and Caterpillar have taken innovative, concerted approaches to introducing evidence-based strategies to protect, support, and respond to employee mental health and mental health concerns. However, these companies are still among the minority; as a result, far too many employees are struggling without necessary support and resources. To help propel progress, we must continue to research and understand the complexities of workplace mental health. We must understand how and why stigma manifests and to what extent the identity of mental illness can be shifted toward a positive, empowered lens; we must understand the experiences of employees with mental illnesses, as well as the experiences of those they work with; and finally, we must understand the process-related challenges and contextual barriers to successful mental health program implementation and management.

References

American Institute of Stress (2005). *Workplace Stress*. Accessed on August 27, 2015. Retrieved from http://www.stress.org/workplace-stress/

American Psychiatric Association (2010). *Caterpillar Builds Healthy Employees.* Accessed 1 August 2020. Retrieved from http://workplacementalhealth.org/Case -Studies/Caterpillar-2

American Psychiatric Association (2016). *American Express: Embracing a Culture of Mental Health.* Accessed January 2020. Retrieved from http://workplaceme ntalhealth.org/Case-Studies/American-Express

American Psychological Association [APA] (2007). *Stress Survey: Stress a Major Health Problem in the U.S.* Retrieved from http://www.apahelpcenter.org/articles/article/ php?id=165>.

American Psychological Association [APA] (2012). *The Impact of Stress.* Retrieved from http://www.apa.org/news/press/releases/stress/2011/impact.aspx. Accessed March 2016.

American Psychological Association [APA] (2020). *Resources for Employers.* Retrieved from https://www.apaexcellence.org/resources/creatingahealthyworkplace/. Accessed January 2020

Attridge, M. & Wallace, S. (2010). *Return to work and accommodations for workers on disability leave for mental disorders.* Human Solutions Report.

Attridge, M., Cahill, T., Granberry, S.W., & Herlihy, P.A. (2013). The National Behavioral Consortium industry profile of external EAP vendors. *Journal of Workplace Behavioral Health, 28*(4), 251–324.

Bakker, A. B., & Demerouti, E. (2007). The job demands–resources model: State of the art. *Journal of Managerial Psychology, 22*(3), 309–328.

Canadian Medical Association (2013). *Mental Health.* Accessed on August 3, 2015. Retrieved from https://www.cma.ca/En/Pages/mental-health.aspx

Canadian Mental Health Association. (2013). *Fast Facts about Mental Illness.* Retrieved from www.cmha.ca/media/fast-facts-about-mental-illness/

Center for Disease Control (2014). *Workplace Health Promotion: Depression.* Retrieved from http://www.cdc.gov/workplacehealthpromotion.html

Chandrashekar, P. (2018). Do mental health mobile apps work: Evidence and recommendations for designing high efficacy mental health mobile apps. *mHealth, 4, 6.*

Chisholm, D., Sweeny, K., Sheehan, P., Rasmussen, B., Smit, F., Cuijpers, P., & Saxena, S. (2016). Scaling-up treatment of depression and anxiety: A global return on investment analysis. *The Lancet Psychiatry, 3*(5), 415–424.

Clement, S., Schauman, O., Graham, T., Maggioni, F., Evans-Lacko, S., Bezborodovs, N., & Thornicroft, G. (2015). What is the impact of mental health-related stigma on help-seeking? A systematic review of quantitative and qualitative studies. *Psychological Medicine, 45*(1), 11–27.

Conference Board of Canada (2016). *Healthy Brains at Work: Employer Sponsored Mental Health Benefits and Programs.* Retrieved from https://www.conferenceboard .ca/temp/20a6d2e4-e665-45fc-81fd-ddec71d13e79/7707_Healthy_Brains_Benefits -and-Programs_BR_EN.pdf

Cooper, A. E., Corrigan, P. W., & Watson, A. C. (2003). Mental illness stigma and care seeking. *Journal of Nervous and Mental Disease, 191*, 339–341.

Corrigan, P. (2004). How stigma interferes with mental health care. *American Psychologist, 59*, 614–625.

Craig, T., Garety, P., Power, P., Rahaman, N., Colbert, S., Fornells-Ambrojo, M., & Dunn, G. (2004). The Lambeth Early Onset (LEO) team: Randomized controlled trial of the effectiveness of specialized care for early psychosis. *British Medical Journal, 329*, 1–5.

Day, N. E., & Schoenrade, P. (1997). Staying in the closet versus coming out: Relationships between communication about sexual orientation and work attitudes. *Personnel Psychology, 50*(1), 147–163.

Demerouti, E., Bakker, A. B., Nachreiner, F., & Schaufeli, W. B. (2001). The job demands–resources model of burnout. *Journal of Applied Psychology, 86*(3), 499–512.

Dewa, C. S., Goering, P., Lin, E., & Paterson, M. (2002). Depression-related short-term disability in an employed population. *Journal of Occupational and Environmental Medicine, 44*(7), 628–633.

Dimoff, J. K., & Kelloway, E. K. (2013). Bridging the gap: Workplace mental health research in Canada. *Canadian Psychology/Psychologie Canadienne, 54,* 203–212.

Dimoff, J. K. & Kelloway, E. K. (2017). Leaders as resources: How managers and supervisors can socially support employees towards better mental health and wellbeing. In E. K. Kelloway, K. Nielsen, & J. K. Dimoff (Eds.), *Leading to Occupational Health and Safety: How Leadership Behaviours Impact Organizational Safety and Well-Being.* Wiley.

Dimoff, J. K., & Kelloway, E. K. (2018a). With a little help from my boss: The impact of workplace mental health training on leader behaviors and employee resource utilization. *Journal of Occupational Health Psychology, 24*(1), 4–9.

Dimoff, J. K., & Kelloway, E. K. (2018b). Signs of struggle (SOSb): The development and validation of a behavioural mental health checklist for the workplace. *Work & Stress,* 1–19.

Dimoff, J. K. & Kelloway, E. K. (2019). Mental health problems are management problems: Exploring the critical role of managers in supporting employee mental health. *Organizational Dynamics, 48*(3), 105–112.

Dimoff, J. K., Kelloway, E. K., & Burnstein, M. D. (2016). Mental health awareness training (MHAT): The development and evaluation of an intervention for workplace leaders. *International Journal of Stress Management, 23*(2), 167–189.

Ekeland, A.G., Bowes, A., & Flottorp, S. (2010). Effectiveness of telemedicine: A systematic review of reviews. *International Journal of Medical Information, 79*(11), 736–771.

Everest College (2013). *Work Stress Survey.* Retrieved from www.cci.edu.

Follmer, K. B., & Jones, K. S. (2018). Mental illness in the workplace: An interdisciplinary review and organizational research agenda. *Journal of Management, 44,* 325–351.

Frank, R. G., Conti, E. M., & Goldman, H. H. (2005). Mental health policy and psychotropic drugs. *Milbank Quarterly, 83*(2), 271–298.

Fried, Y., & Ferris, G. R. (1987). The validity of the job characteristics model: A review and meta-analysis. *Personnel Psychology, 40*(2), 287–322.

Gayed, A., Bryan, B. T., LaMontagne, A. D., Milner, A., Deady, M., Calvo, R. A., ... & Harvey, S. B. (2019). A cluster randomized controlled trial to evaluate HeadCoach: an online mental health training program for workplace managers. *Journal of Occupational and Environmental Medicine, 61*(7), 545–551.

Gayed, A., Tan, L., LaMontagne, A. D., Milner, A., Deady, M., Milligan-Saville, J. S., & Goetzel, R. Z., Ozminkowski, R. J., Sederer, L. I., & Mark, T. L. (2002). The business case for quality mental health services: Why employers should care about the mental health and well-being of their employees. *Journal of Occupational and Environmental Medicine, 44,* 320–330.

Hammer, L. B., Wan, W. H., Brockwood, K. J., Bodner, T., & Mohr, C. D. (2019). Supervisor support training effects on veteran health and work outcomes in the civilian workplace. *Journal of Applied Psychology, 104*(1), 52–69.

Hargrave, G.E., Hiatt, D., Alexander, R., & Shaffer, I.A. (2008). EAP treatment impact on presenteeism and absenteeism: Implications for return on investment. *Journal of Workplace Behavioral Health*, 3(28), 283–293.

Haukka, E., Martimo, K. P., Kivekäs, T., Horppu, R., Lallukka, T., Solovieva, S., & Viikar Juntura, E. (2015). Efficacy of temporary work modifications on disability related tomusculoskeletal pain or depressive symptoms – study protocol for a controlled trial. *BMJ Open*, 5(5), e008300.

Hepburn, C. G., Kelloway, E. K, & Franche, R.-L. (2010). Early employer response to workplace injury: What injured workers perceive as fair and why these perceptions matter. *Journal of Occupational Health Psychology*, 15, 409–420.

Hobfoll, S.E. (1989). Conservation of resources: A new attempt at conceptualizing stress. *American Psychologist*, 44, 513–524.

Hobfoll, S. E. (2001). The influence of culture, community, and the nested-self in the stress process: Advancing conservation of resources theory. *Applied Psychology*, 50, 337–421.

Hobfoll, S.E. (2011). Conservation of resource caravans and engaged setting. *Journal of Occupational and Organizational Psychology*, 84, 116–122.

Holdsworth, L., & Cartwright, S. (2003). Empowerment, stress and satisfaction: An exploratory study of a call centre. *Leadership & Organization Development Journal*, 24(3), 131–140.

House, J. S. (1981). *Work Stress and Social Support*. Reading, MA: Addison Wesley.

Hunsley, J., Elliott, K., & Therrien, Z. (2013). The efficacy and effectiveness of psychological treatments. *Canadian Psychology/Psychologie canadienne*, 55(3), 161–176. https://doi.org/10.1037/a0036933

Jahoda, M. (1982). *Employment and Unemployment: A Social-Psychological Analysis* (Vol. 1). CUP Archive.

Jones, K. P. (2017). To tell or not to tell? Examining the role of discrimination in the pregnancy disclosure process at work. *Journal of Occupational Health Psychology*, 22(2), 239.

Kelloway, E. K., & Barling, J. (2010). Leadership development as an intervention in occupational health psychology. *Work & Stress*, 24(3), 260–279.

Kitchener, B. A., & Jorm, A. F. (2002). Mental health first aid training for the public: Evaluation of effects on knowledge, attitudes and helping behavior. *BMC Psychiatry*, 2(1), 10.

Kitchener, B. A., & Jorm, A. F. (2004). Mental health first aid training in a workplace setting: A randomized controlled trial [ISRCTN13249129]. *BMC Psychiatry*, 4(1).

Kitchener, B. A., & Jorm, A. F. (2008). Mental health first aid: An international programme for early intervention. *Early Intervention in Psychiatry*, 2(1), 55–61.

Langford, C. P. H., Bowsher, J., Maloney, J. P., & Lillis, P. P. (1997). Social support: A conceptual analysis. *Journal of Advanced Nursing*, 25(1), 95–100.

Lim, K. L., Jacobs, P., Ohinmaa, A., Schopflocher, D., & Dewa, C. S. (2008). A new population-based measure of the economic burden of mental illness in Canada. *Chronic Dis Can*, 28(3), 92–98.

Lyons, B. J., Martinez, L. R., Ruggs, E. N., Hebl, M. R., Ryan, A. M., O'Brien, K. R., & Roebuck, A. (2018). To say or not to say: Different strategies of acknowledging a visible disability. *Journal of Management*, 44, 1980–2007.

Martinez, L. R., White, C. D., Shapiro, J. R., & Hebl, M. R. (2016). Selection BIAS: Stereotypes and discrimination related to having a history of cancer. *Journal of Applied Psychology*, 101(1), 122–128.

Mental Health Commission of Canada [MHCC] (2012). *Changing Directions, Changing Lives: The Mental Health Strategy for Canada*. Calgary, AB.

Mental Health Commission of Canada [MHCC] (2013). *Making the Case for Investing in Mental Health in Canada*. Ottawa, ON: Mental Health Commission of Canada.

National Alliance on Mental Illness [NAMI] (2019). *Mental Health by the Numbers*. Retrieved from https://www.nami.org/learn-more/mental-health-by-the-numbers

National Joint Council/Disability Insurance Plan Board of Management. (2008). Annual Report 2008. Available from: http://www.njc-cnm.gc.ca/aux_bin.php?auxid =448

Nielsen, K., & Randall, R. (2009). Managers' active support when implementing teams: The impact on employee well-being. *Applied Psychology: Health and Well-Being, 1*(3), 374–390.

Nittrouer, C. L., Trump, R. C. E., O'Brien, K. R., & Hebl, M. (2014). Stand up and be counted: In the long run, disclosing helps all. *Industrial and Organizational Psychology: Perspectives on Science and Practice, 7,* 235–241.

Oakie, T., Smith, N. A., Dimoff, J. K., & Kelloway, E. K. (2018). Coworker health awareness training: An evaluation. *Journal of Applied Biobehavioral Research, 23*(1–14, 4).

Odle-Dusseau, H. N., Hammer, L. B., Crain, T. L., & Bodner, T. E. (2016). The influence of family-supportive supervisor training on employee job performance and attitudes: An organizational work–family intervention. *Journal of Occupational Health Psychology, 21*(3), 296–308.

Onken, S. J., & Slaten, E. (2000). Disability identity formation and affirmation: The experiences of persons with severe mental illness. *Sociological Practice, 2,* 99–111.

Ragins, B. R. (2008). Disclosure disconnects: Antecedents and consequences of disclosing invisible stigmas across life domains. *Academy of Management Review, 33*(1), 194–215.

Ragins, B. R., Singh, R., & Cornwell, J. M. (2007). Making the invisible visible: Fear and disclosure of sexual orientation at work. *Journal of Applied Psychology, 92*(4), 1103.

Rosch, P. J. (2001). The quandary of job stress compensation. *Health and Stress, 3*(1), 1–4.

Ryan, R. M., & Deci, E. L. (2000). Self-determination theory and the facilitation of intrinsic motivation, social development, and well-being. *American Psychologist, 55*(1), 68–78.

Saint-Arnaud, L., Saint-Jean, M., & Damasse, J. (2007). Towards an enhanced understanding of factors involved in the return-to-work process of employees absent due to mental health problems. *Canadian Journal of Community Mental Health, 25*(2), 303–315.

Sauter, S. L., Murphy, L. R., and Hurrell Jr., J. J. (1990). Prevention of work-related psychological disorders. *American Psychologist, 45,* 1146–1153.

Smith, N. A., Dimoff, J. K., Fox, S., Vogel, W. E. S., & Getzen, S. (2019, April). Mental illness stigma at work: Development of a measurement scale. Symposium presentation at the 34th annual meeting of the Society for Industrial and Organizational Psychology, Washington, DC.

Stephens, T., & Joubert, N. (2001). The economic burden of mental health problems in Canada. *Chronic Dis Can, 22*(1), 18–23.

Tajfel, H., & Turner, J. C. (1986). The social identity theory of intergroup behavior. In S. Worchel & W. G. Austin (Eds.), *Psychology of Intergroup Relations* (2nd ed.). Chicago, IL: Nelson-Hall Publishers.

Vogel, W. E. S., Dimoff, J. K., & Smith, N. A. (2019, April). To call or not to call? The impact of manager training on employee well-being. Symposium presentation at the

34th annual meeting of the Society for Industrial and Organizational Psychology, Washington, DC.

Watson Wyatt Worldwide/National Business Group on Health (2010). *2009/2010 North American Staying@Work Report. The Health and Productivity Advantage.* Toronto, ON: Watson Wyatt Worldwide. Available from: http://www. watsonwyatt. com

Wells, J. D., Hobfoll, S. E., & Lavin, J. (1999). When it rains, it pours: The greater impact of resource loss compared to gain on psychological distress. *Personality and Social Psychology Bulletin, 25,* 1172–1182.

World Health Organization (2002). *Prevention and Promotion in Mental Health.* Accessed on January 20, 2020. Retrieved from https://www.who.int/mental_health/media/en/545.pdf

World Health Organization (2004). *The Summary Report on Promoting Mental Health: Concepts, Emerging Evidence, and Practice.* Geneva, Switzerland: World Health Organization.

World Health Organization (2019). *Depression.* Accessed on January 20, 2020. Retrieved from https://www.who.int/news-room/fact-sheets/detail/depression

9. Managing work stress: the research agenda

Sheena Johnson and Elinor O'Connor

Introduction

The term 'stress management intervention' (SMI) covers a wide array of organisational activities and initiatives designed to reduce the stress that people experience at work and to improve the well-being of employees. However, although some SMIs have been shown to be useful in addressing stress and promoting well-being, there are many interventions in use that are of uncertain efficacy. There is often a dearth of evidence to show whether or not specific interventions are effective, and limited understanding of the factors – contextual and individual – that might influence their efficacy. The aim of this chapter is to highlight some of the things we do not know about SMI and to consider the areas where future research might be targeted to fill these gaps in our knowledge. In doing this, the chapter will review some of the existing evidence in relation to SMI, but it is not intended to be an exhaustive review of the literature. The chapter instead focuses on considering what we do not yet know about SMI efficacy to develop an agenda for future research that may serve to increase and improve our understanding of interventions to enhance psychological well-being at work.

The chapter starts by presenting a typology of SMI that includes the level and focus of the intervention before giving a brief overview of the evidence regarding SMI effectiveness with reference to this typology. We then consider a number of areas where there are identifiable gaps in the research evidence, including more recent approaches to SMI (e.g. creative arts-based interventions); the role of individual differences in SMI efficacy, which has received only limited attention in the literature to date; the use of biofeedback in SMI, which is emerging as a focus of interest as a result of advances in technology; and the nature of resilience, which many interventions – explicitly or implicitly – seek to promote. The chapter moves on to consider the need to focus on researching multi-modal SMI given that the approach of many organisations is to implement more than one SMI at the same time. Multi-modal SMI studies are required to provide insight into the relative effectiveness of multiple interventions rather than focusing on individual interventions as many studies have done to date. Consideration is then given to methodological issues when investigating SMI efficacy, with sections covering the ways in which SMI are implemented, the importance of considering contextual variables, the need for longitudinal research designs, the ways in which SMI data are sourced, and what outcomes should be considered for inclusion in studies of SMI effectiveness. The chapter concludes by considering the changes that have occurred in work and employment and the potential implications of these for SMI implementation and effectiveness.

Before detailing SMI and the approaches taken to researching them, it is appropriate to comment briefly on the potential role publication bias may play in our understanding of SMI. As is recognised more broadly in the psychological literature (e.g. Ferguson & Heene, 2012), it is our contention that studies showing a positive effect of SMI are more likely to be published. What this means, of course, is that there is less known about what does not work and yet this is clearly important information for effective occupational stress management. It is encouraging that some journals are moving in the direction of agreeing publication based on study design, rather than study findings, and we strongly endorse this approach as a means of gaining better insight into SMI efficacy.

Typology of stress management interventions

There are many different types of SMI. Table 9.1 illustrates the typology proposed by Holman et al. (2018), with examples of SMI in each category.

Table 9.1   A typology of stress management interventions

Type of intervention	Primary	Secondary	Tertiary
Individual	• Selection & assessment • Pre-employment medical examination	• Mindfulness training • Health promotion, e.g., exercise • Cognitive behavioural therapy (CBT) • Relaxation • Meditation • Personal and interpersonal skill training • Acceptance and commitment therapy • Psychosocial intervention training • Coping skills training • Resilience training	• Employee Assistance Programme (EAP) • Counselling • Posttraumatic stress assistance • Disability management
Organisational	• Job redesign • Working time and schedules • Management training, e.g. mentoring	• Improving communication and decision making • Conflict management • Peer support groups • Coaching & career planning	• Vocational rehabilitation • Outplacement

Source: based on Holman et al. (2018).

The typology is based on two of the most commonly used classifications of interventions:

- Individual or organisational level:
  - Individual level interventions focus on people and are designed to help reduce people's stress, improve their coping mechanisms when faced with stressful situations in particular, and generally to better manage their stress levels overall;
  - Organisational level interventions focus on places and situations and are designed to change systematically workplace practices in order to remove or reduce any sources of stress arising from them.
- Stress management focus:
  - Primary interventions seek to prevent or reduce stress from occurring;
  - Secondary interventions are designed to reduce the stress experienced by individuals. They do not stop stress from happening but are designed to help people to cope better with the stress they experience;
  - Tertiary interventions seek to help people recover from stress once it has occurred.

Overview of evidence relating to SMI effectiveness

Holman et al. (2018) discussed the evidence regarding SMI efficacy in relation to the typology in Table 9.1 and drew a number of conclusions regarding the effectiveness of individual and organisational interventions.

The strongest evidence for SMI efficacy lies with secondary, individual interventions where much of the SMI research has been conducted to date. There is also a growing evidence base for individual-level, tertiary interventions (see McLeod, 2008; Richmond et al., 2017), with counselling and employee assistance programmes demonstrated to be effective stress management tools. Much less is known about the impact of primary, individual interventions on stress and well-being, in part because they are implemented relatively rarely; this represents a gap in the evidence base and an area where future research could usefully be focused. In doing this, careful consideration would need to be given to potential ethical issues, for example, if selection procedures based on individual stress propensity were to be used for appointing – or not appointing – job applicants to roles.

Primary organisational interventions such as job redesign are reasonably well researched, with the evidence showing that changing the characteristics of a job can reduce stress and improve well-being (e.g. Ahola et al., 2012; Holman and Axtell, 2016). Similarly there is evidence to show that secondary organisational interventions such as conflict management can be effective (e.g. Leiter et al., 2011). Finally, with regard to tertiary organisational interventions such as vocational rehabilitation and outplacement, there is limited evidence available. For example, a detailed report on vocational rehabilitation concluded that although there is generally a strong evidence base for vocational rehabilitation for physical conditions (e.g. musculoskeletal conditions), there is a lack of scientific clarity about stress and a dearth of related evidence for work outcomes (Waddell et al., 2008). The report authors called for an urgent need to improve vocational rehabilitation interventions for mental health conditions. There is, therefore, a clear scope for research to improve the evidence base in this specific domain.

Some gaps in the SMI research evidence base

In addition to more 'traditional' SMI, some of which are reported in Table 9.1, there is a range of additional intervention approaches that are 'new' in the sense of being innovative; are becoming more practicable to implement as a result of technological advances (e.g. biofeedback); or have been relatively under-researched. There are identifiable gaps in the evidence base, which provide potential focal points for future research. Below, we discuss four key areas in which research evidence is as yet relatively limited.

Creative art-based SMI

An emerging and interesting field of study proposes that creative art therapy may be an innovative way to prevent or reduce stress. Broadly speaking, creative art therapy covers art, music, dance/movement and drama. A recent systematic review identified 37 studies, with almost three quarters using robust, randomised controlled trial (RCT) methodological designs, and concluded that creative arts-based interventions were associated with a significant reduction in participant stress (Martin et al., 2018). However, the authors noted that a lack of quality and consistency in the reporting of studies precluded the conduct of a meta-analysis, and the wide variety of different interventions investigated in the literature prevented clear-cut conclusions about the elements of creative art-based interventions that are associated with improved well-being.

Biofeedback

Recent reviews of biofeedback conclude that it can be an effective intervention to reduce stress and enhance well-being and performance (Kennedy & Parker, 2019; De Witte et al., 2019). However, there are only limited empirical studies that have looked at biofeedback as an intervention in relation to workplace stress specifically. In addition, a lack of consistency in approaches hinders comparison across studies and in turn makes conclusions about the consistency of outcomes problematic. In particular, it would be valuable to conduct longitudinal studies to enable identification of the durability of positive outcomes of biofeedback-based SMI beyond the intervention implementation stage when participants may no longer have access to biofeedback devices.

Individual differences

Many studies have investigated individual variables that influence the relationships among stressor appraisal, stress coping, and strain. These include trait variables such as Type A personality, neuroticism, and locus of control (Bliese et al., 2017), and demographic variables such as gender (e.g. Gyllensten & Palmer, 2005) and age (e.g. Johnson et al., 2013). However, relatively little is known about the impact of individual variables on SMI outcomes and we suggest that this is an important avenue for future research. It is to be expected that personality and attitudes will be important in terms of whether or not, and to what extent, people engage with SMI, and a number of studies have indicated that individual differences play a role in SMI effectiveness. For example, research has reported that willingness to change, openness and positive appraisal have a positive effect on job design interventions (e.g. Bond et al., 2008; Cunningham et al., 2002; Nielsen et al., 2007). There is a clear requirement for future research to investigate the impact of individual differences in personality characteristics as well as demographic variables such as age on SMI outcomes.

Resilience

One strand of research in the occupational stress literature has focused on the concept of resilience. Although resilience has been conceived of by some researchers as an individual difference variable, it is now more commonly understood to be a set of capabilities and resources enabling people to protect their well-being in the face of adverse experiences (Rees et al., 2015). This latter conception of resilience implies that it is an entity that can be developed; indeed many individual, secondary SMI explicitly – or implicitly – seek to foster aspects of resilience by equipping people with skills or resources to protect against the negative impact of stressors. Rees et al. (2015) note that although there is some agreement among researchers on the constituents of resilience, there is no dominant, unified model of resilience in the literature. We propose that the development of a proven model of resilience is a fundamental step in devising theoretically grounded and effective SMI that seek to increase resilience.

A need for a focus on the efficacy of multi-modal SMI

Most SMI evaluation studies focus on one type of intervention, but it is increasingly common for organisations to implement multi-modal SMI that combine individual and organisation interventions at different levels, for example, putting in place job redesign while also promoting mindfulness and relaxation initiatives. It might be expected that multiple interventions would offer the best protection from negative stress outcomes, but relatively little is understood about the combined effect of multiple SMI implementation, in part due to the complexity of studying the impact of multiple interventions simultaneously. A number of researchers (e.g. Anger et al. 2015; Daniels et al., 2017) have advocated 'total worker health interventions' based on implementing multi-modal SMI, but little is known about their relative effectiveness singly and in combination.

Meta-analyses (e.g. Richardson & Rothstein, 2008; van der Klink et al., 2001) provide some information and indicate that the effect sizes of multi-modal, secondary, individual-level interventions are similar in magnitude to single SMI (Holman et al., 2018). On the face of it, this suggests that there is limited value in offering multiple SMI when similar effects may be seen when implementing just one effective SMI. However, it has been argued by Richardson & Rothstein (2008) that multi-modal SMI effects are not only longer lasting but also increase over time, which suggests that longitudinal studies measuring outcomes at multiple time points are needed to give a full picture of the potential effects. We have limited insight into the relative effectiveness of SMI because studies tend not to compare the impact of different interventions within the same study. Future research might consider questions such as whether the use of multi-modal SMI lead to improved outcomes, and if so why? Are there interventions that are best 'matched' and others that might work against each other? Is it cost effective to put in place multiple initiatives or better to implement one SMI that has been proven to be effective and focus resources on this?

Methodological considerations in investigating SMI efficacy

It is common to see randomised control trials (RCT) identified as the 'gold standard' for intervention research. However, when implementing interventions in an organisational setting, researchers have argued that sometimes such randomisation may not be practicable and may even not be ethical as it would, for example, delay or prevent some participants from accessing SMI (e.g. see Nielsen & Miraglia, 2017). It has also been argued that the act of randomisation could be viewed as a workplace change event that could influence how employees perceive the intervention and in turn alter outcomes, compromising the robustness of study findings (e.g. see Nabe-Nielsen et al., 2015). Researchers should, of course, strive to use rigorous research designs to gather good-quality data, but SMI research need not consider RCT as the only acceptable approach. Below we outline a number of research design considerations that are important when studying SMI efficacy.

Process of implementation

Researchers have argued that when looking at SMI the *process* of implementation could be just as important as the intervention itself and the outcomes being assessed (Cox et al., 2007). Frameworks designed to address the importance of the process of implementation have been developed, such as the longitudinal evaluation framework proposed by Nielsen and Abildgaard (2013). Such frameworks suggest that both the process of implementation and multiple outcomes (discussed further below) should be assessed to allow better insight into what SMI affects, and the processes underlying and timescales for these effects. The process of implementation includes factors such as preparation and support for introducing the intervention(s), identification of potential risks, employee participation and the way in which interventions are implemented, all of which are factors that have been shown to influence the likelihood of an intervention being successful (e.g. Holman et al., 2018; Nielsen et al., 2010). Some intervention evaluation studies have begun to look at elements of this, for example by using longitudinal methods, looking at multiple outcomes, and considering process in more detail, but there is much more to be done in this area before we can claim to have good understanding of how implementation processes influence SMI effectiveness.

Importance of context

Holman et al. (2018) describe how a variation in effect sizes is evident for some secondary-level SMI and briefly consider the possible influence of context when noting that the positive effects of SMI are not realised in all contexts. Daniels et al. (2017) also discussed how organisational context, for example, downsizing or poor HR practices, can negatively affect SMI effectiveness. However, there is limited research that has directly looked at how the context in which an SMI is implemented can influence SMI outcomes. This is another area where additional research could make an important contribution, and future studies investigating SMI efficacy would benefit from considering and investigating the impact context has on their uptake and success.

Longitudinal research design

Research in occupational psychology has rightly increased emphasis on the importance of longitudinal research, with cross-sectional studies criticised due to their inability to determine the direction of cause and effect. There are a number of things to note in relation to this in terms of a future research agenda on SMI efficacy. Firstly, and fundamentally, it could be argued that there are theories and models that are accepted in the literature but which are built primarily on cross-sectional research. There could, therefore, be a need to conduct more rigorous longitudinal research in order to demonstrate that currently accepted knowledge still holds true. Such research could make an important contribution in terms of supporting, or rejecting, current 'wisdom'. Secondly, as discussed earlier, considerations such as process, context and implementation can be addressed using longitudinal research. Thirdly, as we discussed when considering multi-modal SMI, the effects of some interventions may strengthen (or weaken) over time; this is something of which we at present have limited knowledge and yet it is of vital importance when identifying which SMI are most effective in terms of outcomes and efficient in terms of resource demands.

Data sources

Considering data sources, whether in terms of outcomes or factors such as workers' engagement with SMI, is a potentially fruitful area of research. The richest data in relation to SMI are likely to be multi-source data, for example, measuring performance outcomes by asking participants to rate their performance and also obtaining objective performance data, or asking participants to report their engagement with SMI while also objectively measuring time committed to the intervention (e.g. measuring time spent using a mindfulness app). Rich data such as these are rare because it is difficult, time-consuming, and potentially costly to design studies that include multi-source data measurement. In addition, depending on the type of work being studied, reliable, objective data may simply not be available. Multi-source data collection is challenging, but studies that can achieve this are valuable, with the potential to provide better insight into the efficacy of SMI and also to facilitate comparison of different data sources, for example, establishing the relative robustness of self-reported, manager-reported and objective performance data.

In addition to advocating greater use of multi-source data, researchers have also called for more SMI evaluation studies to implement a multi-level approach (e.g. Martin et al., 2016). It is argued that studies looking at the interaction of individual workers, work groups, organisational factors and even wider societal factors are rare but are needed to enhance understanding of employee health and to support the development of effective well-being interventions.

Determining and measuring outcomes

When evaluating the effectiveness of SMI, a key consideration is determining what outcomes should be measured. An important factor impeding conclusions about SMI effectiveness is that research studies frequently look at different outcomes. For example, research on SMI efficacy has considered a range of outcomes, including:

- Health outcomes such as burnout, depression, anxiety, physical health, psychological health (and these are often defined in different ways in different studies);
- Job-related attitudes such as job satisfaction, organisational citizenship behaviour or workplace commitment;
- Job-related outcomes such as performance, sickness and absenteeism, or turnover.

What would be beneficial to our understanding are studies that explore several outcomes simultaneously, for example by measuring health, attitudes and job outcomes within the same study. This could offer insight into which outcomes are most influenced by SMI, and also potentially the degree to which the outcomes affect and influence each other. Studies should aim to look at multiple outcomes and to assess causal effects. For example, we might expect that an SMI that leads to a positive health outcome would also be likely to increase job satisfaction and to lower absenteeism and turnover. What we do not know is what is influenced first: attitudes or health? Is it better for an intervention to seek to improve health and by doing so change attitudes? Or would an intervention designed to improve job attitudes be more effective in improving health? And over what time period do these effects become evident? Studies that assess multiple outcomes, ideally over an extended period of time, would help to tease out some of the interactions we anticipate occurring across SMI outcomes.

We also need greater clarity in terms of what is meant when reporting on outcomes; for example, a SMI study looking at psychological health outcomes might or might not measure anxiety, depending on the researchers' model and operational definition of psychological health. This lack of consensus in the definitions and measurement tools used in different SMI evaluation studies can make the comparison of findings difficult. Studies that seek to develop a consensus in terms of the measurement of outcomes and reporting of findings have the potential to make a significant contribution to the literature on SMI effectiveness.

Changes in work and employment in the 21st century: implications for SMI

The period from the late 20th to early 21st century has seen a myriad of changes both in the nature of work and in employment patterns. Examples include the emergence of the 'portfolio' career and 'dual practice' (e.g. Russo et al., 2018), involving working with two or more organisations simultaneously, and growing interest in establishing the 'four-day' week as the standard pattern of work (Ashton, 2019).

Gallie (2017) identifies three key trends in the evolution of work in OECD countries in the 21st century: changes in the types of skills required by employers (with growth in professional, technical and service occupations and a reduction in manufacturing and manual occupations); a reduction in the 'quality' of work; and a reduction in job security. Work quality is commonly defined in terms of job control and work intensity (Gallie, 2017), and it is well established that low levels of job control combined with high job demands are associated with physical ill-health and poorer subjective well-being (e.g. Karesek and Theorell, 1990). With regard to job security, there is a general consensus in the labour literature that employment has become less secure since the 1990s, with an increase in temporary contracts, an increase in precarious employment in the form of freelance work or uncertain hours of work associated with 'zero-hours' contracts, and lower pay levels. In a study involving more than 7,000 workers in Canada, Lewchuk (2017) reported that insecure employment was associated with poorer physical and mental health. Lower quality jobs and insecure employment are pertinent to well-being as they are potential sources of stress in their own right, but we propose they may also have implications for the implementation or effectiveness of SMI. Of course, workers may opt for temporary or zero-hours roles entirely by choice and this underlines the importance of research evaluating SMI taking into account individual and contextual factors, as discussed earlier.

A key factor in the changing nature of work and employment from the late 20th century to date is the significant development of information and communication technology (ICT) during this period. ICT development underpins the emergence of new business models such as the 'gig economy', which is characterised by freelance working and zero-hours contracts in app-based service organisations, as well as new types of work, such as teleworking. ICT development has also led to more flexible working arrangements in existing sectors and roles, such as home working. Although this flexibility can be beneficial both to organisations and workers, it has also resulted in permeability of the boundaries between work and personal life domains with mobile devices and job-related technology creating 'constant connectivity' to work, which has implications for well-being. For example, after-work recovery, which plays an important role in reducing psychological strain caused by stressful experiences at work (e.g. Sonnentag & Fritz, 2015), may be compromised by remaining connected to work. Individual differences in managing the boundaries between work and personal life domains are evident, with some preferring to keep them segmented and separate, and others choosing greater integration of the two (Campbell-Clark, 2000). The requirement to remain connected to work due to organisational expectations or workload demands may be more detrimental to well-being in those with a preference for segmentation (e.g. Sonnentag and Pundt, 2017). Sonnentag (2018) emphasises that after-work recovery does not necessarily occur automatically and needs to be actively pursued, and we suggest that there is merit in developing individual and organisational SMI that specifically seek to support after-work recovery.

The last decade has seen a general trend in society towards increased awareness of psychological well-being, including greater openness about mental health difficulties. This general trend is reflected in the workplace, and a number of occupational sectors have introduced targeted initiatives to support psychological well-being and mental health at work, including occupational stress management measures. In the UK, examples include the *Mind Matters* initiative established to support psychological well-being in the veterinary profession (Vet Mind Matters, 2020) and the 'And Me' mental health awareness and support initiative for medical doctors (British Medical Association, 2020). Increased awareness of psychological well-being at work is potentially an important contextual factor influencing the implementation and outcomes of SMI that should be taken into account in future research.

Conclusions

It is thanks to collective research efforts over many years that SMI are currently as widely accepted and promoted within organisations as they are. However, it is also apparent from this review and proposed research agenda that although there is much that is already understood about SMI and their effectiveness, there are also gaps in our knowledge and a range of areas in which future research is necessary to develop the evidence base. There are several issues of which our understanding is currently limited, for example, in relation to the effectiveness of multi-modal SMI, and how the process of implementation and the context in which they take place can impact intervention outcomes. Additionally, changes in society and in the nature of work, as well as technological developments, have potentially important implications for occupational stress management that merit investigation. Designing and conducting research to address these evidence gaps has the potential to make a significant contribution to our understanding of SMI and their effectiveness. This is important not only from a theoretical research perspective, but also in terms of enabling organisations to identify effective and efficient interventions, as well as how they should be implemented to maximise their contribution to reducing stress and enhancing well-being.

References

Ahola, K., Vuori, J., Toppinen-Tanner, S., Mutanen, P., & Honkonen, T. (2012). Resource-enhancing group intervention against depression at workplace: Who benefits? A randomised controlled study with a 7-month follow-up. *Occupational Environmental Medicine, 69*, 870–876. doi.org/10.1136/oemed-2011-100450

Anger, W. K., Elliot, D. L., Bodner, T., et al., (2015). Effectiveness of total worker health interventions. *Journal of Occupational Health Psychology, 20*, 226–247. doi.org/10.1037/a0038340

Ashton, J. R. (2019). The public health case for the four-day working week. *Journal of the Royal Society of Medicine, 112*(2), 81–82.

Bliese, P. D., Edwards, J. R., & Sonnentag, S. (2017). Stress and well-being at work: A century of empirical trends reflecting theoretical and societal influences. *Journal of Applied Psychology, 102*(3), 389–402.

Bond, F. W., Flaxman, P. E., & Bunce, D. (2008). The influence of psychological flexibility on work redesign: Mediated moderation of a work reorganization intervention. *Journal of Applied Psychology, 93*, 645–654. doi.org/10.1037/0021-9010.93.3.645

British Medical Association (2020), bma.org.uk, accessed 30 January 2020.

Campbell-Clark, S. (2000). Work/family border theory: A new theory of work/family balance. *Human Relations, 53*(6), 747–770.

Cox, T., Karanika, M., Griffiths, A., & Houdmont, J. (2007). Evaluating organizational-level work stress interventions: Beyond tradition methods. *Work & Stress, 21*, 348–362. doi.org/10.1080/02678370701760757

Cunningham, C. E., Woodward, C. A., Shannon, H. S., et al. (2002). Readiness for organizational change: A longitudinal study of workplace, psychological and behavioural correlates. *Journal of Occupational and Organizational Psychology, 75*, 377–392. doi.org/10.1348/096317902321119637

Daniels, K., Gedikli, C., Watson, D., Semkina, A., & Vaughn, O. (2017). Job design, employment practices and well-being: A systematic review of intervention studies. *Ergonomics*, doi: 10.1080/00140139.2017.1303085

De Witte, N. A., Buyck, I., & Van Daele, T. (2019). Combining biofeedback with stress management interventions: A systematic review of physiological and psychological effects. *Applied Psychophysiology and Biofeedback, 44*(2), 71–82.

Ferguson, C. J., & Heene, M. (2012). A vast graveyard of undead theories: Publication bias and psychological science's aversion to the null. *Perspectives on Psychological Science, 7*(6), 555–561.

Gallie, D. (2017). The quality of work in a changing labour market. *Social Policy and Administration, 51*(2), 226–243.

Gyllensten, K. & Palmer, S. (2005) The role of gender in workplace stress: A critical literature review. *Health Education Journal, 64*(3), 747–770.

Holman, D. & Axtell, C. (2016). Can job redesign interventions influence a broad range of employee outcomes by changing multiple job characteristics? A quasi-experimental study. *Journal of Occupational Health Psychology, 3*, 284–295. doi.org/10.1037/a0039962

Holman, D., Johnson, S., & O'Connor, E. (2018). Stress management interventions: Improving subjective psychological well-being in the workplace. In E. Diener, S. Oishi, & L. Tay (Eds.), *Handbook of Well-being*. Salt Lake City, UT: DEF Publishers. http://nobascholar.com/chapters/44

Johnson, S. J., Holdsworth, L., Hoel, H., & Zapf, D. (2013). Customer stressors in service organizations: The impact of age on stress management and burnout, *European Journal of Work and Organizational Psychology, 22*(3), 318–330.

Karesek, R. & Theorell, T. (1990). *Healthy Work: Stress, Productivity and the Reconstruction of Work Life*. New York: Basic Books.

Kennedy, L., & Parker, S. H. (2019). Biofeedback as a stress management tool: A systematic review. *Cognition, Technology & Work, 21*(2), 161–190.

Leiter, M.P., Laschinger, H.K., Day, A., & Oore, D.G. (2011). The impact of civility interventions on employee social behavior, distress, and attitudes. *Journal of Applied Psychology, 96*, 1258–1274. doi.org/10.1037/a0024442

Lewchuk, W. (2017). Precarious jobs: Where are they and how do they affect well-being? *Economic and Labour Relations Review, 28*(3), 402–419.

Martin, A., Karanika-Murray, M., Biron, C., & Sanderson, K. (2016). The psychosocial work environment, employee mental health and organizational interventions: Improving research and practice by taking a multilevel approach. *Stress and Health*, *32*(3), 201–215.

Martin, L., Oepen, R., Bauer, K., Nottensteiner, A., Mergheim, K., Gruber, H., & Koch, S. C. (2018). Creative arts interventions for stress management and prevention – a systematic review. *Behavioral Sciences*, *8*(2), 1–28.

McLeod, J. (2008). *Counselling in the Workplace: A Comprehensive Review of the Research Evidence* (2nd edition). British Association for Counselling and Psychotherapy. Accessed 29 January 2020, http://www.bacp.co.uk/docs/pdf/12453 _workplace_systematic_review.pdf

Nabe-Nielsen, K., Persson, R., Nielsen, K., Olsen, O., Carneiro, I., & Garde, H. (2015). Perspective on randomization and readiness for change in a workplace intervention study. In M. Karanika-Murray and C. Biron (Eds.), *Derailed Organizational Stress and Well-being Interventions: Confessions of Failure and Solutions for Success* (pp. 201–208). Dordrecht: Springer.

Nielsen, K. & Abildgaard, J.S. (2013). Organizational interventions: A research-based framework for the evaluation of both process and effects. *Work & Stress*, 27, 278–297. doi.org/10.1080/02678373.2013.812358

Nielsen, K., & Miraglia, M. (2017). What works for whom in which circumstances? On the need to move beyond the 'what works?' question in organizational intervention research. *Human Relations*, *70*, 40–62. doi.org/10.1177/0018726716670226

Nielsen, K., Randall, R., & Albertsen, K. (2007). Participants' appraisals of process issues and the effects of stress management interventions. *Journal of Organizational Behavior*, *28*, 793–810. doi.org/10.1002/job.450

Nielsen, K., Randall, R., Holten, A. L., & González, E. R. (2010). Conducting organizational-level occupational health interventions: What works? *Work & Stress*, *24*, 234–259. doi.org/10.1080/02678373.2010.515393

Rees, C. S., Breen, L. J., Cusack, L., & Hegney, D. (2015). Understanding individual resilience in the workplace: The international collaboration of workforce resilience model. *Frontiers in Psychology*, *6*, article 73.

Richardson, K. M., & Rothstein, H. R. (2008). Effects of occupational stress management intervention programs: A meta-analysis. *Journal of Occupational Health Psychology*, *13*, 69–93. doi.org/10.1037/1076-8998.13.1.69

Richmond, M. K., Pampel, F. C., Wood, R. C., & Nunes, A. P. (2017). The impact of employee assistance services on workplace outcomes: Results of a prospective, quasi-experimental study. *Journal of Occupational Health Psychology*, *22*(2), 170–179.

Russo, G., Fronteira, I., Silva-Jesus, T. & Buchan, J. (2018). Understanding nurses' dual practice: A scoping review of what we know and what we still need to ask on nurses holding multiple jobs. *Human Resources for Health*, *16*(14), doi:10.1186/s12960-018 -0276-x

Sonnentag, S. (2018). The recovery paradox: Portraying the complex interplay between job stressors, lack of recovery, and poor well-being. *Research in Organizational Behavior*, *38*, 169–185.

Sonnentag, S., & Fritz, C. (2015). Recovery from job stress: The stressor-detachment model as an integrative framework. *Journal of Organizational Behavior*, *36*(1), 72–103.

Sonnentag, S., & Pundt, A. (2017). Media use and well-being at the work–home interface. In L. Reinecke & M. B. Oliver (Eds.), *The Routledge Handbook of Media Use and Well-being: International Perspectives on Theory and Research on Positive Media Effects* (pp. 341–354). New York: Routledge/Taylor & Francis Group.

van der Klink, J. J., Blonk, R. W., Schene, A. H., & Van Dijk, F. J. (2001). The benefits of interventions for work-related stress. *American Journal of Public Health, 91,* 270–276. doi.org/10.2105/ajph.91.2.270

Vet Mind Matters (2020), vetmindmatters.org, accessed 30 January 2020.

Waddell, G., Burton, A. K., & Kendall, N. A. (2008). *Vocational Rehabilitation: What Works, for Whom, and When?*(Report for the Vocational Rehabilitation Task Group). London: TSO. Accessed 29 January 2020, https://assets.publishing.service .gov.uk/government/uploads/system/uploads/attachment_data/file/209474/hwwb -vocational-rehabilitation.pdf

10. Cautions for mindfulness research in organisations: taking stock and moving forward

Maree Roche, Michelle R. Tuckey and Ute R. Hülsheger

Introduction

In recent years interest in mindfulness has increased immensely in many different research fields, and in a variety of public domains. Mindfulness has found application first and foremost in the field of clinical psychology in Western settings (Kang & Whittingham, 2010). Recently, however, it has attracted the attention of organisational researchers and practitioners, as it has shown to have positive outcomes in the workplace (Thomasson, 2018). Despite the increased interest in the application of mindfulness in organisational environments, research on mindfulness is still predominantly found in clinical journals rather than in organisational and managerial journals (Roche et al., 2020). While emerging in the workplace, mindfulness research has also demonstrated significant growth and interest.

The existing body of organisational psychological research suggests many benefits of mindfulness for the individual and – more recently – the organisation. For example, mindfulness is negatively associated with burnout, stress and anxiety (Allexandre et al., 2016; Di Benedetto & Swadling, 2014; Grégoire & Lachance, 2015; Ireland et al., 2017) and positively associated with well-being and positive affect (Malinowski & Lim, 2015; Singleton et al., 2014; Zeng & Gu, 2017). In addition to positive outcomes with regards to health, mindfulness also has a positive influence on attitudes and behaviour in the workplace. Mindfulness is positively linked to performance (Dane & Brummel, 2014), affective commitment, job satisfaction and engagement (Andrews et al., 2014; Zivnuska et al., 2016), and negatively related to turnover intentions (Andrews et al., 2014; Dane & Brummel, 2014), counterproductive behaviour (Schwager et al., 2016), and workplace aggression (Liang et al., 2018). These and other personal and professional correlates of mindfulness in the work context have been summarised in a recent meta-analysis (Mesmer-Magnus et al., 2017).

Taking these outcomes into account, there is a clear rationale in studying mindfulness in organisational settings. However, mindfulness is not a straight-forward concept in definition, measurement, intervention, or application in workplace environments. The aim of this chapter is to examine some of the emerging issues regarding mindfulness at work, and thus guide readers' and researchers' insights into this developing field.

Approaches in the way we work with mindfulness

The majority of this chapter focuses on mindfulness via two fundamental aspects of consciousness: awareness and attention. In particular, it examines present-focussed non-judgemental awareness of and attention to experience (Brown et al., 2007). This concept of mindfulness can be described and examined in different ways deriving from these core elements; these different lenses on mindfulness influence how mindfulness at work is understood and investigated (Roche et al., 2020). First is *state mindfulness* – the momentary experience of present-focussed non-judgemental attention and awareness that changes from day to day and even from instant to instant. People differ in how regularly and reliably they experience state mindfulness, reflecting its *trait*-like quality. State and trait mindfulness can also be cultivated through *practice*, such as through meditation, and taught through mindfulness training *interventions* or therapies. Jamieson and Tuckey (2017) have discussed the differences between these different ways of thinking about mindfulness, and the connections between them (see Figure 10.1). All four concepts are studied in the mindfulness literature. On the one hand, exploring mindfulness in these four distinct ways can yield important and parsimonious insights regarding mindfulness at work. On the other hand, the challenge of integrating research findings across four different streams makes understanding the bigger picture on workplace mindfulness more complex, and is reflected in a lack of clarity in how mindfulness is operationalised in the research evidence and implemented at work (as discussed in the following sections).

Against this backdrop, we start this chapter by unpacking the definition and measurement of mindfulness, and we then review mindfulness intervention research conducted in workplace settings. Finally, we conclude with the

Figure 10.1   Different conceptualisations of mindfulness, and their inter-connections

impact of the work environment on employees' potential to be mindful. Our focus is on individual mindfulness as a personal experience in the workplace, which has a range of potentially beneficial effects for individual well-being and performance and, thus, benefits for employer organisations too. However, other perspectives on mindfulness at work acknowledge a more collective dimension, as discussed by Badham and King (2019), but these fall beyond the scope of this chapter.

Definitions and measures of mindfulness

While mindfulness research has experienced a groundswell in recent years, mindfulness research started in the 1970s with Ellen Langer, who developed a socio-cognitive definition of mindfulness, proposing that mindful individuals are able to draw novel distinctions. Seeing novelty keeps individuals in the present and also helps to see the context as well as the perspective of one's actions, which reduces the probability of drawing from categories, routines and situations from the past (Langer & Moldoveanu, 2000).

This definition of mindfulness was the first to acknowledge mindfulness as part of the 'cognitive revolution' in the 1970s. In actuality, Langer initially conducted research on *mindlessness*; for example, the tendency to ignore information in favour of hypotheses confirming data (Langer & Abelson, 1974). Langer hypothesised that humans are more likely to express the tendency to be mindless than they are to be mindful. For example, she demonstrated the biased effect due to mindless processing in a study where the same individual was judged differently during an interview depending on the label the individual was given (Langer & Abelson, 1974). It is argued that these behaviours as observed in these studies are associated with mindlessness, being influenced by cues, primes and expectations rather than an individual's conscious sense of control and awareness of the context and all information given (Langer, 2014).

Drawing from this cognitive perspective, mindfulness within this conceptualisation is viewed as the ability to *draw novel distinctions* (Langer & Moldoveanu, 2000). This definition of mindfulness, which some refer to as Western mindfulness, is also reflected in its measurement (which differs significantly from the measurement of mindfulness that is regarded as a form of awareness and attention as conceptualised by Brown and Ryan (2003), and further outlined below). The Langer Mindfulness Scale (LMS14; Pirson et al., 2015) consists of the three dimensions of (1) novelty-seeking, (2) novelty-producing, and (3) engagement. These dimensions capture an individual's tendency to be open to new novelty, to generate novelty, and to notice novelty and changes in the environment, which are considered to contribute to greater flexibility (Pirson et al., 2015). Yet this is in contrast to more recent research, definition and measurement in mindfulness.

In recent years, interest and cognitive conceptualisation of mindfulness have surged and largely there has been a 'redefinition of mindfulness'. More recent conceptualisations of mindfulness have their roots in Buddhism and Eastern culture. Mindfulness as conceptualised this way, and outlined in the opening paragraphs and further below, involves non-reactive and non-evaluative awareness and attention to the present – it is the conscious monitoring of one's awareness and attention in a non-judgemental manner (Brown & Ryan, 2003). While this conceptualisation of mindfulness is drawn from Eastern philosophy, in terms of psychological processing and definition it involves enhanced awareness and attention to the present moment. Experiential processing forms an essential part of being mindful, which involves observation and attention to stimuli and inner reactions without attaching any meanings to them. This mode of processing requires individuals to mentally distance themselves from evaluations that might affect themselves in order not to bias situations and perceptions through previous learning, personal memories, or projections regarding the future (*including* novelty seeking). Definitions of mindfulness incorporate awareness and attention to both internal *and* external phenomena (Brown et al., 2007). Fundamentally, Western (and Langerian) and Eastern mindfulness differ in the type of cognitive processing involved: awareness and attention, or novelty seeking. Clearly, researchers need to be clear on how they 'define' mindfulness and be aware that mindfulness does not have a single, unified definition.

The growth in mindfulness research stemming from the Eastern-informed definition – awareness and attention to both internal and external phenomena, without judgement – is aligned in an ontological sense, but measuring mindfulness in this sense can also be problematic. There are currently more than ten different mindfulness scales that show minimal convergent validity (see Choi & Leroy, 2015). The various mindfulness scales also differ with regards to their construct validity. Some mindfulness scales such as the Mindful Attention Awareness Scale (MAAS; Brown & Ryan, 2003) regard mindfulness as a unidimensional construct assessing awareness and attention – and item analysis has led some to argue that it is actually a measure of mindlessness, not mindfulness. Yet, this measure appears, at present, to be the most widely used measure of mindfulness at work (see Sutcliffe et al., 2016). Other scales like the Five-Facet Mindfulness Questionnaire (FFMQ) by Baer et al. (2006) see mindfulness as multidimensional, including the factors: Awareness, Describing, Non Judging of Experience, Non Reactivity to Inner Experience and Observing. Measuring mindfulness, therefore, requires caution, and measures should reflect the researcher's hypothesis and research design. As such the first and fundamental questions for researching mindfulness at work should be – How do I define mindfulness? Followed by: How do I measure mindfulness? Finally (the following question is expanded in sections below): Is the research capturing trait, state, mindfulness interventions, or workplace environments? These issues are explored in the following two sections.

Mindfulness interventions in the workplace

While mindfulness can be viewed as a trait and state, and as a form of daily practice, a number of therapeutic interventions aimed at developing greater mindfulness have been developed. These include Mindfulness-Based Stress Reduction (MBSR; Kabat-Zinn, 2009), Mindfulness-Based Cognitive Therapy (MBCT; Segal et al., 2013), Dialectical Behavior Therapy (DBT; Linehan, 1993), and Acceptance and Commitment Therapy (ACT; Hayes et al., 2006). Table 10.1 highlights the key features of these rigorously studied interventions

Table 10.1   Key features of major clinically oriented mindfulness
              interventions

Intervention	Description	Core content
Mindfulness-Based Stress Reduction	An approach that develops present moment awareness in order to illuminate and change habitual reactions and response patterns, especially in stressful situations.	Intensive group training in mindfulness techniques, such as meditation, body scan, yoga, and diaphragmatic breathing.
Mindfulness-Based Cognitive Therapy	A type of psychotherapy that fosters increased awareness of thoughts and feelings and teaches ways to interrupt automatic patterns of thinking and feeling, originally designed to provide clients with skills to assist in the prevention of depressive relapse.	A combination of cognitive behaviour therapy and training in mindfulness techniques, delivered in a group format.
Dialectical Behavior Therapy	A type of cognitive behaviour therapy used to address maladaptive behaviours through validation and problem solving.	Integration of cognitive behaviour therapy with Zen principles and mindfulness techniques, delivered through group skills training, individual psychotherapy, and phone consultation.
Acceptance and Commitment Therapy	A mindfulness-oriented behaviour therapy that increases psychological flexibility and enhances alignment between behaviour and values.	A treatment model that emphasizes present moment awareness, acceptance, cognitive defusion, the observing self, values, and committed action.

(for more detail see the review by Jamieson & Tuckey, 2017). Although created with different clinical applications in mind, each of these approaches typically involves intense guided development and application of mindfulness skills with a specialist practitioner, and utilises a combination of mindfulness techniques with other therapeutic methods in order to aid individuals in managing symptoms of psychological distress and ill-health.

As overviewed by Keng et al. (2011), there is a growing body of empirical evidence for all four of these major mindfulness interventions – MBSR, MBCT,

DBT, and ACT. The findings of quantitative meta-analyses, which take into account all of the scholarly evidence, support the positive effects of: meditation on the reduction of anxiety, depression, and pain (Goyal et al., 2014); mindfulness therapeutic interventions for improvement in anxiety and depression (Hofman et al., 2010); and mindfulness therapeutic interventions in general, across a wide range of physical and psychological health conditions (Khoury et al., 2013) in *clinical* samples.

More recently interest has gone beyond the clinical domain towards understanding the role of mindfulness interventions in promoting employee health and well-being and, to a lesser degree, the potential for mindfulness to improve critical organisational outcomes. Jamieson and Tuckey (2017) searched for published studies of workplace mindfulness interventions (i.e., those conducted in occupational settings or with employee samples) and found 40 journal articles published from 2003 to 2015. According to their review of these studies, three-quarters had examined MBSR (typically a modified form of MBSR for use with employees) or elements of MBSR in conjunction with those from another established intervention framework (e.g., MBCT). A diverse range of other approaches were used in the remaining 25 per cent of studies, such as ACT and a variety of mindfulness practices, such as meditation, loving kindness meditation, contemplative practice, yoga, and mindful reflection.

As evidenced in their review, much of the initial mindfulness intervention research focussed on individual employee health and well-being; nearly all studies have looked at outcomes such as stress, burnout, psychological distress, depression, anxiety, mood, positive and negative affect, or emotion regulation. Research on organisational outcomes continues to grow; close to half of the studies reviewed looked at one or more organisational outcomes like job satisfaction, absenteeism, quality and safety of care, and empathy and compassion towards clients. Looking across the findings of all the intervention studies, there are widespread benefits of mindfulness interventions for employee health and well-being, together with consistent emerging evidence for the role of mindfulness in enhancing organisational outcomes.

It should be noted that the picture is not entirely positive; a small number of studies have reported results inconsistent with the generally positive trends. For instance, there were no significant effects of mindfulness in a few studies utilising physiological outcome measures such as cortisol (Galantino et al., 2005; Klatt et al., 2009; Roeser et al., 2013), blood pressure, and heart rate variability (Roeser et al., 2013). It seems likely that changes evident initially in mental and emotional terms take longer to be seen in the body's physiological systems. Further, one study that evaluated a six-month bespoke mindfulness intervention did not find any significant effects (van Berkel et al., 2014), highlighting the need for caution in ensuring that key mindfulness ingredients are not diluted. At this point, more research is needed to identify whether the positive effects seen in most intervention studies are due to the characteristics of mindfulness in particular (Chiesa & Serretti, 2011) or to more general treatment effects. Finally, the authors of another study highlighted the potential for mindfulness training to increase awareness of negative emotional states experienced, which might lead to an increase in employees reporting those states during the early months of training (Brooker et al., 2013). In that study, the only aspect of mindfulness enhanced by the training was observation. The other aspects of mindfulness – awareness, describing, non-judging, and non-reactivity – would arguably be important for reducing negative emotional states after becoming aware of them. Though measured, they were not influenced by the training within the measurement timeframe of the research. Together, these studies highlight some of the complexities in the evaluation of mindfulness interventions at work, and the challenges for drawing simple and clear conclusions about potential applications.

Challenges in the research on mindfulness interventions at work

When seeking to understand the research findings regarding mindfulness interventions at work and guide the use of mindfulness training in workplaces in an evidence-based way, it is important to unpack a number of issues. First, as discussed earlier, mindfulness can be conceptualised as a state, trait, practice, or intervention, and these conceptualisations are fundamentally interconnected (Jamieson & Tuckey 2017; Roche et al., 2020). In the intervention literature there is substantial variation on which of these conceptualisations of mindfulness have been studied within and across studies; in some cases the conceptualisation of interest has not been made clear at all. Without clarity in the frame of reference within which mindfulness is being investigated, it is difficult to draw conclusions about how, when, and for whom mindfulness interventions work when applied to occupational health, well-being, and performance.

Second, there is variation in the quality of the evidence. In Jamieson and Tuckey's (2017) review, they reported that just over half of the studies in the sample were based on randomised controlled trials (RCTs). RCTs incorporate the random allocation of participants to an intervention group or control condition. The rigorous RCT methodology reduces the risk of variation between research groups because of unknown factors that might substantially influence the study outcomes (e.g., individual factors such as age, tenure, and gender; work-related factors such as job demands and supervisor support); these RCTs thus provide strong support for the benefits of mindfulness for employee and organisational outcomes. When controlled comparison is not a feature of the study design, or when participants self-select into groups rather than being randomly allocated, it is difficult to isolate the effects of the intervention from other influences. The quality of the study design should thus be considered when reviewing existing and new studies on mindfulness interventions.

Third, there may be potential risks arising from the implementation of modified versions of mindfulness interventions for use in workplace settings. As noted above, two studies deviated in their approach to the mindfulness interventions undertaken. Interventions that deviate from the procedures robustly studied in clinical settings may not actually produce changes in mindfulness. This may have been the case in the two studies mentioned above that reported null or negative findings: the intervention utilised by van Berkel et al. (2014) was not grounded in an established mindfulness-based approach; and Brooker et al. (2013) used a modified form of MBSR. When mindfulness training is being implemented, care should be taken to maintain the key elements of established mindfulness protocols. Additionally, care is needed to ensure that the training is delivered by experienced mindfulness instructors. When interventions are put in place in the clinical domain it is usually delivered by a trained psychologist. No such training is expected in workplace interventions. As such the skill and expertise of those running interventions also needs greater attention.

A further complication of interventions at work is that, while the general techniques that form part of established protocols are known, it not yet clear exactly what the active ingredients of mindfulness interventions are when applied at work. Very few studies have compared mindfulness training in the workplace with other interventions (see Wolever et al., 2012, for an exception). It would thus be useful in future research to identify whether and when mindfulness training has advantages beyond other types of approaches. Studies should also check whether the intervention actually leads to changes in mindfulness itself – both momentary experiences (state mindfulness) and more enduring changes to the capacity for mindfulness (trait mindfulness) over a longer period. This practice of assessing changes in mindfulness was evident in only half of published evaluation studies reviewed by Jamieson and Tuckey (2017).

Finally, at this stage it is largely unknown whether or not the effects of mindfulness training are sustained over time. This incomplete picture is linked to a related gap regarding whether or not, and to what extent, employees continue to engage in mindfulness practice after the formal intervention has concluded. One study found that most participants – up to 75 per cent of nurses – did continue to engage in mindfulness practice (Bazarko et al., 2013). Likewise, another study reported that, two months after completing mindfulness training employees indicated that they were still practising, on average, one to two times a week (Walach et al., 2007). Hence, although the data are limited, it seems that employees are likely to continue to practice mindfulness after the formal training has ended, and therefore continue to gain benefit. Indeed, as noted above, continued practice actually brings about changes in the way that the systems of the body and brain function, to sustain the positive impacts. However, much more research is needed to be confident in these emerging findings. Consideration can then be given as to how best to support workers to derive optimum benefit from the training over time, and with respect to their work environment (as discussed in the next section).

Workplace antecedents of mindfulness

While the success of a mindfulness programme depends on the individual's motivation to engage in any training services offered by the employer, organisations may do more to promote mindfulness among their workforce than offering mindfulness training. In this section we examine what various aspects of organisational life may do to develop (or thwart) mindfulness, other than offering trainings/interventions, to promote mindful working. To answer these questions, we need to learn more about how mindfulness *naturally* develops and we need to identify the internal and external factors that help or hinder the experience of mindfulness in general as well as in the work context. Yet, while research on the consequences of mindfulness is abundant, and research on mindfulness interventions is growing (Bartlett et al., 2019; Jamieson & Tuckey, 2017), much less is known about these antecedents of mindfulness in terms of workplace characteristics (cf. Sutcliffe et al., 2016). In the next sections we will review existing evidence in this area and suggest future areas of research.

As described in the first section, mindfulness can be seen as a trait as well as a state. While trait mindfulness refers to a person's general level of mindfulness across time and situations, state mindfulness refers to momentary levels of mindfulness and the extent to which the experience of mindfulness fluctuates from moment to moment. Thus, on the one hand, individuals differ in the extent to which they tend to generally be mindful at work (i.e. trait differences; e.g. overall, person A tends to be more mindful than person B). On the other hand, mindfulness at work fluctuates from moment to moment, day to day (i.e. state differences; e.g. some days person A is more mindful, some days less than she usually is) (see Hülsheger et al., 2013). In seeking to understand what factors drive the development and experience of mindfulness, one should consider both trait as well as state mindfulness. There may be factors that explain why some individuals are generally more mindful than others and other factors may help understand what drives the day-to-day ups and downs in mindfulness. In the following we will consider antecedents of trait mindfulness first, and then turn to the factors that drive day-to-day or moment-to-moment fluctuations in mindfulness.

Individuals naturally differ in the extent to which they generally tend to be mindful. These differences are not only driven by previous experience with mindfulness meditation or other meditative practices. Research suggests that, just as individuals naturally differ regarding their level of general mental abilities or personality traits, individuals also differ in their tendency to be mindful. A behaviour–genetic study (Waszczuk et al., 2015) investigated the genetic and environmental underpinnings of trait mindfulness and revealed that mindfulness is 32 per cent heritable, while 66 per cent is due to non-shared environmental influences, i.e. environmental influences that are not shared between family members. In contrast, shared environmental influences played no role. This study did not, however, reveal which specific non-shared environmental factors help or hinder mindfulness, and these factors may be manifold. They may reside in a person's private environment and family situation and include life events, friends and cultural exposure, as well as prior experience with or regular engagement in meditative practices. However, such environmental factors may also reside in a person's work environment where most individuals spent a considerable amount of their time. Mindfulness scholars have suggested that aspects of work and the work environment that require resources limit employees' ability to perform their work mindfully, while factors that provide employees with resources allow individuals to focus on the present moment and thereby facilitate mindfulness at work (Olafsen, 2017; Reb et al., 2015). Supporting this idea, organisational constraints were negatively related, while supervisor support was positively related to trait mindfulness (Reb et al., 2015). Similarly, a longitudinal study found that employees with managers who supported their needs by acknowledging their perspectives, providing meaningful information and offering opportunities for choice had higher subsequent levels of mindfulness than employees who did not experience managerial need support (Olafsen, 2017).

Other work has focussed on the situational factors that promote or inhibit momentary experiences of mindfulness at work, thereby focusing on mindfulness as a state. There are a number of work-related situational factors that make it particularly difficult to be mindful at work by disrupting a focus on the present moment. A qualitative study conducted with employees with mindfulness experience highlighted the role of task demands and high workload that provoke automatic thought and leave employees with little room to attend to what they are doing with awareness (Lyddy & Good, 2017). In contrast, employees reported that possibilities to seek out places or a private office where they could shield themselves from distractions helped them attending to their work in a mindful way. These findings are particularly important for organisations, considering that distractions are the norm at many companies with hot desking and open office policies.

Two daily diary studies drew attention to the role of energetic and attentional resources in allowing individuals to be mindful at work (Hülsheger et al., 2018; Lawrie et al., 2018). The authors argued that mindfulness does not come naturally but involves self-regulatory activities to bring and sustain attention and awareness to present-moment experiences. As self-regulatory activities require energetic resources, the degree to which employees are able to act mindfully is contingent on their momentary level of energy and the degree to which other (work) activities and experiences draw on or replenish these resources. Accordingly, on days that employees experienced high workloads, they reported more fatigue and had lower levels of mindfulness than they usually had. In contrast, after nights with high sleep quality allowing them to replenish resources, employees were less fatigued and experienced higher-than-usual levels of mindfulness. Similarly, participants' mindfulness levels increased when they had more control over how to perform their work. Another study looking into the factors that drive moment-to-moment ups and downs in the two mindfulness components of awareness and non-reactivity confirmed that individuals tend to be less likely to be mindful when they are fatigued, busy, and in a hurry, i.e. situations that draw on individuals' attentional resources (Suelmann et al., 2018). Taken together, these findings exemplify how experiences at work as well as at home shape individuals' momentary ability to be mindful. They also show that, irrespective of a person's general trait level of mindfulness, every individual experiences ups and downs in their capacity to be mindful. These ups and downs are a function of available energetic and attentional resources and they are therefore influenced by work circumstances such as workload, time pressures, job control, and/or leadership.

Summary

The purpose of this chapter was to draw together emerging issues related to mindfulness at work in order to guide researcher, practitioner and organisational understanding and application moving forward. While clearly there are benefits to mindfulness, we summarise some of the complex issues here. While mindfulness is an advantage for employees and their managers in coping with a very demanding work environment, we advise researchers in mindfulness to work with caution as they highlight the strengths, and unknowns, with clarity and awareness. That is, there are a number of complex issues associated with mindfulness research at work as we move forward with research.

Firstly, research would benefit by having greater clarity of definition around mindfulness. This is not straightforward, as it can refer to state, trait, intervention or practice. Differing perspectives of mindfulness (West v East) exist, and within these differing measurements. Thus, mindfulness is a broad construct, with multiple ways of measuring the phenomena. We suggest researchers provide clarity here before embarking on research. As such, there is a need to be very clear what mindfulness is (not), and – where possible – to avoid vague and metaphorical language that muddies the concept of mindfulness. While being precise in one's definition may sound limiting, we believe this could remove some of the initial confusion over what mindfulness is and is not.

Secondly, when thinking about mindfulness interventions at work, research is currently behind practice. The quality of this line of research, and the information that can be learned from it, can be improved in both design and implementation. In terms of design, the conceptualisation of mindfulness guiding each study should be clearly defined, operationalised, and communicated; changes in mindfulness should be assessed to check the efficacy of mindfulness training before drawing conclusions about the effects on outcomes of interest; and comparison conditions should be used to explore whether it is indeed mindfulness training that is beneficial, rather than a more general treatment effect. In terms of implementation, the active ingredients in mindfulness interventions; the role and characteristics of training providers; and the mode, duration, and composition of training should be explicitly studied as important topics in their own right. As the research field progresses in these ways, practitioners and organisations will increasingly be able to make intelligence-led decisions about delivering mindfulness training in work settings.

Finally, we are only just beginning to understand how the workplace itself may impact on a person's ability to be mindful. The work context predominantly fosters a mode that is characterised by goal-directed cognitions and behaviour. In contrast, mindfulness involves a cognitive mode of present-ness – that is, being with whatever happens in the present and attending to momentary experiences as they are (Lyddy & Good, 2017). While these modes may seem incompatible at first sight, they can co-exist and thereby foster workplace functioning and well-being (see Lyddy & Good, 2017). Research evidence on being mindful while working is, however, still scarce. The workplace is a unique environment for mindfulness research generally, and it can aid, or detract from one's ability to be mindful at work. Researchers could also ask how the workplace environment affects one's ability to be mindful. Furthermore, they could investigate whether the workplace is one that drains psychological resources, that does not allow for quiet time, and that obliges workers to take on tasks that are depleting, or to endure abusive supervision. These questions seem to be gaining importance in our growing understanding of 'successful' mindfulness at work. More research into the antecedents of mindfulness at work is also indispensable to ensure that mindfulness at work is not only considered an issue for the individual, but also a responsibility of organisational decision makers, who should consider mindfulness in work design and leadership development initiative.

While the above research areas are outlined as cautions to guide readers, we are strong advocates of promoting mindfulness at work. The mounting evidence is that mindfulness at work has tremendous value for individuals and organisations. We believe the current evidence is merely scratching the surface of the potential impacts of mindfulness. We also believe that mindfulness should be researched with clarity and caution so that we can continue to advocate, in an evidenced-based way, for the potentially profound impacts on human functioning that we believe mindfulness offers.

References

Allexandre, D., Bernstein, A. M., Walker, E., Hunter, J., Roizen, M. F., & Morledge, T. J. (2016). A web-based mindfulness stress management program in a corporate call center. *Journal of Occupational and Environmental Medicine, 58*(3), 254–264. http://doi.org/10.1097/JOM.0000000000000680

Andrews, M. C., Kacmar, K. M. & Kacmar, C. (2014). The mediational effect of regulatory focus on the relationships between mindfulness and job satisfaction and turnover intentions. *Career Development International, 19*(5), 494–507.

Badham, R., & King, E. (2019). Mindfulness at work: A critical re-view. *Organization.* https://doi.org/10.1177/1350508419888897

Baer, R. A., Smith, G. T., Hopkins, J., Krietemeyer, J., & Toney, L. (2006). Using self-report assessment methods to explore facets of mindfulness. *Assessment, 13*(1), 27–45. http://doi.org/10.1177/1073191105283504

Bartlett, L., Martin, A., Neil, A. L., Memish, K., Otahal, P., Kilpatrick, M., & Sanderson, K. (2019). A systematic review and meta-analysis of workplace mindfulness training randomized controlled trials. *Journal of Occupational Health Psychology, 24,* 108–126.

Bazarko, D., Cate, R. A., Azocar, F., & Kreitzer, M. J. (2013). The impact of an innovative mindfulness-based stress reduction program on the health and well-being of nurses employed in a corporate setting. *Journal of Workplace Behavioral Health, 28,* 107–133.

Brooker, J., Julian, J., Webber, L., Chan, J., Shawyer, F., & Meadows, G. (2013). Evaluation of an occupational mindfulness program for staff employed in the disability sector in Australia. *Mindfulness, 4,* 122–136.

Brown, K. W., & Ryan, R. M. (2003). The benefits of being present: Mindfulness and its role in psychological well-being. *Journal of Personality and Social Psychology, 84*(4), 822–848. http://doi.org/10.1037/0022-3514.84.4.822

Brown, K. W., Ryan, R. M., & Creswell, J. D. (2007). Mindfulness: Theoretical foundations and evidence for its salutary effects. *Psychological Inquiry, 18,* 211–237. http://dx.doi.org/10.1080/10478400701598298

Chiesa, A., & Serretti, A. (2011). Mindfulness based cognitive therapy for psychiatric disorders: A systematic review and meta-analysis. *Psychiatry Research, 187,* 441–453.

Choi, E., & Leroy, H. (2015). Methods of mindfulness: How mindfulness is studied in the workplace. In J. Reb & P. W. B. Atkins (Eds.), *Mindfulness in Organizations: Foundations, Research, and Applications* (pp. 67–99). London, UK: Cambridge University Press. http://doi.org/10.1017/CBO9781107587793.006

Dane, E., & Brummel, B. J. (2014). Examining workplace mindfulness and its relations to job performance and turnover intention. *Human Relations, 67*(1), 105–128. http://doi.org/10.1177/0018726713487753

Di Benedetto, M., & Swadling, M. (2014). Burnout in Australian psychologists: Correlations with work-setting, mindfulness and self-care behaviours. *Psychology, Health and Medicine, 19*(6), 705–715. https://doi.org/10.1080/13548506.2013.861602

Galantino, M. L., Baime, M., Maguire, M., Szapary, P. O., & Farrar, J. T. (2005). Association of psychological and physiological measures of stress in health-care professionals during an 8-week mindfulness meditation program: Mindfulness in practice. *Stress & Health, 21,* 255–261.

Goyal, M., Singh, S., Sibinga, E., Bould, N. F., Rowland-Seymour, A., … Haythornthwaite, J. A. (2014). Meditation programs for psychological stress and well-being: A systematic review and meta-analysis. *JAMA Internal Medicine, 174,* 357–368.

Gregoire, S. & Lachance, L. (2015) Evaluation of a brief mindfulness-based intervention to reduce psychological distress in the workplace. *Mindfulness, 6*(4), 836–847.

Hayes, S. C., Luoma, J. B., Bond, F. W., Masuda, A., & Lillis, J. (2006). Acceptance and commitment therapy: Model, processes and outcomes. *Behaviour Research and Therapy, 44,* 1–25.

Hofman, S.G., Sawyer, A.T., Witt, A.A., & Oh, D. (2010). The effect of mindfulness-based therapy on anxiety and depression: A meta-analytic review. *Journal of Consulting and Clinical Psychology, 78*(2), 169-183. DOI: 10.1037/a0018555

Hülsheger, U. R., Alberts, H. J. E. M., Feinholdt, A., & Lang, J. W. B. (2013). Benefits of mindfulness at work: The role of mindfulness in emotion regulation, emotional exhaustion, and job satisfaction. *Journal of Applied Psychology, 98,* 310–325.

Hülsheger, U. R., Walkowiak, A., & Thommes, M. S. (2018). How can mindfulness be promoted? Workload and recovery experiences as antecedents of daily fluctuations in mindfulness. *Journal of Occupational and Organizational Psychology, 91*, 261–284.

Ireland, M. J., Clough, B., Gill, K., Langan, F., O'Connor, A., & Spencer, L. (2017). A randomized controlled trial of mindfulness to reduce stress and burnout among intern medical practitioners. *Medical Teacher, 39*(4), 409–414. http://doi.org/10.1080/0142159X.2017.1294749

Jamieson, S. D., & Tuckey, M. R. (2017). Mindfulness interventions in the workplace: A critique of the current state of the literature. *Journal of Occupational Health Psychology, 22*, 180–193.

Kabat-Zinn, J. (2009). *Full Catastrophe Living: Using the Wisdom of your Body and Mind to Face Stress, Pain, and Illness* (15th anniv. ed.). New York, NY: Random House.

Kang, C., & Whittingham, K. (2010). Mindfulness: A dialogue between Buddhism and clinical psychology. *Mindfulness, 1*(3), 161–173. http://doi.org/10.1007/s12671-010-0018-1

Keng, S. L., Smoski, M. J., & Robins, C. J. (2011). Effects of mindfulness on psychological health: A review of empirical studies. *Clinical Psychology Review, 31*, 1041–1056.

Khoury, B., Lecomte, T., Fortin, G., Masse, M., Therien, P., Bouchard, V., Chapleau, M., Paquin, K., & Hofmann, S. G. (2013). Mindfulness-based therapy: A comprehensive meta-analysis. *Clinical Psychology Review, 33*, 763–771.

Klatt, M. D., Buckworth, J., & Malarkey, W. B. (2009). Effects of low-dose mindfulness-based stress reduction (MBSR-ld) on working adults. *Health Education & Behavior, 36*, 601–614.

Langer, E. J. (2014). Mindfulness forward and back. In A. Ie, C. T. Ngnoumen, & E. J. Langer (Eds.), *The Wiley Blackwell Handbook of Mindfulness* (pp. 8–20). London: John Wiley and Sons.

Langer, E. J., & Abelson, R. P. (1974). The semantics of asking a favor: How to succeed in getting help without really dying. *Journal of Personality and Social Psychology, 24*, 26–32.

Langer, E. J., & Moldoveanu, M. (2000). The construct of mindfulness. *Journal of Social Issues, 56*(1), 1–9. http://doi.org/10.1111/0022-4537.00148

Lawrie, E. J., Tuckey, M. R., & Dollard, M. F. (2018). Job design for mindful work: The boosting effect of psychosocial safety climate. *Journal of Occupational Health Psychology, 23*, 483–495. https://doi.org/http://dx.doi.org/10.1037/ocp0000102

Liang, L. H., Brown, D. J., Ferris, D. L., Hanig, S., Lian, H., & Keeping, L. M. (2018). The dimensions and mechanisms of mindfulness in regulating aggressive behaviors. *Journal of Applied Psychology, 103*, 281–299. https://doi.org/10.1037/apl0000283

Linehan, M. M. (1993). *Cognitive-Behavioral Treatment of Borderline Personality Disorder*. New York, NY: Guilford Press

Lyddy, C. J., & Good, D. J. (2017). Being while doing: An inductive model of mindfulness at work. *Frontiers in Psychology, 7*, 1–18.

Malinowski, P., & Lim, H. J. (2015). Mindfulness at work: Positive affect, hope, and optimism mediate the relationship between dispositional mindfulness, work engagement, and well-being. *Mindfulness, 6*, 1250–1262. http://doi.org/10.1007/s12671-015-0388-5

Mesmer-Magnus, J., Manapragada, A., Viswesvaran, C., & Allen, J. W. (2017). Trait mindfulness at work: A meta-analysis of the personal and professional correlates of trait mindfulness. *Human Performance, 30*, 79–98. https://doi.org/10.1080/08959285.2017.1307842

Olafsen, A. H. (2017). The implications of need-satisfying work climates on state mindfulness in a longitudinal analysis of work outcomes. *Motivation and Emotion, 41*, 22–37.

Pirson, M., Langer, E. J., Bodner, T., & Zilcha, S. (2015). The development and validation of the Langer Mindfulness Scale – enabling a socio-cognitive perspective of mindfulness in organizational contexts. *Academy of Management Annual Meeting Proceedings, 2015*(1): 11308–11308.

Reb, J., Narayanan, J., & Ho, Z. W. (2015). Mindfulness at work: Antecedents and consequences of employee awareness and absent-mindedness, *Mindfulness, 6*(1), 111–122.

Roche, M. , Good, D., Lyddy, C., Tuckey, M.R., Grazier, M., Leroy, H., & Hülsheger, U (2020). A Swiss army knife? How science challenges our understanding of mindfulness in the workplace. *Organizational Dynamics, 49*(4). http://doi.org/10.1016/j.orgdyn.2020.100766

Roeser, R. W., Schonert-Reichl, K. A., Jha, A., Cullen, M., Wallace, L., Wilensky, R., ... Harrison, J. (2013). Mindfulness training and reductions in teacher stress and burnout: Results from two randomized, waitlist-control field trials. *Journal of Educational Psychology, 105*, 787–804.

Schwager, I. T. L., Hülsheger, U. R., & Lang, J. W. B. (2016). Be aware to be on the square: Mindfulness and counterproductive academic behavior. *Personality and Individual Differences, 93*, 74–79. http://doi.org/10.1016/j.paid.2015.08.043

Segal, Z. V., Williams, J. M. G., & Teasdale, J. D. (2013). *Mindfulness-Based Cognitive Therapy for Depression* (2nd ed.). Retrieved from http://search.library.unisa.edu.au/record/UNISA_ALMA51112906170001831

Singleton, O., Hölzel, B. K., Vangel, M., Brach, N., Carmody, J., & Lazar, S. W. (2014). Change in brainstem gray matter concentration following a mindfulness-based intervention is correlated with improvement in psychological well-being. *Frontiers in Human Neuroscience*. doi: 10.3389/fnhum.2014.00033

Suelmann, H., Brouwers, A., & Snippe, E. (2018). Explaining variations in mindfulness levels in daily life. *Mindfulness, 9*(6), 1895–1906.

Sutcliffe, K. M., Vogus, T. J., Dane, E., & Jones, J. H. (2016). Mindfulness in organizations: A cross-level review. *Annual Review of Organizational Psychology and Organizational Behavior, 3*, 55–81. https://doi.org/10.1146/annurev-orgpsych-041015-062531

Thomasson, E. (2018, May 17). At Germany's SAP, employee mindfulness leads to higher profits. Retrieved June 24, 2018, from https://www.reuters.com/article/us-world-work-sap/at-germanys-sap-

van Berkel, J., Boot, C. R. L., Proper, K. I., Bongers, P. M., & van der Beek, A. J. (2014). Effectiveness of a worksite mindfulness-related multi-component health promotion intervention on work engagement and mental health: Results of a randomized controlled trial. *PloS One, 9*, 1–10.

Walach, H., Nord, E., Zier, C., Dietz-Waschkowski, B., Kersig, S., Schüpbach, H., ... Violanti, J. M. (2007). Mindfulness-based stress reduction as a method for personnel development: A pilot evaluation. *International Journal of Stress Management, 14*, 188–198.

Waszczuk, M. A., Zavos, H. M. S., Antonova, E., Haworth, C. M., Plomin, R., & Eley, T. C. (2015). A multivariate twin study of trait mindfulness, depressive symptoms, and anxiety sensitivity. *Depression and Anxiety, 8*, 1–8. https://doi.org/10.1002/da.22326

Wolever, R. Q., Bobinet, K. J., McCabe, K., Mackenzie, E. R., Fekete, E., Kusnick, C. A., & Baime, M. (2012). Effective and viable mind–body stress reduction in the workplace: A randomized controlled trial. *Journal of Occupational Health Psychology, 17,* 246–258.

Zeng, W., & Gu, M. (2017). Relationship between mindfulness and positive affect of Chinese older adults: Optimism as mediator. *Social Behavior and Personality: An International Journal, 45*(1), 155–162. http://doi.org/10.2224/sbp.5606

Zivnuska, S., Kacmar, K. M., Ferguson, M., & Carlson, D. S. (2016). Mindfulness at work: Resource accumulation, well-being, and attitudes. *Career Development International, 21*(2), 106–124. http://doi.org/10.1108/CDI-06-2015-0086

11. Organizational interventions – fitting the intervention to the context to ensure the participatory process

Karina Nielsen, Carolyn Axtell and Glorian Sorensen

Participatory organizational interventions – how can we create a context for participation?

Participatory organizational interventions can be defined as interventions that aim to change the way work is organized, designed and managed to improve employee wellbeing with the engagement of multiple stakeholders across different levels in the organization focusing on changing work practices, procedures and policies (LaMontagne et al., 2007; Nielsen, 2013). A key element of this type of intervention is that they employ a participatory design where employees and managers jointly decide on the design, content and the process of the intervention (Nielsen & Noblet, 2018). These types of interventions are widely recommended as they address the root causes of stress and poor wellbeing, rather than the symptoms (ETUC, 2004; EU-OSHA, 2010; ILO, 2001).

Participatory organizational interventions often employ a problem-solving cycle design where employees and management, together with other key stakeholders such as Human Resources and/or Occupational Health work together to decide on the process and the content of the intervention. In the first phase, the intervention is set up with a steering group that decides on the intervention design and sometimes also the content. Leadership support and commitment to the process is important in these early stages. Next, identification of the areas that need to be addressed takes place (screening). Workers and managers provide input regarding the main problematic working conditions, along with information about their health and wellbeing that may be consequences of adverse working conditions. Surveys are the preferred method for obtaining this information, but other interactive methods could also be used (Nielsen et al., 2018). In some cases, existing data regarding outcomes (e.g., injury rates, absence) as well as working conditions (e.g., work hours, schedule) may also inform the screening process. Based on the results of the screening process, managers and workers jointly develop and prioritize actions to reduce or eliminate adverse working conditions. Once action plans have been agreed, their implementation should be closely monitored and finally, it should be evaluated whether the participatory organizational intervention achieved its intended outcomes, i.e. reduction of stress and improvement of employee wellbeing (McLellan et al., 2017; Nielsen & Noblet, 2018).

Some reviews of participatory organizational interventions focusing on only effects have questioned the effectiveness of such interventions (e.g. Richardson & Rothstein, 2008), however, others have argued that the intervention process and context play a key role in determining intervention outcomes and it is crucial to understand how the context influences intervention processes and how these processes bring out intended and unintended outcomes (Nielsen, 2013; Nielsen & Miraglia, 2017).

Although we call them participatory organizational interventions, action plans may in fact address multiple levels of intervention. A meta-analysis by Nielsen et al. (2017) found that resources at the individual, group, leader, and organizational (IGLO) levels can be linked to performance and wellbeing and suggested that organizational interventions need to address all four levels, proposing the IGLO model of interventions, i.e. that activities to improve employee wellbeing need to be developed for individuals, groups, leaders and to change organizational practices and procedures. As such, organizational interventions can focus on changes to job design, e.g. increasing job autonomy and social support, changes in HR policies (organizational level initiatives); building leaders' resources through leadership training (leader level initiatives); introducing collective decision making procedures of self-managing work teams or civility training of groups (group level initiatives); or training workers in how to deal with their work and nonwork demands (individual level initiatives; Day & Nielsen, 2017). Such recommended strategies might be prioritized according to the potential for impact; using a Hierarchy of Controls framework, the greatest impact may be achieved by first eliminating or reducing exposure to those working conditions that contribute to poor worker health outcomes (National Institute for Occupational Safety and Health, 2016).

Participatory organizational interventions in context

It has been argued that the organizational context plays an important role in determining the intervention's outcomes (Nielsen & Randall, 2015). Organizational interventions have their roots in the randomized, controlled trial evaluation paradigm where context may be seen as noise and something that should be kept stable and controlled for (Nielsen, 2013; Nielsen & Miraglia, 2017). Real-life research, however, has amply demonstrated that this is not always possible in organizational settings (Nielsen & Noblet, 2018). A book on derailed interventions provide plentiful examples of how the context is difficult to control and keep stable (Karanika-Murray & Biron, 2015). We therefore argue that we need to consider context rather than ignoring it.

The IGLOO model provides a useful framework for this approach. Prior work has similarly attended to the role of context. The Social Contextual Model provides a framework for incorporating the social context to guide intervention planning and research (Sorensen et al., 2003). This model distinguishes between a set of modifying conditions that independently influence outcomes, but which are not influenced by the intervention, from a set of mediating mechanisms, defined as those factors that may be targeted by the intervention process. Using a social ecological framework, this model conceptualizes social contextual modifiers and mediators as cutting across multiple levels of influence, including individual, interpersonal, organizational, and community, and societal factors. In this way, the model guides intervention planning to target those social contextual factors that may be amenable to change; in addition, the intervention can be shaped by understanding the social contextual modifying conditions, thereby increasing the responsiveness to the setting. This model complements the IGLO model described here by further illustrating the central importance of understanding the social context as part of organizational interventions.

A key element of participatory organizational interventions is of course participation. Participation is assumed to work through a number of mechanisms. First, participation is assumed to bring about a positive intervention outcome as it makes use of workers' expertise of what the key issues are and which actions can be realistically implemented in a particular workplace. Second, participation ensures that workers and managers at all levels feel ownership of the intervention process and the actions planned, and therefore are more likely to proactively integrate changes to work practices and procedures into existing practices. Third, as workers and managers go through the collaborative process and jointly develop actions and implement these, they are more likely to be

able to make sense of the why and how of changes to work practices and procedures (Abildgaard & Nielsen, 2018). Although there have been developments
in the mechanisms related to participation that make interventions work (e.g.
Abildgaard et al., 2018; von Thiele Schwarz et al., 2017), there is still limited
understanding of contextual factors that may help ensure successful intervention outcomes. Nielsen and Randall (2015) suggested that organizational
interventions need to consider the individual and the organizational context.
In the present chapter, we build on these thoughts and propose a framework
for the contextual factors that may be important for the mechanisms of participation to be triggered. We propose that interventions need to be designed and
implemented in a way that considers the context at five levels. First, the characteristics of workers, e.g. demographics and personality factors, may influence
the extent to which it is possible to implement an organizational intervention
using a participatory approach. Second, characteristics at the group level may
also need to be considered. Third, we propose that leaders must possess certain
characteristics and enact certain leadership behaviours for the participatory
process to work. Finally, existing practices and policies within the organization may also influence the extent to which the participatory process will run
smoothly. We thus build the framework on the IGLO model (Nielsen et al.,
2017), and based on a recent call to also consider the overarching context, i.e.
the context outside the organization (Nielsen et al., 2018), we propose contextual factors at the IGLOO levels. As little research has explicitly focused on the
context at these levels, we base our model partly on a review of the literature,
partly on psychological and sociological theories and models that can help us
identify factors, which may be of importance. An overview of the contextual
factors we propose may be important to make organizational interventions
work can be found in Table 11.1.

Individual level context

A number of individual-level factors can be expected to influence the extent
to which participation mechanisms are triggered. First, these relate to the
demographics of the participants. Age and education levels may play a role.
Tsutsumi et al. (2009) found that workers close to retirement resisted the
intervention and Busch et al. (2017) found that migrant workers found it hard
to engage fully with the participatory process as they lacked the necessary
language skills. Furthermore, Nielsen et al. (2006) found that in a low-skilled
employee group, workers preferred a more directive process facilitator as they
found it challenging to engage in the participatory process.

Table 11.1   Contextual factors to make organizational interventions work

Level	Contextual factors
Individual	Demographics: age, education Self-esteem Self-efficacy
Group	Relational coordination Social relations Participative safety Task orientation Support for innovation Geographic location
Leader	Trust Conflicting priorities Health-promoting leadership
Organization	Organizational characteristics Existing policies Readiness for change
Overarching context	National legislation Sector-specific factors, e.g. understaffing, subcontracting Weather conditions Economic, legal, cultural context

There is little research to suggest which personal characteristics may trigger the mechanism of participation. Tsutsumi et al. (2009) found that employees with low self-esteem found it hard to engage in the participatory process. Building on this research, we suggest that self-efficacy, i.e. the belief that one can successfully influence the situations one finds oneself in (Bandura, 1986), may also be an important contextual factor. Workers high in self-efficacy sustain and heighten their efforts when facing challenges as they believe they can influence the change of events (Bandura, 1986). When implementing changes to work practices and procedures it is important to continually review progress and make adjustments if necessary (von Thiele Schwartz et al., 2017) and individuals high in self-efficacy are more likely to pursue progress. If workers have low self-efficacy, they may not feel confident coming forward with suggestions for actions as they are not confident they can come up with viable solutions.

A higher order construct encompassing self-efficacy is the concept of psychological capital (PsyCap) which also comprises hope, resilience and optimism (Luthans et al., 2007). Although rarely considered in organizational level interventions, PsyCap may be an important contextual factor. Workers who are not only efficacious, but are optimistic about the potential gains relating to the intervention, possess hope in a better end state and are resilient to the setbacks that may happen during an intervention process, may be better positioned to engage in the participatory process.

Group level

The characteristics of the work group may play an important role in triggering the participatory mechanisms. To date, little research has explored the group contextual factors that may influence the intervention process. Tsutsumi et al. (2009) found that poor relationships in the intervention group prevented participants from engaging in the participatory process. This finding suggests that group processes may be important.

To understand the group contextual factors that may trigger the participatory process, relational coordination (Gittell, 2006) may be used as an underlying framework. Key elements of the relational coordination include on the one hand, communication, and on the other, relationship ties. In order for the participatory process to be a success, a group context where members communicate frequently and in a timely manner, and are accurate in their exchanges at the same time as focusing on problem solving rather than blaming each other for problems (Gittell, 2006), may be crucial for action plans to be developed and implemented. Likewise, in groups where relationship ties are strong, i.e. where the goals of the group are clear, members mutually respect each other and they share knowledge (Gittell, 2006), the participatory process may be facilitated as the group will find it easier to develop the targets for intervention and apply the necessary knowledge to develop and implement appropriate action plans.

Specifically, from the team literature we can identify a number of group level factors, which may be important for worker participation. First, in extension of Tsutsumi et al. (2009), and inspired by the team innovation literature (Anderson & West, 1998), we propose that where groups have previous experience engaging in collective decision-making processes and openly share information, they will more easily be able to engage in participatory decision making processes to develop and implement actions to address adverse working conditions. Groups where participative safety is high, i.e. interpersonal interactions are characterized by non-threatening trust and support (Anderson & West, 1998), workers are more likely to feel encouraged to suggest solutions to work-related issues.

Task orientation, i.e. the extent to which the group members hold each other mutually accountable for completing the group's tasks and have systems in place for reviewing and making adjustments to achieve high performance, may also be important for the participatory process to happen (Anderson & West, 1998). Focusing on developing and reviewing action plans and making the necessary adjustments for the action plans to be implemented successfully is likely to increase the intervention's success.

Similarly, support for innovation, i.e. the group's acceptance and support of members' attempts to introduce new ways of working (West, 1990) is likely to be important for the participation process to lead to the intended outcomes. In order to make changes to the way work is organized, designed and managed to reduce stress and improve worker wellbeing, groups need to actively work towards integrating changes to work practices and procedures.

In a context where groups are dispersed across different locations, participatory interventions may be a particular challenge. The dispersed locations may impair the group's ability to interact and participate in collective decision making compared to teams that are in the same location. The distribution of workers can impact on social identity processes and sub-group formation. Fault-lines can develop between team members at separate locations, which has a negative effect on team dynamics, information sharing and decision making (Polzer et al., 2006). These fault-lines are most likely in situations where there are two equally sized subgroups at separate locations and where the team members within each location are homogeneous (O'Leary & Cummings, 2007; O'Leary and Mortensen, 2010). Therefore, the configuration of the team across different locations will have implications for the success of participatory interventions. In addition, geographical distance implies a reliance on communication technologies for team interaction. Leaner, text-based communications media are considered less appropriate for interactions that involve emotions or where misunderstandings are likely (Daft & Lengel, 1986). The richest type of communication is face to face, as an array of non-verbal and social cues is available to help team members understand the meaning of communications and the immediate feedback cues allow misunderstandings to be corrected in a timely manner (Sproull & Keisler, 1986), which may facilitate the participatory process. Video conferencing and telephone communications are not as rich as face-to-face communications but are richer than email. Therefore, an organizational context that does not support the use of 'richer' communications media or face-to-face meetings for dispersed team members is likely to impair the ability of the team to participate fully in these interventions.

Having task interdependence and frequent interaction within a dispersed team is also likely to help enhance the effectiveness of any participatory interventions. Frequency of interaction and use of richer technologies is associated with greater perceived support when communications media are relied upon (Merrit & Havill, 2016). Moreover, interdependence within dispersed teams promotes team cohesion, trust and indispensability of individual contributions to the team (Hertel et al., 2004). Therefore, a team that has already developed this greater interdependence will likely have a better ability to engage in participative interventions.

Leader level

Studies have found that leaders play a key role in successful participatory organizational interventions (Parry et al., 2013; Randall et al., 2005; Stansfeld et al., 2015). Leadership supporting the intervention is important at all levels of the organization (Nielsen, 2017; Nielsen & Noblet, 2018). Senior leaders set the overall direction and mission of the organization, and have the power to set priorities around worker health and wellbeing (McLellan et al., 2017). Senior and mid-level leaders also can channel resources toward those priorities, and can ensure accountability for action. For example, Sabbath et al. (2014) suggested that leaders may help to shape the overall social context of interactions among workers, and in this way may provide protective strategies to reduce the potential for workplace verbal abuse.

Conflicting priorities is often an issue at this level. Swindler and Eschleman (2015) reported how a line manager stalled the process as he was both responsible for the intervention and for a competing larger initiative, which was prioritized by the line manager. Randall et al. (2005) found that line managers failed to communicate a change in responsibilities, as the change would have a negative impact on their key performance indicators. Where there is a lack of trust between line management and workers, workers may feel uncomfortable speaking up and making suggestions for improvements during workshops where managers are present (Nylén et al., 2017).

In recent years, the concept of health-promoting leadership has gained traction focusing at the health-promoting behaviours of line managers. Contrary to existing leadership frameworks that focus on worker performance (Nielsen & Taris, 2019), these leadership frameworks have been developed that focus directly on the behaviours leaders should enact to promote worker health and wellbeing (Nielsen & Taris, 2019). A recent review of these leadership frameworks identified four main characteristics of health-promoting leadership: engagement in workers' health promotion, taking responsibility for action to improve worker health, maintaining open communication about health-related issues and ensuring workers' participation in change processes (Akerjordet et al., 2018). In a context where the leader already engages in such behaviours, the participatory process is more likely to run smoothly as leaders and workers already are accustomed to addressing health-related issues. Leaders who have previously demonstrated engagement in workers' health promotion are likely to have gained the trust of their workers and thus these workers are more likely to have faith in the leader taking the intervention seriously and thus workers are more likely to engage in the participatory process. Leaders who have demonstrated openness with communication about health-related issues are more likely to have workers who are willing to discuss adverse working conditions and what actions to take to reduce or eliminate those to improve worker wellbeing. In a context where leaders have previously taken action to improve worker health, workers and managers are more likely to have an understanding of what needs to change and what can realistically be implemented. Finally, workers whose leaders have previously engaged them in participatory processes are more likely to be able to make sense of the participatory process and understand how to engage in the problem-solving cycle.

Leader support at all levels within the organization thus is an important contextual factor that may act as a precursor that may or may not trigger the participatory mechanisms of organizational interventions.

Organizational level

Ultimately, participatory organizational interventions aim to affect change at the organizational level, including changes in the organization of work, job tasks and demands, and psychosocial factors at work (Sorensen et al., 2016). Existing organizational factors may shape implementation of these organizational interventions, including: (1) organizational characteristics; (2) existing policies that are likely to shape future priorities; and (3) readiness for change.

Characteristics of the organization, such as industry sector and size, influence the working conditions workers face, and are likely to factor into the implementation of organizational interventions (Sorensen et al., 2016). Across employers, disparities in available resources may contribute to the extent to which worker protections are already in place (Occupational Safety and Health Administration (OSHA), 2015), thereby providing a baseline context for workers' participation. Similarly, concurrent changes have often been found to be a barrier to a successful intervention outcome (von Thiele Schwarz et al., 2017). Labour practices, such as downsizing, cost cutting, and work intensification that is increasingly common as part of globalization, shape the overall work environment. Downsizing, often accompanied by increased outsourcing and contract work, may contribute to mounting demands for productivity, increasing pressures on workers, and employers' ability to engage in improvements in the work organization. Importantly, the presence of a labour union in the workplace provides a structure for collective bargaining that can form the basis for improving working conditions, structuring work standards and policies, and providing workers with a voice in decision making (Landsbergis, 2000), which may facilitate their involvement in the participatory process.

The pre-existing methodology of change used within the organization is likely to affect the success of participatory interventions. Many organizations use continuous improvement methodologies. There are mixed findings regarding the effect of these on employee outcomes with some showing improvements in skills and employee involvement in decisions and others showing negative outcomes like work intensification and disempowerment (Bamber et al., 2014). Nevertheless, in organizations that already take an approach to change that involves employees (such as within continuous improvement methodologies based on 'lean' philosophies), managers and employees may be used to suggesting ideas for change and implementing them (von Thiele Schartz et al., 2017) thus enabling them to transfer this knowledge to a participatory intervention context. Being familiar with collective decision-making processes such as those applied in continuous improvement, is likely to enable workers to engage with the participatory decision making process (Nielsen & Noblet, 2018).

The organization also structures the way jobs are designed, and in this way may also influence the success of participatory interventions. Employees who have simplified work and a narrow range of responsibilities may feel less able to engage in collective decision making. Those employees who report higher ownership of their work, higher role breadth self-efficacy (in relation to performing broader activities beyond the core job) and higher job control are more likely to make suggestions for change (Axtell et al., 2000). Similarly, workers who report autonomy in influencing changes in work practices and procedures are likely to feel more able to participate in change processes (Parry et al., 2013).

A recently published review presented evidence of the importance of worker health and safety policies and suggested that the types of policies organizations already have in place may shape the design and implementation of the participatory organizational intervention process (Gómez et al., 2019). For example, work scheduling policies may define the parameters of job flexibility, determine times when required business meetings may be scheduled, or structure shift characteristics (e.g., length of shifts, total hours worked, rotating or night, required overtime), and thus also structuring opportunities for worker participation. Policies that define the frequency and length of meal breaks may contribute to lowering psychological distress (Kim et al., 2013), allow for fatigue recovery (Hurtado et al., 2015) and thus improve workers' ability to participate in organizational changes. Similarly, organizations that have clear sickness absence policies may find it easier to analyze existing sickness absence data to identify which departments or teams may be at particular risk of ill health and where intervention is needed. Policies or practices that ensure adequate staffing, including regular assessments to align job demands with available resources, may contribute to managing workloads and work intensity, and enabling workers to engage in the participatory process. The culture of the workplace is further shaped by policies towards workplace harassment and abuse, including policies that communicate zero tolerance of harassment, encourage workers to report incidents and suggest ways to prevent them, and affirm management commitment to worker health and safety (Occupational Safety and Health Administration (OSHA), 2009). Where such policies have been successfully implemented, workers may feel more comfortable engaging in the participatory process because they do not fear harassment or abuse from their colleagues or leaders. Benefit structures, including policies that determine pay scales, work hours, health care or related benefits, further influence the existing organizational climate and may contribute to workers' trust in the participatory process (Baron et al., 2014). Taken together, these policies may improve the organizational climate toward a culture of health and a willingness to engage in further organizational change (Pfeffer, 2018).

Organizational readiness for change is a precursor to implementing successful organizational interventions (Weiner, 2009). This readiness may reflect leaders' commitment and efficacy to implement change (Herscovitch & Meyer, 2002). In addition to the propensity of individual leaders, however, organizational readiness encompasses organizational structures and resource allocations that shape the ability to act and the ability to engage fully in the participatory process. Readiness for change may be improved by increasing the value organizational members place on the targeted organizational change, for example by increasing perceptions of need for the change, identifying likely successful pathways to change, and improving access to available resources. Contextual conditions clearly influence readiness for change, and may include an organizational culture that values innovation and tolerates risk-taking

(Weiner, 2009) in order for workers to feel comfortable coming forward with suggestions for improvements.

Overarching context

At the overarching contextual level, i.e. the context outside the organization, a number of factors may play a role.

National contexts may influence conditions within the organization. A large body of literature demonstrates the critical roles played by governmental policies in ensuring protections of worker safety and health, including benefit structures, work hours, and compensation after work-related injuries (Wagner & Spieler, 2017). Such policies clearly shape employers' implementation of organizational changes. For example, the Danish work environment legislation stipulates that work environment risk management must be organized and managed in a dialogue between employer, managers and employees (Arbejdsmiljoloeven, 2017) and thus directly emphasizes the importance of a participatory approach involving employees.

In some countries such as the UK, concrete guidance on how to design and implement participatory organizational interventions has been provided by the national health and safety policy body, the Health and Safety Executive (HSE). This guidance known as the Management Standards (2004) outlines a four-phase process with suggested tools to support the participatory process. Such guidance may support and encourage organizations to embark on the journey of improving working conditions through the process of participation.

Economic downturn may influence organizations' commitment to improving employee health and wellbeing. In the period 2004–2012, the UK HSE rolled out a major national initiative to implement the Management Standards. As part of the initiative, the HSE monitored risks in a large national survey in this period. They found that control decreased in the period 2009–2010 and suggested it may be caused by the recession and the related job insecurity that arose at the end of 2008.

The changing nature of work presents a range of challenges for participatory organizational interventions. Many sectors in modern society have complex structures with subcontractors that each carry some responsibility for worker health and wellbeing, making it challenging to implement interventions in worksites where multiple organizations are interdependent and boundaries are fuzzy. One such sector is the construction sector, where many small organizations may work on the same site at the same time (Brunette, 2004). Peters et al. (2018) found the subcontracting structure to be a barrier. Although the foreman of the subcontracting companies was trained as part of the intervention, subcontractors did not have the necessary systems in place to change working conditions.

The healthcare sector in many countries is under pressure due to understaffing as insufficient healthcare staff are trained and many leave the occupation due to poor working conditions (Coombs et al., 2007). Previous research has found that high work pressures due to understaffing resulted in workers failing to engage with the participatory intervention process (Madede et al., 2017; Schneider et al., 2019).

Although rarely considered in organizational interventions, external factors such as the weather may also be an important contextual factor. Bad weather may increase time pressure and detract attention from the intervention (Abildgaard & Nielsen, 2018; Peters et al., 2018).

Discussion

In this chapter we argue that rather than controlling for context we need to understand and integrate our interventions into the organizational context to ensure a successful intervention outcome. We need to give up the illusion that we can keep the context stable and control for it, we need to ensure that our interventions align with the context. This alignment may require we develop initiatives to support the organizational intervention, or we make changes to our intervention, e.g. adapt participatory processes to the population. For example, the contextual factors of the large, multi-national food service company that services canteens in other organizations such as hospitals may influence the participatory process. Such organizations employ workers with little formal education and these are often migrant workers with limited language skills and limited understanding of health and safety issues, potentially making it challenging for these workers to engage in group discussions. At the same time, as the work is simplified and does not involve collective decision making, workers may not feel comfortable engaging in the participatory process at the team level. At the leader level, line managers may not be accustomed to considering the workers' perspectives and may not know how to support collective decision making. At the organizational level, the policies and practices that are developed centrally at the company's headquarters may not be known by line managers and workers if the communication channels do not support access to these policies. Finally, multi-national organizations often face the challenge of meeting the requirements of different national legislation on health and safety management. Together, all these contextual factors call for a structured approach to the participatory process where workers are given a clear description of what is required and provided with tools to engage in the process.

In this chapter we have listed a number of contextual factors classified according to the IGLOO levels. The list of contextual factors outlined in this chapter is far from exhaustive, but we hope it will stimulate debate on how we can consider context differently in our interventions when designing and implementing participatory, organizational interventions. It is important to be aware that these levels interact: the way work is already designed is likely to influence the amount of confidence and energy employees apply to participating in changes. For instance, Xanthopolou et al. (2007) found that job resources such as autonomy, support and supervisory coaching activate personal resources such as self-efficacy, self-esteem and optimism, which in turn influence employee engagement and exhaustion. Enhanced personal resources like self-efficacy enable employees to feel more able to control their work environment (Luthans et al., 2006) and are therefore likely to be benefi-cial for engagement in participatory interventions. Or taking our multinational company as an example, low-skilled workers may have less power or lack trust in their line managers and may therefore not feel empowered to engage in the participatory process.

We hope this preliminary framework for the contextual factors will inspire scholars to rethink the role of context in participatory organizational inter-ventions, and rather than seeing context as 'noise', will analyze the contextual challenges pre-intervention and take measures to address these in order to ensure a successful intervention outcome.

References

Abildgaard, J. S. & Nielsen, K. (2018). The interplay of sensemaking and material artefacts during interventions: A case study. *Nordic Journal of Working Life Studies*, 8(3), 5–26.
Abildgaard, J. S., Hasson, H., von Thiele Schwarz, U., Løvseth, L., Ala-Laurinaho, A., & Nielsen, K. (2018). Forms of participation – the development and appli-cation of a conceptual model of participation in work environment interven-

tions. *Economic and Industrial Democracy*, 41(3), 746–769. https://doi.org/10.1177/0143831X17743576

Akerjordet, K., Furunes, T., & Haver, A. (2018). Health-promoting leadership: An integrative review and future research agenda. *Journal of Advanced Nursing*, 74(7), 1505–1516.

Anderson, N. R., & West, M. A. (1998). Measuring climate for work group innovation: development and validation of the team climate inventory. *Journal of Organizational Behavior*, 19(3), 235–258.

Arbejdsmiljoeloven (2017). https://amid.dk/regler/love-og-eu-forordninger/arbejdsmiljoe-sam-1084/ retrieved 5th December, 2019.

Axtell, C. M., Holman, D., Unsworth, K., Wall, T., Waterson, P., & Harrington, E. (2000). Shopfloor innovation: Facilitating the suggestion and implementation of ideas. *Journal of Occupational & Organizational Psychology*, 73, 265–285.

Bamber, G. J., Stanton, P., Bartram, T., & Ballardie, R. (2014). Human resource management, lean processes and outcomes for employees: Towards a research agenda, *International Journal of Human Resource Management*, 25, 2881–2891. DOI:10.1080/09585192.2014.962563

Bandura, A. (1986). *Social Foundations of Thought and Action: A Social Cognitive Theory*. Englewood Cliffs, NJ: Prentice-Hall.

Baron, S. L., Beard, S., Davis, L. K., Delp, L., Forst, L., Kidd-Taylor, A., & Welch, L. S. (2014). Promoting integrated approaches to reducing health inequities among low-income workers: Applying a social ecological framework. *American Journal of Industrial Medicine*, 57(5), 539–556.

Brunette, M. J. (2004). Construction safety research in the United States: Targeting the Hispanic workforce. *Injury Prevention*, 10, 244–248. https://doi.org/10.1136/ip.2004.005389

Busch, C., Koch, T., Clasen, J., Winkler, E., & Vowinkel, J. (2017). Evaluation of an organizational health intervention for low-skilled workers and immigrants. *Human Relations*, 70(8), 994–1016.

Coombs, C. R., Arnold, J., Loan-Clarke, J., Wilkinson, A., Park, J., & Preston, D. (2007). Improving the recruitment and return of nurses and allied health professionals: A quantitative study. *Health Services Management Research*, 20(1), 22–36.

Daft, R. L., & Lengel, R. H. (1986) Organizational information requirements, media richness and structural design. *Management Science*, 32(5), 554–571.

Day, A. & Nielsen, K. (2017). What does our organization do to help our well-being? Creating healthy workplaces and workers. In Nik Chmiel, Franco Fraccaroli, & Magnus Sverke (eds), *An Introduction to Work and Organizational Psychology* (pp. 295-314). London: Wiley Blackwell.

ETUC (2004). *Framework agreement on work-related stress*. Brussels: European Trade Union Confederation.

EU-OSHA [European Agency for Safety and Health at Work] (2010). *European Survey of Enterprises on New and Emerging Risks, 2010*. Available at: www.esener.eu

Gittell, J.H. (2006). Relational coordination: coordinating work through relationships of shared goals, shared knowledge and mutual respect. In O. Kyriakidou and M. Ozbilgin (eds), *Relational Perspectives in Organizational Studies: A Research Companion*, Cheltenham, UK and Northampton, MA, USA: Edward Elgar Publishers, 74–94.

Gómez, M. A. L., Sparer-Fine, E., Sorensen, G., & Wagner, G. (2019). Literature review of policy implications from findings of the center for work, health, and well-being. *Journal of Occupational and Environmental Medicine*, 61(11), 868–876.

Herscovitch, L., & Meyer, J. P. (2002). Commitment to organizational change: Extension of a three-component model. *Journal of Applied Psychology, 87*(3), 474–487.

Hertel, G., Konradt, U., & Orlikowski, B. (2004). Managing distance by interdependence: Goal setting, task interdependence and team-based rewards in virtual teams. *European Journal of Work and Organizational Psychology, 13,* 1–28.

Hurtado, D. A., Nelson, C. C., Hashimoto, D., & Sorensen, G. (2015). Supervisors' support for nurses' meal breaks and mental health. *Workplace Health & Safety, 63*(3), 107–115.

ILO (2001). *Guidelines on Occupational Safety and Health Management Systems.* Geneva: International Labor Office.

Karanika-Murray, M., & Biron, C. (2015). *Derailed Organizational Interventions for Stress and Well-being.* Dordrecht: Springer.

Kim, S. S., Okechukwu, C. A., Buxton, O. M., Dennerlein, J. T., Boden, L. I., Hashimoto, D. M., & Sorensen, G. (2013). Association between work–family conflict and musculoskeletal pain among hospital patient care workers. *American Journal of Industrial Medicine, 56*(4), 488–495.

LaMontagne, A. D., Keegel, T., Louie, A. M., Ostry, A., & Landsbergis, P. A. (2007). A systematic review of the job-stress intervention evaluation literature, 1990–2005. *International Journal of Occupational and Environmental Health, 13*(3), 268–280.

Landsbergis, P. (2000). Legal and legislative issues – collective bargaining to reduce CVD risk factors in the work environment. *State of the Art Reviews: Occupational Medicine, 15*(1), 287–290.

Luthans, F., Avey, J. B., Avolio, B. J., Norman, S. M., & Combs, G. M. (2006). Psychological capital development: Toward a micro-intervention. *Journal of Organizational Behavior, 27,* 387–393.

Luthans, F., Youssef, C. M., & Avolio, B. J. (2007). *Psychological Capital: Developing the Human Competitive Edge.* New York: Oxford University Press.

Madede, T., Sidat, M., McAuliffe, E., Patricio, S. R., Uduma, O., Galligan, M., & Cambe, I. (2017). The impact of a supportive supervision intervention on health workers in Niassa, Mozambique: A cluster-controlled trial. *Human Resources for Health, 15*(1), no. 58.

Management Standards (2004). https://www.hse.gov.uk/stress/standards/ retrieved 6th December, 2019.

Marine, A., Ruotsalainen, J. H., Serra, C., & Verbeek, J. H. (2006). Preventing occupational stress in healthcare workers. *Cochrane Database of Systematic Reviews,* (4). DOI: 10.1002/14651858.CD002892.pub5

McLellan, D, Moore, W, Nagler, E, & Sorensen, G. (2017). *Implementing an Integrated Approach: Weaving Worker Health, Safety, and Well-being into the Fabric of your Organization.* Boston, MA: Dana-Farber Cancer Institute.

Merritt, S. M. & Havill, L. (2016). Electronic and face-to-face communication in mentoring relationships: Recommendations on communication media and frequency of interaction, *Development and Learning in Organizations: An International Journal, 30,* 17–19.

National Institute for Occupational Safety and Health (2016). *Total Worker Health: Let's Get Started.* Retrieved from: https://www.cdc.gov/niosh/twh/letsgetstarted .html., Accessed 22 July 2021.

Nielsen, K. (2013). How can we make organizational interventions work? Employees and line managers as actively crafting interventions. *Human Relations, 66,* 1029–1050.

Nielsen, K. (2017). Leaders can make or break an intervention – but are they the villains of the piece. In E. K. Helloway, K. Nielsen, and J. K. Dimoff (eds), *Leading to*

Occupational Health and Safety: How Leadership Behaviours Impact Organizational Safety and Well-being (pp. 197–210). Chichester, West Sussex, UK: John Wiley & Sons.

Nielsen, K. & Miraglia, M. (2017). Critical essay: What works for whom in which circumstances? On the need to move beyond the 'what works?' question in organizational intervention. *Human Relations, 70*(1), 40–62.

Nielsen, K. & Noblet, A. (2018). Introduction: Organizational interventions: Where we are, where we go from here? In K. Nielsen, & A. Noblet (eds), *Organizational Interventions for Health and Well-being: A Handbook for Evidence-Based Practice*. Oxon: Routledge, pp. 1–23.

Nielsen, K., & Randall, R. (2015). Assessing and addressing the fit of planned interventions to the organizational context. In M. Karanika-Murray & C. Biron (eds), *Derailed Organizational Interventions for Stress and Well-being* (pp. 107–113). Dordrecht: Springer.

Nielsen, K., & Taris, T. W. (2019). Leading well: Challenges to researching leadership in occupational health psychology – and some ways forward. *Work & Stress, 33*(2), 107–118.

Nielsen, K., Birk Jorgensen, M., Milczarek, M., & Munar, L. (2018). *Healthy Workers, Thriving Companies – a Practical Guide to Wellbeing at work. Tackling Psychosocial Risks and Musculoskeletal Disorders in Small Businesses*. Luxembourg: EU-OSHA.

Nielsen, K., Fredslund, H., Christensen, K. B., & Albertsen, K. (2006). Success or failure? Interpreting and understanding the impact of interventions in four similar worksites. *Work & Stress, 20*(3), 272–287. https://doi.org/10.1080/02678370601022688

Nielsen, K., Nielsen, M. B., Ogbonnaya, C., Känsälä, M., Saari, E., & Isaksson, K. (2017). Workplace resources to improve both employee well-being and performance: A systematic review and meta-analysis. *Work & Stress, 31*(2), 101–120.

Nielsen, K., Yarker, J., Munir, F. & Bültmann, U. (2018). IGLOO: An integrated framework for sustainable return to work in workers with common mental disorders. *Work & Stress, 32*(4), 400–417.

Nylén, E. C., Lindfors, P., Ishäll, L., Göransson, S., Aronsson, G., Kylin, C., & Sverke, M. (2017). A pilot-study of a worksite based participatory intervention program: Its acceptability and short-term effects on work climate and attitudes in human service employees. *Work, 56*(4), 625–636.

O'Leary M. B., & Cummings J. N. (2007). The spacial, temporal and configurational characteristics of geographic dispersion in teams. *MIS Quarterly, 31*, 433–452.

O'Leary, M. B., & Mortensen, M. (2010). Go (con)figure: Subgroups, imbalance and isolates in geographically dispersed teams. *Organization Science, 21*, 115–131.

Occupational Safety and Health Administration (OSHA) (2015). *Adding Inequality to Injury: The Costs of Failing to Protect Workers on the Job*. http://www.dol.gov/osha/report/20150304-inequality.pdf., Accessed 22 July 2021.

Occupational Safety and Health Administration (OSHA) (2009). *Recommendations for Workplace Violence Prevention Programs in Late-Night Retail Establishments*. Retrieved from https://www.osha.gov/sites/default/files/publications/osha3153.pdf, Accessed 22 July 2021.

Parry, S., Straker, L., Gilson, N. D., & Smith, A. J. (2013). Participatory workplace interventions can reduce sedentary time for office workers – a randomised controlled trial. *PloS One, 8*(11), e78957.

Peters, S., Grant, M., Rodgers, J., Manjourides, J., Okechukwu, C., & Dennerlein, J. (2018). A cluster randomized controlled trial of a Total Worker Health® intervention on commercial construction sites. *International Journal of Environmental Research and Public Health*, *15*(11), 2354.

Pfeffer, J. (2018). *Dying for a Paycheck: How Modern Management Harms Employee Health and Company Performance – and What We Can Do About It*. HarperCollins.

Polzer, J. T., Crisp, C. B., Jarvenpaa, S. L. & Kim, J. W. (2006). Extending the faultline model to geographically dispersed teams: How collocated subgroups can impair group functioning. *Academy of Management Journal*, *49*, 679–692.

Randall, R., Griffiths, A., & Cox, T. (2005). Evaluating organizational stress-management interventions using adapted study designs. *European Journal of Work and Organizational Psychology*, *14*(1), 23–41.

Richardson, K. M., & Rothstein, H. R. (2008). Effects of occupational stress management intervention programs: A meta-analysis. *Journal of Occupational Health Psychology*, *13*(1), 69– 93. https://doi.org/10.1037/1076-8998.13.1.69

Sabbath, E. L., Hurtado, D. A., Okechukwu, C. A., Tamers, S. L., Nelson, C., Kim, S. S., & Schneider, A., Wehler, M., & Weigl, M. (2019). Effects of work conditions on provider mental well-being and quality of care: A mixed-methods intervention study in the emergency department. *BMC Emergency Medicine*, *19*(1), 1.

Sorensen, G., Emmons, K., Hunt, M. K., Barbeau, E., Goldman, R., Peterson, K., & Berkman, L. (2003). Model for incorporating social context in health behavior interventions: Applications for cancer prevention for working-class, multiethnic populations. *Preventive Medicine*, *37*(3), 188–197.

Sorensen, G., McLellan, D. L., Sabbath, E. L., Dennerlein, J. T., Nagler, E. M., Hurtado, D. A., & Wagner, G. R. (2016). Integrating worksite health protection and health promotion: A conceptual model for intervention and research. *Preventive Medicine*, *91*, 188–196.

Sproull, L., & Kiesler, S. (1986). Reducing social-context cues – electronic mail in organizational communication. *Management Science*, *32*, 1492–1512.

Stansfeld, S. A., Kerry, S., Chandola, T., Russell, J., Berney, L., Hounsome, N., Lanz, D., Costelloe, C., Smuk, M. & Bhui, K. (2015). Pilot study of a cluster randomised trial of a guided e-learning health promotion intervention for managers based on management standards for the improvement of employee well-being and reduction of sickness absence: GEM study. *BMJ Open*, *5*(10), e007981.

Swindler, S., & Eschleman, K. J. (2015). In Line for takeoff... and waiting: Challenges with getting a wellness intervention started in the military. In M. Karanika-Murray & C. Biron (eds), *Derailed Organizational Interventions for Stress and Well-Being* (pp. 101–106). Dordrecht: Springer.

Tsutsumi, A., Nagami, M., Yoshikawa, T., Kogi, K., & Kawakami, N. (2009). Participatory intervention for workplace improvements on mental health and job performance among blue-collar workers: A cluster randomized controlled trial. *Journal of Occupational and Environmental Medicine*, *51*(5), 554–563.

von Thiele Schwarz, U., Nielsen, K. M., Stenfors-Hayes, T., & Hasson, H. (2017). Using kaizen to improve employee well-being: Results from two organizational intervention studies. *Human Relations*, *70*(8), 966–993.

Wagner, G., & Spieler E. (2017). The roles of government in protecting and promoting occupational and environmental health. In B. S. Levy, D. H. Wegman, S. L. Baron, & R. K. Sokas (eds), *Occupational and Environmental Health*. 7th ed. USA: Oxford University Press, doi: 10.1093/oso/9780190662677.001.0001.

Weiner, B. J. (2009). A theory of organizational readiness for change. *Implementation Science*, *4*, 67. doi:10.1186/1748-5908-4-67.

West, M. A. (1990). The social psychology of innovation in groups. In M. A. West & J. L. Farr (eds), *Innovation and Creativity at Work: Psychological and Organizational Strategies* (pp. 4–36). Chichester: Wiley.

Xanthopoulou, D., Bakker, A. B., Demerouti, E. & Schaufeli, W. B. (2007). The role of personal resources in the job demands–resources model. *International Journal of Stress Management, 14,* 121–141.

12. COVID-19: short- and long-term impacts on work and well-being

Gary W. Ivey, Jennifer E.C. Lee, Deniz Fikretoglu, Eva Guérin, Christine Frank, Stacey Silins, Donna I. Pickering, Megan M. Thompson and Madeleine T. D'Agata

As we write, Coronavirus disease (COVID-19) has infected more than 11 million people in 216 countries, and it is responsible for the deaths of more than 500,000 people (WHO, 2020). Beyond the direct threat of infection, the impacts and drastic changes associated with the pandemic pose various psychosocial and physical challenges that can affect the health and well-being of employees, and the organizations they work for. This chapter expands on a series of high-level scientific briefs by a team of Defence scientists whose varied expertise in the social, behavioural, and health sciences were applied to COVID-19. The aim of the briefs was to provide timely assistance to senior leaders within the Canadian Department of National Defence on how personnel may react during this unusual and stressful situation, and in its aftermath, as well as how the organization could support its people through it to maintain operational readiness and effectiveness. To do so, we reviewed the scientific literature and available data that (in)directly related to COVID-19, and we distilled the information to a manageable set of recommendations deemed relevant to the organizational context.

Whereas the scientific briefs were intended as high-level findings and recommendations for senior military and civilian leaders in Defence, this chapter provides a broader and more integrated discussion of the research that informed those briefs, as well as research conducted since, and it is intended for the wider organizational and academic communities. Specifically, our objective here is to summarize some of the central risks and consequences of COVID-19 and highlight specific considerations for organizations in several key areas, including (a) impacts *of disasters*, (b) impacts *on work*, (c) impacts on *family life*, (d) *(non-)compliance* with public health directives, (e) *reintegration* into the workplace, and (f) *crisis communication* and *management*. We offer evidence-informed recommendations for how organizations might mitigate the potential harmful psychosocial effects of COVID-19 (see Appendix) and future crises, and we offer a research agenda to fill knowledge gaps.

Impacts of disasters

A global study found that over 40 percent of people have experienced a decline in their mental health since the start of COVID-19 (Greenwood et al., 2020), and other data suggest those estimates could be higher. For instance, a Canadian study (Angus Reid Institute, 2020a) reported that 50 percent of people reported a worsening of their mental health since the COVID-19 shutdown (especially women aged 18–54), and 42 percent (especially young men) reported a decline in their physical well-being. Many report feeling worried, anxious, and bored, and many are struggling financially.

These findings are in line with past research indicating that natural (e.g., pandemics) and human-made (e.g., terrorist attacks) disasters can elicit a range of negative psychological and emotional states (i.e., fear, anxiety, hopelessness, helplessness, denial, guilt, sadness, frustration, uncertainty) that can impact mental health (Brooks et al., 2019; Canadian Psychological Association, 2020; Inter-Agency Standing Committee, 2020; U.S. Department of Health and Human Services, n.d.). For pandemics in particular, research has shown that being quarantined for any amount of time is associated with loneliness, depression, stress, anger, anxiety, and post-traumatic stress disorder (PTSD) symptoms (Brooks et al., 2020b). While such effects seem to fade over time in most cases (Jeong et al., 2016), some situations appear to increase the risk of experiencing distress in the short term. Specifically, those experiencing longer quarantine periods and those with lower household incomes (i.e., under $40,000 per year) appear to be impacted to a higher degree (Hawryluck et al., 2004). The associated financial strain has been negatively associated with mental health (Frank et al., 2014).

Beyond their impacts on mental health, however, disasters have been characterized by their ripple effects on communities and society at large, for example, through their disproportionate impacts on certain individuals or groups, potential to engender discrimination and conflict, and consequences to a wide range of individual behaviours (Amaratunga & O'Sullivan, 2006), in addition to their repercussions on the economy (Nicola et al., 2020). Thus, it is important for organizational leaders to recognize and understand that the lives of all employees may be touched by these effects to varying degrees, especially given the potential work-related impacts.

Impacts on work

Physical distancing and other imposed restrictions related to the COVID-19 pandemic have substantially altered the way in which most employees carry out their work. Most so-called "non-essential workers" were restricted from working on site since the early stages of the pandemic, and many of those who have not lost their employment are currently either working from home or self-isolating. Research has shown that telework can have positive impacts on people and their productivity (Bloom et al., 2015; Mercer, 2019), and research suggests workers in Canada and the U.S. have generally adjusted well to working from home (Brenan, 2020; Statistics Canada, 2020a). However, telework can result in adverse effects—particularly when it is imposed or forced (Harris, 2003; Lyonette & Baldauf, 2019; Canadian Press, 2020). Many individuals perceive their connection with their coworkers as equally important, or more important, than the work itself (Airtasker, 2020). Separation from colleagues at a time when individuals are also unable to maintain their usual social networks outside of work may be particularly difficult.

In addition to feelings of social isolation and loneliness (Buckner, 2019), working from home presents a risk of work–life imbalance (Airtasker, 2020). Forty percent of surveyed Canadians new to working from home as a result of COVID-19 reported *work–life balance* challenges (Statistics Canada, 2020a). There is evidence that individuals feel a heightened pressure to perform when working remotely, which can result in prolonged work hours (Digital Ocean, 2019). For some, this pressure may be driven by fears that coworkers or managers do not believe they are working hard (Wilkie, 2017). Remote workers with household responsibilities, such as caring for children or elderly family members, may experience anxiety or guilt over not being able to match the productivity of their peers without such responsibilities. Similar sentiments may be experienced by those who face a limited capacity to work from home and collaborate with their team due to technological barriers or the nature of their work. Being unable to contribute to team or organizational efforts in a meaningful way could negatively impact the well-being of employees. Meaningful work emerged as a key driver of global workplace well-being among military personnel (Blais et al., 2020), and it has been identified as an important buffer against the negative effects of job stress among emergency healthcare workers (Ben-Itzhak et al., 2015; Sinclair et al., 2020).

Also, as a consequence of the COVID-19 restrictions, hiring freezes and pauses in professional development and promotion practices (including international assignments) may leave many individuals unsure of their career prospects and the longer-term impact this may have. In the short term, interruptions to work flow for any number of reasons may intensify concerns about productivity and career progression. During these times, those who are unable to contribute to organizational efforts to the same extent as others may feel particularly vulnerable.

Impacts on family life

In addition to the impacts of COVID-19 restrictions on work, organizational leaders/managers must recognize the many ways they could be affecting the personal/family lives of their employees. Physical distancing measures to restrict the spread of COVID-19 have greatly reduced social contact with loved ones. Social isolation may be extensive for employees who live alone or away from loved ones due to imposed public health restrictions or quarantine. Although living alone is generally associated with poorer mental health (Therrien et al., 2016), prolonged forced proximity to immediate family while simultaneously reducing or eliminating interactions with external social networks can still lead to feeling isolated and emotionally disconnected, even in the presence of others (Brooks et al., 2020b; Nickell et al., 2004; Van Bavel et al., 2020). Furthermore, research suggests that having a partner may not be protective in times of quarantine, with symptoms of depression and PTSD being similar between married and single individuals (Hawryluck et al., 2004). Relationships may be impacted by increased conflict, due in part to the negative effects of isolation on mood (Brooks et al., 2020b) and the strain associated with constant physical proximity over an extended period of time, particularly for those in small living quarters.

People who carry out essential work outside of the home may be living with stress or anxiety about exposing members of their household to COVID-19. This may be particularly salient among medical staff (Nickell et al., 2004) and other frontline workers (i.e., emergency response crews, military personnel responding to COVID-19) assisting with patient management during the pandemic. Studies also show that individuals living with someone working on the front line of the pandemic may be impacted due to changes to work routine or heightened stress, anxiety, and anger (Nickell et al., 2004; Van Bavel et al., 2020; Ying et al., 2020). Frontline workers may be exposed to multiple stressors and ethical dilemmas (e.g., increased risk of infection, tending to the sick and dying, decisions about how to prioritize care), which may increase their risk of mental health problems, including moral injury and PTSD (Brooks et al., 2020b).

Millions of people around the world have lost their jobs—some temporarily, some permanently—as a result of COVID-19 restrictions and are now coping with reduced income of their own, or of other members of their family. Unemployment rates rose to 13.7 percent in Canada (Statistics Canada, 2020b) and 14.7 percent in the U.S. (Rugaber, 2020) during the pandemic, and 28 percent of European Union survey respondents reported losing their job (Eurofound, 2020). Financial insecurity has been linked to work–family conflict, stress, and negative health outcomes (Odle-Dusseau et al., 2018). Individuals who experience financial hardship (or those with lower income) during the pandemic may also experience greater psychological distress (Brooks et al., 2019, 2020b; Frank et al., 2014).

Employees who have had to adjust to working from home may have encountered unique challenges related to their family (Brooks et al., 2020b; Harris, 2003; Nickell et al., 2004; Van Bavel et al., 2020; Ying et al., 2020). Specifically, they may feel strained as a result of the spillover effect of their work onto their family life and vice versa (Liu et al., 2020; O'Sullivan et al., 2009). In Europe, it has been estimated that more than one third (36 percent) of those working from home live in households with children under 17 (Eurofound, 2020). Having to negotiate childcare and work, parents may experience guilt due to loss of productivity and/or fears of parenting oversight. Despite progress with regard to gender role expectations, women may experience particular stresses around caregiving and work–life conflict (McElwain et al., 2005; Shockley & Clark, 2020), and they may be especially disadvantaged in balancing the provision of informal care with professional demands (O'Sullivan et al., 2009; Sinclair et al., 2020; Wenham et al., 2020).

As of May, 2020, more than 1.5 billion children and youths in 190 countries were impacted by nationwide school closures (UNESCO, 2020). Concerns by workers about how to handle school closures during outbreaks have been noted, including routine disruptions, homeschooling struggles, and the need for childcare among those who perform essential duties (O'Sullivan et al., 2009; Szabo et al., 2020). School and daycare closures place a significant amount of pressure on parents (Wang et al., 2020) as they must monitor their child(ren)'s academic progress in addition to addressing their psychosocial needs. A study of Canadian children aged 10–17 found that 71 percent reported feeling "bored" and older children were more likely to feel angry (Angus Reid Institute, 2020b), and 29 percent of American Gallup poll parent respondents said social distancing and school closures have caused harm to their children's mental health (Calderon, 2020). Missing out on school and not being able to socialize with friends were common concerns.

Sudden changes to normal roles and routines can create stress for the entire family unit (Robertson et al., 2004). In some instances, such pressures can create an environment that fosters domestic violence (Abramson, 2020; Serrata & Alvarado, 2019). Since COVID-19 social isolation and quarantine measures were implemented, reports of domestic abuse and family violence increased around the world (Bradbury-Jones & Isham, 2020; Usher & Bhullar, 2020). Furthermore, these impacts may be exacerbated by alcohol use (Campbell, 2020), which is estimated to have increased in some countries (Statista, 2020; Statistics Canada, 2020c).

Finally, those with elderly parents or family members at increased risk may experience heightened anxiety due to concerns of their loved one becoming ill (Holmes et al., 2020). Having to care for someone who has become sick with COVID-19 may intensify caregiving for children or other dependents. Thus, employees who are also caregivers may experience fatigue, discomfort, and helplessness with the new added responsibilities, accompanied by fear, anxiety and concern for the family member (Sun et al., 2020). Again, women may be disproportionately impacted owing to their tendency to play a more prominent role in caregiving.

(Non-)Compliance

Although the majority of Canadians are following public health guidelines during the COVID-19 pandemic (e.g., physical distancing, self-isolation, hand washing), a substantial and increasing minority of the population (up to 35 percent) has reported that they have not complied with certain measures (Leger, 2020). In the U.S., similar reports of non-compliance are as high as 52 percent (Leger, 2020). A great deal of research has focused on the psychological factors underlying individual motivation to comply with directives during public health crises. This work has largely evolved from health behaviour theories, which vary in their components but commonly propose that individuals' responses to potential health hazards are a function of their perceptions of the potential risks associated with these hazards, and their evaluations of prescribed responses aimed at reducing these risks (Vaughn, 2011).

Research has shown that individuals will not act to protect themselves from potential health hazards if they do not believe they pose a threat. During past outbreaks (i.e., SARS, avian flu, pandemic influenza), perceived susceptibility to these viruses was associated with adherence to prescribed protective behaviours (Bish & Michie, 2010; Rizzo et al., 2013; Timpka et al., 2014). In the case of COVID-19, compliance with mitigation strategies may be stronger if individuals believe there is a significant likelihood of catching or spreading the virus, and that this would have serious consequences.

Even if a hazard is seen as threatening, individuals' subsequent evaluations of prescribed responses play a key role in their compliance with them. This includes whether they believe that the recommended measures are feasible and whether performing them will reduce the threat. For example, compliance with physical distancing guidelines during pandemics has been linked to one's belief that they can personally cope with the threat, and that their actions will effectively reduce the risks associated with the viruses (Rizzo et al., 2013; Timpka et al., 2014).

Compliance has also been linked to confidence in emergency management personnel and institutional responses (DiGiovanni et al., 2004; Rubin et al., 2009), as individuals may believe that their efforts will be more effective if they feel better supported. Compliance with COVID-19 mitigation directives might, therefore, partly depend on the perceived effectiveness of physical distancing, self-isolation, and other prescribed measures, as well as the extent to which people consider such actions feasible based on their unique personal circumstances.

A number of other individual characteristics have been found to be associated with compliance to public health guidelines in past research. Emotional responses, such as boredom and loneliness, may hinder compliance with directives (DiGiovanni et al., 2004). Understandably, individuals with pre-existing physical health conditions (e.g., auto-immune disorders) or other personal risk factors (e.g., older age) that increase the risk of severe COVID-19 symptoms may be more anxious about getting infected. While worrying about the possibility of becoming ill has been associated with a greater likelihood of complying with directives (Rizzo et al., 2013), individuals with health anxiety may experience heightened COVID-19 worry and may engage in excessive safety behaviours (e.g., visits to hospital emergency rooms to seek reassurance; Asmundson & Taylor, 2020). Although they may be adaptive in keeping individuals safe (or feeling safe) in the short term, such reactions may be maladaptive when excessive and persistent (Brooks et al., 2019).

Certain personality traits have been associated with compliance. Individuals scoring higher on extraversion, for example, were found to be less likely to adhere to social distancing guidelines during the COVID-19 pandemic, suggesting that reducing social proximity to others may be more challenging for this group (Carvalho et al., 2020). In contrast, individuals with higher scores on conscientiousness reported greater compliance, suggesting these individuals have a higher propensity for accepting safety recommendations (Carvalho et al., 2020).

A recent survey (Leger, 2020) and two systematic reviews (Bish & Michie, 2010; Moran & Del Valle, 2016) have also noted consistent results linking gender to social distancing and other non-pharmaceutical directives, with men being less likely than women to comply with these guidelines. Non-compliance was also less likely among younger individuals and those with lower levels of education (Bish & Michie, 2010). Sectors dominated by lower earning young males (e.g., military, public safety, construction), therefore, may be particularly at risk for disease transmission given this demographic group's lower likelihood of complying with public health directives.

Social influences on individual behaviour are also relevant to whether individuals comply. These may be particularly relevant to the COVID-19 pandemic since the success of mitigation efforts require collective compliance with public health directives. For instance, seeing others engage in protective behaviours can facilitate individual compliance, especially when these actions are observed within one's own social networks (Wood et al., 2011). During the 2009 H1N1 (swine flu) pandemic, vaccine uptake was found to be greater as the number of one's social contacts encouraging vaccination increased (Kumar et al., 2011). Another study found that U.S. soldiers whose leaders actively encouraged health-promoting behaviours had more positive attitudes towards quarantine during the Ebola crisis (Adler et al., 2018). Research during natural disasters demonstrated that engagement in protective behaviours is tied to having strong social ties within a community and the existence of social norms that support such behaviours (Becker et al., 2012; Solberg et al., 2010). Managers and organizational leaders can reinforce such norms by encouraging health-promoting behaviours.

The scientific literature on implementing behaviour change emphasizes the importance of personal motivation (both automatic and reflective), capability (both physical, and psychological), and opportunities (both social and physical; Michie et al., 2011). As efforts begin to shift toward reintegration into the workplace, adherence to public health guidelines and new directives will become all the more integral to prevent subsequent waves of infection. For effective reintegration to the workplace, employees will have to change old workplace behaviours (e.g., taking breaks or eating lunch in a shared space) and adapt to new ones (e.g., maintain social distance, frequent hand washing, avoid touching face).

Reintegration

Research in the stress and coping domain characterizes the COVID-19 pandemic as a traumatic event, suggesting potential longer-term consequences for mental health and well-being world-wide (Horesh & Brown, 2020). This is complicated by a concern that COVID-19 will continue to circulate globally and a resurgence is possible (Garfin et al., 2020; Horesh & Brown, 2020). Thus, reintegration in this context is not a traditional return to the workplace.

A May 2020 survey of North Americans reinforced the persistent impact of COVID-19 (Leger, 2020); 55 percent of Canadians and 65 percent of U.S. respondents reported being afraid that they themselves will contract COVID-19, and 67 percent of respondents from both countries reported that they continue to be afraid that a family member will contract the disease. Employees' attitudes related to factors that can impact how they work have also been impacted by COVID-19. For instance, many respondents reported commuting to work daily (44 percent Canadian, 45 percent U.S.), and a large proportion indicated that they now work from home due to COVID-19 (44 percent Canadian, 33 percent U.S.). Importantly, of those who currently work from home, 39 percent indicated that they would prefer to return to their commute with the option of working from home more often, and almost as many (36 percent Canadian, 30 percent U.S.) indicated that they would prefer to continue to work primarily from home, commuting to work only when necessary once the pandemic ends. Results such as these are important sources to consider when creating return-to-work policies and procedures. Teleworking may continue to be a prominent feature of the new normal (Sinclair et al., 2020).

Return-to-work approaches

Many countries and organizations have developed plans and guidance for returning to work (e.g., Centers for Disease Control and Prevention, 2020;

Government of Ontario, 2020; Government of Scotland, 2020). The consistent themes across their plans include a regard for human health and well-being, comprehensive testing and tracking, thoughtful, phased approaches based on the latest scientific evidence, and an acknowledgment that the situation may evolve rapidly, perhaps necessitating a reinstatement of lifted protections. Large and dispersed organizations also need to consider regional (country, provincial, state, etc.) variations in terms of lock-down and reopening policies that might impact individuals' capacity to return to work.

As we prepare this chapter, employees in several countries have started to return to work. Many of these countries have used a phased approach (Coleman et al., 2020). In addition to considering whether a position is critical (or not) as criteria for who returns, and when they return, some businesses have used employee vulnerability factors (e.g., age, health conditions, home situation; Coleman et al., 2020). Chinese businesses implemented: staggered shifts; the use of infrared cameras (i.e., security staff checking temperatures when people arrive on location); decontamination three times per day; wearing face masks at all times; restrictions in gatherings (e.g., people in elevators, social gatherings); tape on floors showing where people should stand, and encouraging efforts to social distance (Wiles, 2020). Despite the implementation of these health and safety precautions, combined with more frequent hand washing, employees returning to their workplace had concerns about possible COVID-19 flare-ups (Knight, 2020). Some countries that have reopened their economies have already encountered consequential increases in the reported number of COVID-19 cases (Sly & Morris, 2020), sparking businesses to create contingency plans (i.e., re-exiting, re-entering workplace phases; Knight, 2020; Sly & Morris, 2020).

Organizational trust

As levels of risk and uncertainty associated with COVID-19 are expected to persist, people's trust in the organization will also be critical to effective reintegration. Where an organization's leaders are seen as competent in their abilities, benevolent in their concern for others, and to have the convictions of their principles (i.e., integrity), organizational trust tends to flourish (Davis et al., 2000; Joseph & Winston, 2005). Organizational trust is also higher when bureaucratic structures are seen as effective, fair, clear, and consistently applied (Allen & Braun, 2013; Searle & Billsberry, 2011).

Although not a panacea, research demonstrates that high organizational trust is associated with an array of benefits, such as higher morale, organizational commitment, and perceived organizational support (Albrecht & Travaglione,

2003; Dirks & Skarlicki, 2004; Fransen et al., 2015; Hermawati, 2014; Mayer et al., 1995). Organizational trust is considered to be especially important during a crisis (Balliet & Van Lange, 2013; Krishnan et al., 2006), contributing to the stability and effectiveness of organizations through higher levels of compliance (i.e., during medical crises; Blair et al., 2017; Vinck et al., 2019), cooperation, the sharing of scarce resources, higher cohesion, lower turnover, and higher overall performance and goal attainment (Balkan et al., 2014; Davis et al., 2000; Farooq & Farooq, 2014; Rich, 1997). High levels of trust provide a protective psychological benefit in the face of actual setbacks, allowing continued confidence that all reasonable efforts were made on one's behalf, even in cases that lead to a poorer than expected outcome (Dirks & Skarlicki, 2004; Robinson, 1996; Tyler, 1994).

As a central component of perceived organizational support, individuals need to believe/feel that their organization is concerned for their well-being (Blais et al., 2020; Eisenberger, 1986). Considering the pervasive nature of COVID-19 restrictions on all spheres of life (e.g., childcare, leisure, travel), supportive leadership (Sinclair et al., 2020), supportive human resources practices, and safe work conditions may be critical to a successful reintegration approach.

Crisis communication and management

Past disasters have raised awareness of the need for organizations to adopt effective practices to enable the exchange of important information during and after a disaster or crisis (McClain, 2007). It has been argued that internal communications take precedence during a crisis, and that organizations can manage crisis communication processes most efficiently if its leaders are highly visible to employees, communicate updates to employees, meet regularly to discuss how people are doing, impart the content of these discussions with workers, and provide employees with a means to check in (Hurley-Hanson & Giannantonio, 2009).

In contrast, ineffective communications in times of crisis can exacerbate people's stress reactions, and undermine adherence to recommended behaviours. For example, inadequate guidelines or misinformation about risks (e.g., conflicting messages across different levels of government, or in the media) can cause anxiety and emotional distress (U.S. Department of Health and Human Services, 2020; Brooks, Webster et al., 2020b). This may be especially salient for COVID-19, as medical health experts struggle with the epidemiology of the disease, and strive to recognize its symptoms and effective treatment.

Withholding information or over-reassuring the public to avoid panic can cause more harm than good (U.S. Department of Health and Human Services, 2020). Under normal circumstances, information overload has been linked to stress and lower overall health (Misra & Stokols, 2012). This may or may not hold during times of high stress and ambiguity, but the psychological effects of crises can be exacerbated by excessive media coverage, even among those indirectly affected by events (Canadian Psychological Association, 2020). As well, it is important to recognize that crises can affect how people process information. According to the U.S. Centers for Disease Control and Prevention, people tend to simplify messages, hold on to current beliefs, seek additional information or opinions, and believe early messages (U.S. Department of Health and Human Services, 2020).

In order to communicate with employees most effectively, it is also recommended that organizations listen to, and understand, the concerns of their workers. Accordingly, managers and organizational leaders need to be cognizant of the various impacts employees face as they adjust to the restrictions related to the COVID-19 pandemic in the workplace (Seeger, 2007).

Discussion

Our objective was to highlight the psychosocial impacts of COVID-19 that could affect the health and well-being of workers and the organizations that employ them. From our review, it is clear that the impact of the COVID-19 pandemic has been intensive, far-reaching, and dynamic. Our research and recommendations underscore the critical role of organizational initiatives for addressing the myriad challenges workers lucky enough to retain their employment may face as they strive to be productive while coping with the threat of infection, new ways of working, and the increasingly blurred line between their work and personal spaces.

Research agenda

It is important to acknowledge that our research was conducted during the pandemic, as a critical review in practice (Grant & Booth, 2009), and under many of the same difficult conditions we report on herein. Still, we conducted a thorough review, covering a broad range of applicable topics, and placing emphasis on higher-quality sources of evidence. Although our recommendations are rooted in the evidence we reviewed, and on the data available at the time of writing, the information pertaining to COVID-19 is continuously evolving. Thus, when the "dust settles", it will be important for researchers to (1) revisit the research and data following the prescribed steps of a systematic review (Grant & Booth, 2009) to verify and build on the key factors and outcomes we and other researchers (e.g., Sinclair et al., 2020) have commented on in real time.

This chapter highlights the tremendous individual variability in reactions to COVID-19, and in terms of its impact on personal situations. Some employees may be particularly susceptible to its negative effects based on their perceptions, demographic characteristics, personal or financial circumstances, family dynamics, pre-existing health conditions, lifestyle habits, and the nature of their work. We acknowledge that there are significant issues around diversity that we did not address, including the unique challenges experienced by those with disabilities, Indigenous and racialized people, and members of the LGBTQ2+ community (Flanagan, 2020; Government of Canada, 2020; Ravanera, 2020). Future research might (2) further explore individual protective and risk factors, including those for (3) diverse groups, and (4) how individual characteristics, personal situations, and diversity intersect to exacerbate risks or strengthen resilience. Given the scope of varied individual responses, it would be prudent to examine (5) how organizations might develop policies, procedures, and accommodations in crisis management that are individualized enough, and sensitive to different realities, but that can be broadly applied.

As mentioned above, COVID-19 has the potential for longer-lasting effects on the well-being of individuals, on the economy and the organizations that drive it, and on how we continue to conduct our work in the aftermath. Accordingly, future research should consider the residual effects of COVID-19, including: (6) the long-term consequences on employee mental health and well-being; (7) the long-term consequences on the mental health and well-being of organizational leaders who bear the burden of responsibility for organizational effectiveness while coping with the effects of COVID-19 themselves; (8) the implications and challenges for organizations, leaders, and employees associated with a more prevalent and continuous work from home posture; (9) the impact of the cumulative effects of living with multiple stressors, including the threat and uncertainty around COVID-19, a depressed economy, personal financial struggles, work–life conflict, job/career impacts, and the overarching uncertainty around what the future holds, to name some.

While the negative impacts of the pandemic have received more scientific attention, there are indications that positive responses, such as a greater appreciation of life, feeling more connected to others, a renewed sense of community, and a sense of pride, relief, elation, and empowerment may also occur following crises (Canadian Psychological Association, 2020; Inter-Agency Standing Committee, 2020; U.S. Department of Health and Human Services, 2020). Preliminary research on COVID-19 has suggested some positive impacts, such as receiving increased support from family and friends, a willingness to share feelings with others, and increased feelings of togetherness and cooperation (Gyasi et al., 2019; Zhang & Ma, 2020). Such examples of post-traumatic growth can unfold both at personal and professional levels, especially if protective factors are in place (Brooks et al., 2020a). To assist organizations through the aftermath of COVID-19 and in mitigating the negative effects of a resurgence or future pandemics, researchers might (10) explore the post-traumatic growth that occurred through COVID-19, including the individual, organizational, and cultural factors that supported it.

Some organizations may have protective factors in place to help them manage the effects of COVID-19 better than others (Brooks et al., 2019). Military organizations, for example, may be bolstered by their comprehensive health services, well-established support networks, an accessible suite of training and support resources, and a workforce that is trained for, and largely experienced in, dealing with stressful and ambiguous situations, from armed conflict to natural disasters. Future research might (11) explore how different organizations or sectors fared in mitigating the negative effects of COVID-19, and the factors (e.g., economy, structure, composition, culture, policies, technology) that helped to protect the well-being of their employees. Along the same line, (12) which factors are most critical to employee well-being and organizational effectiveness, and how might organizations prioritize their actions? Finally, though not exclusively, future research might assess (13) the extent to which successful organizational responses cohere with the evidence-based recommendations presented herein (see Appendix). Indeed, lessons learned from organizational success stories may help others protect themselves against future outbreaks and disasters.

Conclusion

Effective organizational communications that empower employees with timely information to reduce ambiguity and take positive action, that helps to mitigate the effects of COVID-19 stressors and reduce the risk of harm, and that is sensitive to delivery pitfalls (e.g., overload) may help manage the psychosocial effects of COVID-19 on individuals and achieve positive outcomes for organizations and society (Canadian Psychological Association, 2020; Inter-Agency Standing Committee, 2020; U.S. Department of Health and Human Services,

2020). Beyond the provision of credible information, organizational leaders can support their employees by preparing them with the training and resources to remain healthy and resilient (Sinclair et al., 2020), and to meaningfully contribute to the organizational effort (or mission), whether they are working from home or on the frontline supporting their communities. Understanding who is at risk—for experiencing difficulty, for non-compliance—and taking appropriate action to mitigate that risk is also important. Accordingly, leaders can assist their employees in maintaining or enhancing their own well-being, and that of their families, by understanding the risks associated with COVID-19, by demonstrating compassion and support for their employees as they uniquely cope with the psychological strain imposed by the crisis, and by being flexible in recognition of challenges to productivity and work–life balance. Effective organizational responses are critical when the risks are acute, but also in the aftermath of the pandemic given the potential for a COVID-19 resurgence and longer term effects on individuals.

Acknowledgements

The authors would like to thank (in alphabetical order) Robbie Arrabito, Hamid Boland, Angela Febbraro, Joshua Granek, Lieutenant-Commander Jennifer Price, Oshin Vartanian, and Barbara Waruszynski for their contributions to this paper, as well as Eugenia Kalantzis and Sanela Dursun for their insights and support.

Disclaimer

The opinions expressed in this chapter are those of the authors and do not necessarily reflect the official position of the Department of National Defence or Canadian Armed Forces.

References

Abramson, A. (2020, April 8). *How COVID-19 May Increase Domestic Violence and Child Abuse*. American Psychological Association. https://www.apa.org/topics/covid-19/domestic-violence-child-abuse

Adler, A. B., Kim, P. Y., Thomas, S. J., & Sopis, M. L. (2018). Quarantine and the U.S. military response to the Ebola crisis: Soldier health and attitudes. *Public Health, 155,* 95–98. https://doi.org/10.1016/j.puhe.2017.11.020

Airtasker (2020, March 31). *Comparing the Productivity, Spending, and Health of Remote vs. In-office Employees.* https://www.airtasker.com/blog/the-benefits-of -working-from-home/

Albrecht, S. L., & Travaglione, A. (2003). Trust in public-sector senior management. *International Journal of Human Resource Management, 14,* 76–92. https://doi.org/10 .1080/09585190210158529

Allen, C. D., & Braun, W. G. (2013). Trust: Implications for the Army profession. *Military Review, September–October (2013),* 73–85. https://apps.dtic.mil/dtic/tr/ fulltext/u2/a591153.pdf

Amaratunga, C. A., & O'Sullivan, T. L. (2006). In the path of disasters: Psychosocial issues for preparedness, response, and recovery. *Prehospital and Disaster Medicine, 21,* 149–153. https://doi.org/10.1017/S1049023X00003605

Angus Reid Institute (2020a, April 27). *Worry, Gratitude & Boredom: As COVID-19 Affects Mental, Financial Health, Who Fares Better; Who Is Worse?* http://angusreid .org/covid19-mental-health/

Angus Reid Institute (2020b, May 11). *Kids & COVID-19: Canadian Children are Done with School from Home, Fear Falling Behind, and Miss Their Friends.* http:// angusreid.org/covid19-kids-opening-schools/9

Asmundson, G. J. G., & Taylor, S. (2020). How health anxiety influences responses to viral outbreaks like COVID-19: What all decision-makers, health authorities, and health care professionals need to know. *Journal of Anxiety Disorders, 71,* 102211. https://doi.org/10.1016/j.janxdis.2020.102211

Balkan, M. O., Serin, A. E., & Soran, S. (2014). The relationship between trust, turnover intentions and emotions: An application. *European Scientific Journal, 10,* 73–85. http://citeseerx.ist.psu.edu/viewdoc/download?doi=10.1.1.1000.6325&rep=rep1& type=pdf

Balliet, D., & Van Lange, P. A. M. (2013). Trust, conflict, and cooperation: A meta-analysis. *Psychological Bulletin, 139,* 1090–1112. https://doi.org/10.1037/ a0030939

Becker, J. S., Paton, D., Johnston, D. M., & Ronan, K. R. (2012). A model of household preparedness for earthquakes: How individuals make meaning of earthquake information and how this influences preparedness. *Natural Hazards, 64,* 107–137. https:// doi.org/10.1007/s11069-012-0238-x

Ben-Itzhak, S., Dvash, J., Maor, M., Rosenberg, N., & Halpern, P. (2015). Sense of meaning as a predictor of burnout in emergency physicians in Israel: A national survey. *Clinical and Experimental Emergency Medicine, 2*(4), 217–225.

Bish, A., & Michie, S. (2010). Demographic and attitudinal determinants of protective behaviors during a pandemic: A review. *British Journal of Health Psychology, 15,* 797–824. https://doi.org/10.1348/135910710X485826

Blair, R. A., Morse, B. S., & Tsai, L. L. (2017). Public health and public trust: Survey evidence from the Ebola Virus Disease epidemic in Liberia. *Social Science & Medicine, 172,* 89–97. https://doi.org/10.1016/j.socscimed.2016.11.016

Blais, A.-R., Howell, G., Dobreva-Martinova, T., Hlywa, M., Ivey, G. W., Michaud, K., Suurd Ralph, C., & Harding, C. (2020). *2018 Defence Workplace Well-being Survey: L0 results.* Ottawa, Canada: Director General Military Personnel Research and Analysis.

Bloom, N., Liang, J., Roberts, J., & Ying, Z. J. (2015). Does working from home work? Evidence from a Chinese experiment. *Quarterly Journal of Economics*, *130*, 165–218. https://doi.org/10.1093/qje/qju032

Bradbury-Jones, C., & Isham, L. (2020). The pandemic paradox: The consequences of COVID-19 on domestic violence. *Journal of Clinical Nursing*, *29*, 2047–2049. https://onlinelibrary.wiley.com/doi/epdf/10.1111/jocn.15296

Brenan, M. (2020, April 3). *U.S. Workers Discovering Affinity for Remote Work*. https://news.gallup.com/poll/306695/workers-discovering-affinity-remote-work.aspx

Brooks, S. K., Amlôt, R., Rubin, G. J., & Greenberg, N. (2020). Psychological resilience and post-traumatic growth in disaster-exposed organisations: Overview of the literature. *BMJ Military Health*, *166*, 52–56. http://dx.doi.org/10.1136/jramc-2017-000876

Brooks, S. K., Rubin, G. J., & Greenberg, N. (2019). Traumatic stress within disaster-exposed occupations: Overview of the literature and suggestions for the management of traumatic stress in the workplace. *British Medical Bulletin*, *129*, 25–34. https://doi.org/10.1093/bmb/ldy040.

Brooks, S. K., Webster, R. K., Smith, L. E., Woodland, L., Wessely, S., Greenberg, N., & Rubin, G. J. (2020). The psychological impact of quarantine and how to reduce it: Rapid review of the evidence. *The Lancet*, *395*, 912–920. https://doi.org/10.1016/S0140-6736(20)30460-8

Buckner, D. (2019, April 24). *The Working-at-Home Blues: Loneliness, Depression a Risk for Those Who Are Isolated*. CBC News. https://www.cbc.ca/news/business/working-at-home-isolation-1.5103498

Calderon, V. J. (2020, June 6). *U.S. Parents say COVID-19 Harming Child's Mental Health*. https://news.gallup.com/poll/312605/parents-say-covid-harming-child-mental-health.aspx

Campbell, A. M. (2020). An increasing risk of family violence during the Covid-19 pandemic: Strengthening community collaborations to save lives. *Forensic Science International: Reports*, *2*, 100089. https://doi.org/10.1016/j.fsir.2020.100089

Canadian Press (2020, March 31). *Working Remotely During COVID-19 is Stressing Out Quebec Public Servants: Union Poll*. https://montreal.ctvnews.ca/working-remotely-during-covid-19-is-stressing-out-quebec-public-servants-union-poll-1.4876297?cache=yes%3FclipId%3D373266%3FclipId%3D64268

Canadian Psychological Association. (2020, March 20). *"Psychology Works" Fact Sheet: Psychological Impacts of the Coronavirus (COVID-19)*. https://cpa.ca/psychology-works-fact-sheet-psychological-impacts-of-the-coronavirus-covid-19/

Carvalho, L. D. F., Pianowski, G., & Gonçalves, A. P. (2020). Personality differences and the COVID-19: Are extroversion and conscientiousness personality traits associated with engagement in containment measures? *Trends in Psychiatry and Psychotherapy*. Advance online publication. https://doi.org/10.1590/2237-6089-2020-0029

Centers for Disease Control and Prevention (2020, May 7). *Reopening Guidance for Cleaning and Disinfecting Public Spaces, Workplaces, Businesses, Schools, and Homes*. https://www.cdc.gov/coronavirus/2019-ncov/community/reopen-guidance.html

Coleman, C., Ricker, D., & Stull, J. (2002, April 10). *10 Considerations for Transitioning Back to Work in a Post-COVID-19 World*. https://www.gensler.com/research-insight/blog/10-considerations-for-transitioning-back-to-work-in-a-post

Davis, J. H., Schoorman, F. D., Mayer, R.C., & Tan, H. H. (2000). Trusted unit manager and business unit performance: Empirical evidence of a competitive advantage. *Strategic Management Journal*, *21*, 563–576. https://doi.org/10.1002/(SICI)10970266(200005)21:5%3C563::AID-SMJ99%3E3.0.CO;2-0

DiGiovanni, C., Conley, J., Chiu, D., & Zaborski, J. (2004). Factors influencing compliance with quarantine in Toronto during the 2003 SARS outbreak. *Biosecurity and Bioterrorism: Biodefense Strategy, Practice, and Science, 2,* 265–272. https://doi.org/10.1089/bsp.2004.2.265

Digital Ocean (2019). *Currents: Remote Work Edition.* https://www.digitalocean.com/assets/media/currents-research/pdf/DigitalOcean-Currents-Q3-2019.pdf

Dirks, K. T., & Skarlicki, D. (2004). Trust in leaders: Existing research and emerging issues. In R. Kramer & K. Cook (Eds.), *Trust and Distrust in Organizations: Dilemmas and Approaches* (pp. 21–40), Russell Sage Foundation.

Eisenberger, R., Huntington, R., Hutchison, S., & Sowa, D. (1986). Perceived organizational support. *Journal of Applied Psychology, 71,* 500–507. https://doi.org/10.1037/0021-9010.71.3.500

Eurofound (2020, May 6). *Living, Working and COVID-19: First Findings – April 2020.* https://www.eurofound.europa.eu/publications/report/2020/living-working-and-covid-19-first-findings-april-2020

Farooq, M., & Farooq, O. (2014). Organizational justice, employee turnover, and trust in the workplace: A study in South Asian telecommunication companies. *Global Business and Organizational Excellence, 33,* 56–62. https://doi.org/10.1002/joe.21539

Flanagan, R. (2020, April 15). *Does COVID-19 Discriminate? This is How Some Canadians are Harder-hit.* CTV News. https://www.ctvnews.ca/health/coronavirus/does-covid-19-discriminate-this-is-how-some-canadians-are-harder-hit-1.4897298

Frank, C., Davis, C. G., & Elgar, F. J. (2014). Financial strain, social capital, and perceived health during economic revision: A longitudinal survey in rural Canada. *Anxiety, Stress & Coping, 27,* 422–438. https://doi.org/10.1080/10615806.2013.864389

Fransen, K., Haslam, S. A., Steffens, N. K., Vanbeselaere, N., De Cuyper, B., & Boen, F. (2015). Believing in "us": Exploring leaders' capacity to enhance team confidence and performance by building a sense of shared social identity. *Journal of Experimental Psychology: Applied, 21,* 89–100. https://doi.org/10.1037/xap0000033

Garfin, D. R., Silver, R. C., & Holman, E. A. (2020). The novel coronavirus (COVID-2019) outbreak: Amplification of public health consequences by media exposure. *Health Psychology, 39,* 355–357. http://dx.doi.org/10.1037/hea0000875

Government of Canada (2020, May 7). *COVID-19 and People with Disabilities in Canada.* https://www.canada.ca/en/public-health/services/diseases/2019-novel-coronavirus-infection/guidance-documents/people-with-disabilities.html

Government of Ontario (2020, April 27). *A Framework for Re-opening our Province.* https://files.ontario.ca/mof-framework-for-reopening-our-province-en-2020-04-27.pdf

Government of Scotland. (2020, April 23). *COVID-19: A Framework for Decision Making.* https://www.gov.scot/publications/coronavirus-covid-19-framework-decision-making/

Grant, M. J., & Booth, A. (2009). A typology of reviews: An analysis of 14 review types and associated methodologies. *Health Information and Libraries Journal, 26,* 91–108. https://doi.org/10.1111/j.1471-1842.2009.00848.x

Greenwood, K., Bapat, V., & Maughan, M. (2020, May 19). *The Other COVID-19 Crisis: Declining Mental Health.* Forbes. https://www.forbes.com/sites/sap/2020/05/19/the-other-covid-19-crisis-declining-mental-health/#4f7b0cbf3d65

Gyasi, R. M., Yeboah, A. A., Mensah, C. M., Ouedraogo, R., & Addae, A. (2019). Neighborhood, social isolation and mental health outcome among older people in Ghana. *Journal of Affective Disorders, 259,* 154–163. https://doi.org/10.1016/j.jad.2019.08.024

Harris, L. (2003). Home-based teleworking and the employment relationship: Managerial challenges and dilemmas. *Personnel Review, 32*, 422–437. https://doi.org/10.1108/00483480310477515

Hawryluck, L., Gold, W.L., Robinson, S., Pogorski, S., Galea, S., & Styra, R. (2004). SARS control and psychological effects of quarantine, Toronto, Canada. *Emerging Infectious Diseases, 10*, 1206–1212. https://doi.org/10.3201/eid1007.030703

Hermawati, A. (2014). Quality of work life and organizational trust related to job satisfaction and organizational trust related to job satisfaction and organizational commitment at private higher education institutions in Malang-Indonesia. *Journal of Basic and Applied Scientific Research, 4*, 349–357. https://www.textroad.com/pdf/JBASR/J.%20Basic.%20Appl.%20Sci.%20Res.,%204(2)349-357,%202014.pdf

Holmes, E. A., O'Connor, R. C., Perry, V. H., Tracey, I., Wessely, S., Arseneault, L., Ballard, C., Christensen, H., Silver, R. C., Everall, I., Ford, T., John, A., Kabir, T., King, K., Madan, I., Michie, S., Przybylski, A., Shafran, R., Sweeney, A., ... Bullmore, E. (2020). Multidisciplinary research priorities for the COVID-19 pandemic: A call for action for mental health science. *The Lancet Psychiatry, 7*, 547–560. https://doi.org/10.1016/S2215-0366(20)30168-1

Horesh, D., & Brown, A. D. (2020). Traumatic stress in the age of COVID-19: A call to close critical gaps and adapt to new realities. *Psychological Trauma: Theory, Research, Practice, and Policy, 12*, 331–335. http://dx.doi.org/10.1037/tra0000592

Hurley-Hanson, A. E., & Giannantonio, C. M. (2013). Crisis response plans post 9/11: Current status and future directions. *Electronic Business Journal, 12*, 378–392. http://electronic-businessjournal.com/images/2013/5/4.pdf

Inter-Agency Standing Committee (2020, February). *Briefing Note on Addressing Mental Health and Psychosocial Aspects of COVID-19 Outbreak – Version 1.5.* https://interagencystandingcommittee.org/system/files/2020-03/IASC%20Interim%20Briefing%20Note%20on%20COVID-19%20Outbreak%20Readiness%20and%20Response%20Operations%20-%20MHPSS_0.pdf

Jeong, H., Yim, H.W., Song, Y.-J., Ki, M., Min, J.-A., Cho, J., & Chae, J-H. (2016). Mental health status of people isolated due to Middle East respiratory syndrome. *Epidemiology and Health, 38*, e2016048. https://doi.org/10.4178/epih.e2016048

Joseph, E. E., & Winston, B.E. (2005). A correlation of servant leadership, leader trust, and organizational trust. *Leadership & Organization Development Journal, 26*, 6–22. https://doi.org/10.1108/01437730510575552

Knight, W. (2020, March 27). *China Goes Back to Work as Coronavirus Rages on Elsewhere.* https://www.wired.com/story/china-goes-work-coronavirus-rages-elsewhere/

Krishnan, R., Martin, X., & Noorderhaven, N. G. (2006). When does trust matter to alliance performance? *Academy of Management Journal, 49*, 894–917. https://doi.org/10.5465/amj.2006.22798171

Kumar, S., Quinn, S. C., Kim, K. H., Musa, D., Hilyard, K. M., & Freimuth, V. S. (2011). The social ecological model as a framework for determinants of 2009 H1N1 influenza vaccine uptake in the United States. *Health Education & Behavior, 39*, 229–243. https://doi.org/10.1177/1090198111415105

Leger/Association for Canadian Studies (2020, May). *COVID-19 Tracking Survey Results.* https://leger360.com/surveys/stay-informed-covid-19-surveys/

Liu, J. J., Bao, Y., Huang, X., Shi, J., & Lu, L. (2020). Mental health considerations for children quarantined because of COVID-19. *The Lancet Child & Adolescent Health, 4*, 347–349. https://doi.org/10.1016/S2352-4642(20)30096-1

Lyonette, C., & Baldauf, B. (2019). *Family Friendly Working Policies and Practices: Motivations, Influences and Impacts for Employers.* Government Equalities Office. https://assets.publishing.service.gov.uk/government/uploads/system/uploads/attachment_data/file/840061/Warwick_Final_Report_1610.pdf

Mayer, R. C., Davis, J. H., & Schoorman, F. D. (1995). An integrative model of organizational trust. *Academy Management Review, 20,* 709–734. https://doi.org/10.5465/amr.1995.9508080335

McClain, M. (2007). Employee crisis communication and disaster assistance planning: Providing disaster assistance to employees and their families. *Journal of Business Continuity and Emergency Planning, 1,* 213–220. https://www.ingentaconnect.com/content/hsp/jbcep/2007/00000001/00000002/art00009#expand/collapse

McElwain, A. K., Korabik, K., & Rosin, H. M. (2005). An examination of gender differences in work–family conflict. *Canadian Journal of Behavioural Science, 37,* 283–298. https://doi.org/10.1037/h0087263

Mercer, N. (2019, November). *Flexible Work Arrangements in the Canadian Armed Forces (CAF)* [Conference session]. Conference of the Inter-University Seminar on Armed Forces and Society, Reston, VA, United States.

Michie, S., van Stralen, M. M., & West, R. (2011). The behaviour change wheel: A new method for characterizing and designing behaviour change interventions. *Implementation Science, 6,* 42–54. https://doi.org/10.1186/1748-5908-6-42

Misra, S., & Stokols, D. (2012). Psychological health outcomes of perceived information overload. *Environment and Behavior, 44,* 737–759. https://doi.org/10.1177/0013916511404408

Moran, K. R., & Del Valle, S. Y. (2016). A meta-analysis of the association between gender and protective behaviors in response to respiratory epidemics and pandemics. *PLoS ONE, 11,* e0164541. https://doi.org/10.1371/journal.pone.0164541

Nickell, L. A., Crighton, E. J., Tracy, C. S., Al-Enazy, H., Bolaji, Y., Hanjrah, S., Hussain, A., Makhlouf, S., & Upshur, R. E. G. (2004). Psychosocial effects of SARS on hospital staff: Survey of a large tertiary care institution. *Canadian Medical Association Journal, 170,* 793–798. https://doi.org/10.1503/cmaj.1031077

Nicola, M., Alsafi, Z., Sohrabi, C., Kerwan, A., Al-Jabir, A., Iosifidis, C., Agha, M., & Agha, R. (2020). The socio-economic implications of the coronavirus and COVID-19 pandemic: A review. *International Journal of Surgery, 78,* 185–193. https://doi.org/10.1016/j.ijsu.2020.04.018

Odle-Dusseau, H. N., Matthews, R. A., & Wayne, J. H. (2018). Employees' financial insecurity and health: The underlying role of stress and work–family conflict appraisals. *Journal of Occupational and Organizational Psychology, 91,* 546–568. https://doi.org/10.1111/joop.12216

O'Sullivan, T. L., Amaratunga, C., Phillips, K. P., Corneil, W., O'Connor, E., Lemyre, L., & Dow, D. (2009). If schools are closed, who will watch our kids? Family caregiving and other sources of role conflict among nurses during large-scale outbreaks. *Prehospital Disaster Medicine, 24,* 321–325. https://doi.org/10.1017/S1049023X00007044

Ravanera, C. (2020, April). *Primer on the Gendered Impacts of COVID-19.* Institute for Gender and the Economy. https://cdn.gendereconomy.org/wp-content/uploads/2020/04/GATE-COVID19-Primer.pdf

Rich, G. A. (1997). The sales manager as a role model: Effects of trust, job satisfaction, and performance of salespeople. *Journal of the Academy of Marketing Science, 25,* 319–328. https://doi.org/10.1177/0092070397254004

Rizzo, C., Fabiani, M., & Amlôt, R. (2013). Survey on the likely behavioural changes of the general public in four European countries during the 2009/2010 pandemic. In P. Manfredi & A. D'Onofrio (Eds.), *Modeling the Interplay between Human Behavior and the Spread of Infectious Diseases* (pp. 23-41). Springer.

Robertson, E., Hershenfield, K., Grace, S. L., & Stewart, D. E. (2004). The psychological effects of being quarantined following exposure to SARS: A qualitative study of Toronto Health Care Workers. *Canadian Journal of Psychiatry, 49*, 403–407. https:// doi.org/10.1177/070674370404900612

Robinson, S. L. (1996). Trust and breach of the psychological contract. *Administrative Science Quarterly, 41*, 574-599. https://doi.org/10.2307/2393868

Rubin, G. J., Amlôt, R., Page, L., & Wessely, S. (2009). Public perceptions, anxiety, and behaviour change in relation to the swine flu outbreak: Cross sectional telephone survey. *BMJ, 339*, b2651. https://doi.org/10.1136/bmj.b2651

Rugaber, C. (2020, June 5). *U.S. Unemployment Rate Falls to 13.3% in May.* https:// globalnews.ca/news/7029692/us-unemployment-rate-may/

Searle, R., & Billsberry, J. (2011). The development and destruction of organizational trust during recruitment and selection. In R. Searle & D. Skinner (Eds.), *Trust and Human Resource Management* (pp. 67–86). Cheltenham, UK and Northampton, MA, USA: Edward Elgar Publishing Ltd.

Seeger, M. W. (2007). Best practices in crisis communication: An expert panel process. *Journal of Applied Communication Research, 34*, 232–244. https://doi.org/10.1080/ 00909880600769944

Serrata, J. V., & Alvarado, G. H. (2019). *Understanding the Impact of Hurricane Harvey on Family Violence Survivors in Texas and Those Who Serve Them.* The Texas Council on family violence. https://tcfv.org/wp-content/uploads/2019/08/Hurricane -Harvey-Report-FINAL-and-APPROVED-as-of-060619.pdf

Shockley, K. M., & Clark, M. (2020). Work–family balance struggles in the time of COVID-19. *Society for Industrial and Organizational Psychology.* https://www.siop .org/Research-Publications/Items-of-Interest/ArtMID/19366/ArticleID/3454/Work -Family-Balance-Struggles-in-the-Time-of-COVID-19

Sinclair, R. R., Allen, T., Barber, L., Bergman, M., Britt, T., Butler, A., Ford, M., Hammer, L., Kath, L., Probst, T., & Yuan, Z. (2020). Occupational health science in the time of COVID-19: Now more than ever. *Occupational Health Science.* https:// doi.org/10.1007/s41542-020-00064-3

Sly, L., & Morris, L. (2020, May 13). *As Some Countries Ease Up, Others are Reimposing Lockdowns Amid a Resurgence of Coronavirus Infections.* Washington Post.   https://www.washingtonpost.com/world/as-some-countries-ease-up-others -are-reimposing-lockdowns-amid-a-resurgence-of-coronavirus-infections/2020/ 05/12/6373cf6a-9455-11ea-87a3-22d324235636_story.html

Solberg, C., Rossetto, T., & Joffe, H. (2010). The social psychology of seismic hazard adjustment: Re-evaluating the international literature. *Natural Hazards and Earth System Sciences, 10*, 1663–1677. https://doi.org/10.5194/nhess-10-1663-2010

Statista (2020, May). *Impact of the Coronavirus (COVID-19) Pandemic on Alcohol Consumption in the United Kingdom (UK) in 2020.* https://www.statista.com/ statistics/1118716/alcohol-consumption-due-to-coronvirus-uk/

Statistics Canada (2020a, April 17). *Canadian Perspectives Survey Series 1: COVID-19 and Working from Home.* https://www150.statcan.gc.ca/n1/daily-quotidien/200417/ dq200417a-eng.htm

Statistics Canada (2020b, June 24). *Table 14-10-0287-03 Labour Force Characteristics by Province, Monthly, Seasonally Adjusted.* https://doi.org/10.25318/1410028701-eng

Statistics Canada (2020c, April 8). *How are Canadians Coping with the COVID-19 Situation?* https://www150.statcan.gc.ca/n1/pub/11-627-m/11-627-m2020029-eng .htm

Sun, N., Wei, L., Shi, S., Jiao, D., Song, R., Ma, L., Wang, H., Wang, C., Wang, Z., You, Y., Liu, S., & Wang, H. (2020). A qualitative study on the psychological experience of caregivers of COVID-19 patients. *American Journal of Infection Control, 48,* 592–598. https://doi.org/10.1016/j.ajic.2020.03.018

Szabo, T. G., Richling, S., Embry, D. D., Biglan, A., & Wilson, K. G. (2020). From helpless to hero: Promoting values-based behavior and positive family interaction in the midst of Covid-19. *Behavior Analysis in Practice.* Advance online publication. https://doi.org/10.1007/s40617-020-00431-0

Therrien, M. E., Richer, I., Lee, J. E. C., Watkins, K., & Zamorski, M. A. (2016). Family/ household characteristics and positive mental health of Canadian military members: Mediation through social support. *Journal of Military, Veteran and Family Health, 2,* 8–20. https://doi.org/10.3138/jmvfh.4017

Timpka, T., Spreco, A., Gursky, E., Eriksson, O., Dahlström, Ö., Strömgren, M., Ekberg, J., Pilemalm, S., Karlsson, D., Hinkula, J., & Holm, E. (2014). Intentions to perform non-pharmaceutical protective behaviors during influenza outbreaks in Sweden: A cross-sectional study following a mass vaccination campaign. *PLoS ONE, 9,* 91060. https://doi.org/10.1371/journal.pone.0091060

Tyler, T. R. (1994). Psychological models of the justice motive: Antecedents of distributive and procedural justice. *Journal of Personality and Social Psychology, 67,* 850–863. https://doi.org/10.1037/0022-3514.67.5.850

UNESCO (2020, May 13). *Reopening Schools: When, Where and How?* https://en .unesco.org/news/reopening-schools-when-where-and-how

U.S. Department of Health and Human Services, Centers for Disease Control and Prevention. (n.d.). *Crisis + Emergency Risk Communication – Psychology of a Crisis. 2019 Update.* https://emergency.cdc.gov/cerc/ppt/CERC_Psychology_of_a_Crisis .pdf

Usher, K., & Bhullar, N. (2020). Family violence and COVID-19: Increased vulnerability and reduced options for support. *International Journal of Mental Health Nursing, 29*(4), 549–552. https://doi.org/10.111/inm.12735

Van Bavel, J. J., Baicker, K., Boggio, P. S., Capraro, V., Chichocka, A., Cikara, M., Crockett, M. J., Crum, A. J., Douglas, K. M., Druckman, J. N., Drury, J., Dube, O., Ellemers, N., Finkel, E. J., Fowler, J. H., Gelfand, M., Han, S., Haslam, A. S., Jetten, J., … Kitayama, S. (2020). Using social and behavioural science to support COVID-19 pandemic response. *Nature Human Behaviour, 4,* 460–471. https://doi.org/10.1038/ s41562-020-0884-z

Vaughn, E. (2011). Contemporary perspectives on risk perceptions, health-protective behaviors, and control of emerging infectious diseases. *International Journal of Behavioral Medicine, 18,* 83–87. https://doi.org/10.1007/s12529-011-9160-y

Vinck, P., Pham, P. N., Bindu, K. K., Bedford, J., & Nilles, E. J. (2019). Institutional trust and misinformation in the response to the 2018–19 Ebola outbreak in North Kivu, DR Congo: A population-based survey. *The Lancet Infectious Diseases, 19,* 529–536. https://doi.org/10.1016/S1473-3099(19)30063-5

Wang, G., Zhang, Y., Zhao, J., Zhang, J., & Jiang, F. (2020). Mitigate the effects of home confinement on children during the COVID-19 outbreak. *The Lancet, 395,* 945–947. https://doi.org/10.1016/S0140-6736(20)30547-X

Wenham, C., Smith, J., & Morgan, R. (2020). COVID-19: The gendered impacts of the outbreak. *The Lancet, 395,* 846–848. https://doi.org/10.1016/S0140-6736(20)30526-2

Wiles, J. (2020, March 23). *Five Remote Lessons Learned from Asia*. Gartner. https://www.gartner.com/smarterwithgartner/early-covid-19-lessons-learned-from-employers-in-asia/

Wilkie, D. (2017, March 23). *Remote Workers Feel Productive but Also Guilty*. SHRM. https://www.shrm.org/ResourcesAndTools/hr-topics/employee-relations/Pages/remote-workers-feel-guilty-.aspx

Wood, M. M., Mileti, D. S., Kano, M., Kelley, M. M., Regan, R., & Bourque, L. B. (2011). Communicating actionable risk for terrorism and other hazards. *Risk Analysis, 32*, 601–615. https://doi.org/10.1111/j.1539-6924.2011.01645.x

WHO – World Health Organization (2020, June 23). *Coronavirus Disease (COVID-19) Pandemic*. https://www.who.int/emergencies/diseases/novel-coronavirus-2019

Ying, Y., Kong, F., Zhu, B., Ji, Y., Lou, Z., & Ruan, L. (2020). Mental health status among family members of health care workers in Ningbo, China during the Coronavirus disease 2019 (COVID-19) outbreak: A cross-sectional study. *medRxiv, 21*(56). https://doi.org/10.1101/2020.03.13.20033290

Zhang, Y., & Ma, Z. F. (2020). Impact of the COVID-19 pandemic on mental health and quality of life among local residents in Liaoning province, China: A cross-sectional study. *International Journal of Environmental Research and Public Health, 17*, 2381. https://doi.org/10.3390/ijerph17072381

Appendix: Organizational strategies for maintaining employee well-being through COVID-19 and related disasters

	Managing Reactions
☐	Maintain an open and honest flow of information to employees, and release accurate information as soon as it is available. Acknowledge and normalize fears and other emotional responses to avoid stigma and promote help seeking if required.
☐	Encourage adaptive coping strategies, including good hygiene, exercise, and healthy eating, and discouraging negative coping strategies (e.g., drugs, excessive alcohol).
☐	Promote healthy adaptive behaviours with behaviourally specific advice (i.e., who needs to do what, when and how; what should not be done) and provide reasons why, as explanations help people understand and increase motivation to act.
☐	Instill a sense of purpose or meaning by describing how employees' actions contribute to organizational goals and society.
☐	Avoid information overload and standardize communications by setting boundaries and rules of engagement for use of communication tools.
☐	Strive for a consolidated approach to communications. Place resources, relevant applications, updates, etc. in a centralized location that is easily accessible.
☐	Ensure workers responding to COVID-19 are adequately trained for (a) crisis operational tasks and (b) resilience (including discussions of morally challenging scenarios) to increase their sense of preparedness and competence.
☐	Remind personnel to draw on prior psychological resilience training, as applicable, and refer them to online and app-based platforms that can facilitate the use of key concepts and skills during the pandemic. Promote the use of online and app-based resilience training among those who may not have taken it previously.
☐	Advocate for support (peer, leader, friends, family), especially for those deemed at greater risk of negative psychological reactions; e.g., demonstrate empathy towards personnel experiencing stress, and provide flexible work arrangements for those with unique challenges.
☐	Monitor and support the psychological functioning and well-being of employees, especially those at greater risk of negative reactions. Publicize the range of available mental health services (in-person, telephone, web- and app-based) in support of potential moral injury, PTSD, suicidality, and domestic violence during and after the pandemic.

Managing Impacts on Work

☐ Acknowledge barriers to productivity to help alleviate workers' stress; working from home is a learned skill.

☐ Empower employees by adjusting and clarifying work expectations, and by providing opportunities for workers to safely raise concerns and offer suggestions.

☐ Provide clear, consistent, and supportive messaging regarding productivity expectations and accommodations for those who may be experiencing additional challenges and stress.

☐ Encourage work–life balance and flexible schedules.

☐ Discourage working after hours where feasible.

☐ Encourage virtual social interactions between colleagues (e.g., virtual coffee breaks) as a means of checking in.

☐ Encourage engagement in healthy leisure activities, such as reading and exercise.

☐ Provide timely information regarding career implications and job security as a result of COVID-19.

Managing Impacts on Family Life

☐ Provide links to trusted sources of health information on reducing the risk of exposure to COVID-19 within the household.

☐ Inform employees about financial resources and alternative support services (e.g., child or elder care), recognizing vulnerable employees, such as single parents and those experiencing a loss of income.

☐ Normalize tension and stress in family or intimate relationships during this period; encourage employees to alter expectations for themselves and partners/family members.

☐ Recognize parenting stressors and encourage workers to develop a family plan to manage new or altered roles as educators, coaches, nurses, and so on (e.g., lists, agendas, contingencies).

☐ Advocate for peer support networks among coworkers and encourage the sharing of resources (e.g., educational tools, links to online individual and family forums and activities such as exercise classes).

☐ Remind employees of the psychological resources available to them and their family (e.g., family information line) and inform them of crisis hotlines.

☐ Promote family-wide self-care (e.g., sleep, healthy eating, exercise, meditation) and the use of virtual support programs and services.

Encouraging Compliance

☐ Ensure that the severity of the threat associated with COVID-19 is communicated clearly, and that messages about protective behaviours reinforce their effectiveness for mitigating the threat.

☐ Provide directives that are perceived as personally feasible, taking into consideration unique personal circumstances (e.g., caregiving responsibilities, access to resources).

☐ Reinforce social norms of responsibility to support the public interest, and facilitate communication between employees that draws out their conscientiousness and demonstrates collective compliance with public health directives.

☐ Emphasize shared identity and vigilance in diffusing destructive social reactions in crises, such as zero sum thinking (i.e., believing that benefits to others come at the expense to oneself) and inter-group discrimination (i.e., emphasizing the moral aspects of doing the right thing, and modelling cooperative behaviours).

Managing Reintegration

☐ Acknowledge hard work performed to date under extremely difficult conditions, from the everyday contributions by the majority to those deserving formal recognition.

☐ Provide clear communication about new COVID-19 health and safety policies and procedures implemented in the workplace, and the extent to which they are aligned with universal guidelines (e.g., World Health Organization).

☐ Manage expectations for the reality they will be returning to (the "new normal)", and that a resurgence of COVID-19 could mean changes in work arrangements. Doing so may reduce ambiguity and associated stress.

☐ Reinforce feelings of organizational support as people return to their workplaces; e.g., through regular communication, facilitate safe activities that foster group cohesion, and acknowledge and support the use of resources, such as employee assistance programs. Doing so can mitigate the potential negative impact of a variety of stressors, including fear of contagion, uncertainty, and social isolation.

☐ Enable flexibility with respect to scheduling a return to the workplace by taking into account vulnerability criteria (e.g., age, health status, at home situation), along with the nature of the work required. Doing so may reduce stress by providing employees a sense of control, which is important for well-being.

☐ Engage employees in the development, implementation, and assessment of return to work plans (e.g., clarifying how a plan meets their needs, soliciting feedback on implementation) to facilitate buy-in. Employee engagement may also provide personnel the physical and social opportunities, the reflective motivation, and the psychological capability to adopt and adhere to new behaviours.

☐ Keep policies, procedures and processes flexible and adaptable to change. They should be perceived by employees to support and facilitate shared goals and values, and they should minimize emphasis on oversight and punishment, as this can reduce people's trust in the organization and its leaders.

Index